Journey of the Soul

Also by Dr Brenda Davies

Affairs of the Heart
The Rainbow Journey
Total Wellbeing (*with Dr Hilary Jones*)

Journey
of the Soul

Awakening Ourselves to the
Enduring Cycle of Life

Dr Brenda Davies

Hodder & Stoughton

Copyright © 2002 by Dr Brenda Davies

First published in Great Britain in 2002 by Hodder and Stoughton
First published in paperback in 2003 by Hodder and Stoughton
A division of Hodder Headline

The right of Dr Brenda Davies to be identified as the Author
of the Work has been asserted by her in accordance with the
Copyright, Designs and Patents Act 1988.

5 7 9 10 8 6

A CIP catalogue record for this title is available from the British Library

ISBN 0 340 73390 X

Every effort has been made to trace the copyright holders of the extracts
reproduced within this book, the author and publishers apologise to
anyone who has not been contacted in advance or credited.

Typeset in 11/14pt Sabon by
Palimpsest Book Production Limited,
Polmont, Stirlingshire
Printed and bound in Great Britain by
Clays Ltd, St Ives plc

Hodder and Stoughton
A division of Hodder Headline
338 Euston Road
London NW1 3BH

For my mother, Hilda Todd, who made her peaceful transition on 2 February 2001

ACKNOWLEDGEMENTS

Acknowledging all the people who help to bring a book into being is a joy, however I've been blessed with so many wonderful guides and helpers (not only of the soul plane variety!) that it becomes difficult to thank them all individually. So please forgive me if I don't mention you by name. All of you who have helped me know who you are, and I send you my love and deepest gratitude.

My mother deserves special mention since she chose to make her transition while I was writing *Journey of the Soul*, and in doing so, she taught me a great deal. And while my heart ached at her loss, I learned more about love and grief and letting go, which then found its way on to these pages. My father, who as his soul self helped comfort me at that time, has always been my great teacher too. Thank you, Dad. Still in the flesh, thank God, my daughter Lesda is ever willing to spend time with me, support me and cheer me on despite the fact that my work leaves me with less time to spend with her than she would like. Thank you, Angel. And Keith and his lovely wife Elizabeth are always there for me too, and the joy of having my grandchildren, Jonathan and Alex, has healed my heart when it was sore, and I'm ever grateful that they have graced our lives. Les, always the wind under my wings, thank you for being there when I needed you. My sister Pam and her husband Bill have also been supportive, and I thank you too.

Many people have been more than patient and loving with me as I was sometimes neither as available nor as prompt as I could have been as I juggled various commitments while needing to take some time to care for myself: my patients from whom I'm always learning; dear friends and organizers of workshops, master classes, seminars and the media – Kim Arnold and Cheryl van Blerk in the UK, (thank you for your readings too, Kim!), Lisa Powell Watts, my lovely friend and a great colleague in Texas, Wilfried Droste, Dr Christiane Ley and my dear friend Friedrich Schewe in Berlin, Jennie Gorman, Kim Rathmann and Shaun Leyland in Australia, Naoko Miki in Japan, Patric van Blerk and Laurie Adams in South Africa, Erroll Hickey and his lovely wife Ursula in Zambia, who have also been gracious and generous hosts; in California my publicist and friend Sarah Fahey, ever encouraging and with whom I share stories of gardening and Africa; my long-suffering friends and website designers, Wendy Griffiths and Mike Lort at Stackrock Technology, who manage to produce something of beauty for me despite the fact that I fail to answer e-mails and generally try their patience; my ever-helpful secretary Nigel Shakespeare and the lovely Pauline Groman who always accommodates me at Violet Hill Studios in London, and of course Scott Hunt whom I would dearly love to adopt as my second son! Lucie Barnette stepped into the secretarial breach for a while in Texas and without her I would have sunk without trace. Bless you, Lucie. In Brenham, Texas I have a wonderful, supportive band of friends too numerous to mention, who took me into their hearts and with whom I can always discuss matters metaphysical and also share love and humour. And my friend Betty Rainey – always at the end of a phone or an e-mail and filled with wisdom and care. In London, Annie Lionnet, whose amazingly intuitive astrological readings keep me on track and let me know that some of my apparently crazy ideas are grounded in reality after all. All of you were so kind to me when I needed strong shoulders in February 2001 and without you, I would still be struggling to reach my deadline.

Then of course there is Hodder with its great team: my editor Emma Heyworth-Dunn, who has ever so gently chivvied me along, Rowena Webb who is always there when I need her, Kerry Hood whose briefest of notes convey so much, Briar Silich whose faith in me and determination to get my books read around the world is nothing short of heroic, and Diane Banks, who, alongside Briar, keeps pushing me out into the world. The design department has thrilled me with the jacket for *Journey of the Soul* and production have been patient even when the time was getting tight. Also Helen Campbell who undertook the copyediting. Thank you all.

In the midst of all of the ups and downs of 2001, I also had another great teacher who forced me to reassess a great deal about myself, who I am and where I'm going. Thank you, Vickie. I shall never forget the lessons I learned.

To those I haven't mentioned by name, please forgive me. All of you, named or not, have been angels, and I thank you and send you my heartfelt love.

I am certain of nothing but the holiness of the heart's affections and the truth of imagination – what the imagination seizes as beauty must be truth – whether it existed before or not.

John Keats, Letter to Benjamin Bailey, 1817

Brenda Davies
January 2002

CONTENTS

INTRODUCTION

Our soul is on a journey which began eons ago and which, for most of us, will continue for centuries yet. Increasing our understanding of that journey and appreciating who we really are enriches our lives beyond measure. Honouring childbirth and death as equal adventures in life, and giving them both the spiritual status they deserve, enables us to welcome wise, ancient souls at one end of human life and release those who have completed their chosen earthly tasks at the moment we call death. Dr David Reilly of the Glasgow Homeopathic Hospital has said that cellular destruction, illness and death are inherent in the human process. True. But our growth continues throughout. An understanding of death as simply part of life may not necessarily rid us of our grief but can relieve us of any fear of death and bring us a richness and joy even in loss that escapes those who have no such comprehension. The non-physical reality raises a multitude of questions, of course. The answers may challenge our old belief systems, but the evidence is neither conjecture nor fanciful dreams nor confabulation. Judge for yourself. We have already completed many sojourns on the planet, and most of us will have many more yet before we return that final time to that great body of spirit we call God. I am not here to encourage you to rush your return, but to suggest ways of making the learning joyful and loving for yourself and others and to move towards completion in the richest way possible.

While I was writing *Journey of the Soul* my mother passed away. After a dynamic life, filled with love and joy but also trials and tribulations, and having had visits from all of her family, she finally took her leave. It was sad but wonderful to be with her in the last few days before her transition and to live once more that 'healing into death' with someone I love so deeply. Many of the feelings were similar to those when seven years earlier my father passed. But many were different. She had wanted to leave for some time and she, my sister and I had talked a great deal about what death meant to her, what she expected to happen, where she thought she would go afterwards and whether my dad would be waiting for her 'on the other side'. I had such a feeling of peace in those last days as I held her hand, read her favourite poetry and the Native American prayers that she loved, and played recordings that Pam's family had made for her birthday. At the last, I held her and I felt her suspended in a peaceful place as she finally managed to leave her body.

My sister Pam and I shared those last days in peaceful watchfulness, reflecting on all of our lives and how they intertwined. We all talked about what Mum had done in her life, the things she had loved and enjoyed, the grand-children and great-grandchildren, what she would like us to do now and how we would proceed without her. We also laughed as we remembered that a couple of weeks earlier she had announced that she was about to 'let go' and so wouldn't be seeing us again. She said her goodbyes and a few hours later, wide awake after a sound sleep, she announced that she had done as we'd talked about, said to God that she was ready and had 'let go' and she had 'been' but had come back!

In the days that followed her passing, I had such a sense of peace for her, yet experienced that strange aching hole in the middle of my chest as my heart chakra started to deal with the business of healing. It was strange that life simply went on without a blip on its screen despite the fact that this beautiful woman who had been our mother was no longer there. The day after the funeral my sister said quite naturally, 'Wait till I tell Mum about all the people who came.' The following Sunday I picked up the phone to make my usual call to her.

On returning to Texas I felt bereft at leaving England and leaving her there despite the fact that I know she is available to me anywhere in the world. I also had renewed sadness about being so geographically removed from my own children. As I walked in my pastures I tried to talk to her – too early in many ways – and felt the loneliness of not being able to contact her. I had always been able to do so in her lifetime. But then I noticed that the first violets were out under the oak trees, and coming back from my walk with my dog Suki, I stopped to pick some. It was then that I felt her presence for the first time. She was there with me, smiling and softly loving me. I felt her gentle breath as she soothed my grieving and suddenly all was fine. Even though in the days that followed there were still times when my heart hurt, when my body signalled it was time to rest by pulling my energy out from under me, the evidence of her survival, though in many ways I needed none, had comforted me and I began to heal in a different way. I had walked the pasture so many times with my dad since he passed away, and now they were both here. One of the last things my mother said was that one of her few regrets was that she hadn't been able to see my home in Texas. I assured her that she would be there walking with me very soon, and here, under the oak trees with the violets, she had made it at last, and my heart sang for her freedom.

How comforting and reassuring it is, under such circumstances, to know that our soul doesn't die. I hope that through this book, you will gain similar reassurance regarding death.

You'll find that I've divided *Journey of the Soul* into two parts, since our life naturally falls into an earthly phase and a phase taking place on the soul plane. Part I is of a self-help nature, dealing with our earthly life and development, our spiritual growth in the context of our world and the life events that highlight the interface between our physical and spiritual realities. It will help you be more in touch with your own soul and will enrich your contact with the souls of those around you. Part II focuses on the interlife or the interim phase. This is where we go after our body has physically died, and where we continue to be alive and even more vital, though without a physical body. Here I have drawn together channelled wisdom, evidence from those who have had near-death experiences and statements from those who have been closely involved with 'dying' and 'death', as well as some of the teachings from major religions about the survival of the soul and what happens after we die and before we reincarnate again.

Since my commitment is not only to accuracy but also to healing and spiritual growth, *Journey of the Soul* needs to be a practical tool as well. From time to time I shall refer to the chakra system, so I've included a recap on its structure, development, functions and dysfunction in Appendix 2. (However, I would refer you to *The Rainbow Journey* (Dr Brenda Davies, Hodder & Stoughton, 1998) for a more detailed account and clearer understanding.)

The meditation you will find at the end of each chapter is to help consolidate your growth and open to your higher wisdom and understanding. You will probably find it best to have a place where you will not be disturbed to do your meditations – a space where you can be alone unless you wish to invite someone to meditate with you – where you can play gentle music and have a comfortable chair, cushion or meditation stool, perhaps a small table on which you can place some items of particular significance for you, such as flowers, a crystal, a candle and maybe a photograph or an object that reminds you of your spirituality. Have a glass of water with you and perhaps your journal so that you can record any insights or just write for a while and let your soul talk through your writing. (For this to happen you really need to allow yourself at least fifteen minutes to write non-stop, as quickly as you can without editing in any way). Then just date your entry and leave it. You can reread it at some later time when you want to. You can either read the meditations a couple of times, then close your eyes and visualize them, or have a friend read them to you, or record them, then listen to them. Give yourself plenty of time with the phone off the hook. When you're finished, have a drink of water and make sure that you're grounded before you go back to your normal activities. There's a grounding exercise and a visualization for closing down your chakras in Appendix 3.

Verbalizing our gratitude and affirming our intention about what we want to happen in our lives can help us maintain our connection with the Divine and manifest our desires, making our soul's journey as we want it to be. So you will also find at the end of each chapter an affirmation and a prayer that will form a framework which you can build on when you're ready. However, it's important to use our own words if we can, personalizing our message. If you find your own words just pouring forth, please just ignore mine. Yours will be much better.

Just a word about affirmations. These positive statements help counteract negative thinking, facilitating inner changes in a quite amazing way. You don't have to believe in them for them to have power. If you tell your mind enough times that something positive is happening, you will start to create a reality where that is a possibility, so it's important that they're always in the present tense. You'll be surprised how your cognitive processes will change as you see things in a more positive light and start to risk the thought that life can be different. As you do so, your behaviour changes and there is usually an accompanying rise in mood. Of course, this prompts positive feedback from those around you, and as you create new beliefs, you put out different vibrations into the world. Now your positive statement becomes a reality and your journey more fulfilling. So why not just suspend judgment, say them, write them or record them and listen to them, and do it regularly and often? What have you got to lose?

Imagery and visualization are also important and powerful in helping you better your reality and therefore enhance your soul's journey, and we shall use them here and there. These are tools used for example by sportsmen who may practise a particular move in their minds, visualizing a positive outcome long before doing it in reality. If you can suspend any negative belief, for instance that you might be in pain, afraid or that you will fail, and then let go of resistance and view the scenario positively, a more positive outcome is assured. As you will see, such techniques can be used for various life events. And lastly, there is a bibliography which will help provide you with ideas for further reading. Appendix 1 offers you a brief review about angels.

And me? First of all, let me say that I do not propose to know all the answers, and in the end, only you can decide what you believe. But for me, not only is there overwhelming evidence of what I say, but my own personal experiences are also sufficient to convince me that we do survive. I often use the word *knowing* when I receive information via my crown chakra which comes in as a fully formed statement of fact – not something I've worked out or understand, it's more than that. So please forgive me if I use that now. I *know* that we have lived many times and that our souls have survived and always will.

I use all the tools of which I shall be talking, and in the main, I'm enjoying my journey. In some ways I never want it to end, yet I know the time will come when I've learned all I have to learn, taught all I have to teach, given all I have to give and received all I have to receive in this life-time and then it will be time to go. I hope that I shall depart with a similar joy and excitement to that with which I currently devour life. I hope you're enjoying your stay also and that it will become ever more rewarding. Whether you're on your own spiritual quest, grieving for someone who has 'died', are preparing to let someone go or are approaching your own departure, I hope that *Journey of the Soul* will give you some new insights and allay any fears. I wish you new understanding, increased awareness, joy in the know-ledge that neither you nor your loved ones will ever die, and inspiration for the rest of your journey.

Come along and let us begin!

✪

Part I

Experiencing the Human Life

BEFORE WE BEGIN . . .

SETTING OUR INTENTION

Our intention is very powerful in bringing to the forefront of our consciousness what we really want and intend to have in our lives. This not only focuses our minds and sets in motion our heart's desire, but calls in all that we need today to move along our path to our goal of enlightenment and to try our best to resolve issues as they arise rather than setting up any new problems for ourselves. It also calls to our guides and helpers and puts out a powerful and peaceful message to the universe. Thus intention can make an important and positive contribution to our journey.

Every morning I set my intention for the day. At the beginning of workshops or evenings of spiritual conversation, the participants and I almost always do the same. It's a practice I would recommend that you adopt at least every morning, if not several times a day, and one that would be good to do right now before you begin reading this book. I have to say that sometimes I overrule my intention, like overriding the cruise control setting in my car, and let my emotions get in the way. However, when the storm is over, all I need to do is reset my intention and start again.

Beginning to read this book and making a commitment to look at your life afresh and learn more about your soul is a good time to look critically at your intention and be sure that you set in motion whatever it is you truly want. Looking briefly at the options can help us make good choices.

- Do you intend to be open, present and loving to yourself and others and every wonderful possibility the universe offers you?
- Do you intend to have a wonderful, peaceful day, extending into a wonderful, peaceful life?
- Is it your intention to be excited by new challenges that come along to help you expand your awareness and raise your consciousness?
- Do you want to be open and grow today even if that means looking at emotions and hearing constructive criticism you might not like?
- Do you intend to greet every person you meet with love, openness and childlike curiosity, respecting them for who they are even if their beliefs are different to yours?
- Do you intend to give of your very best to all the people you meet today – including yourself?
- Are you willing to have an open mind and update your understanding of the truth if it seems appropriate?
- Are you willing to incorporate some new ideas into your daily life?
- Are you willing to forgive where you're able to and call back those parts of yourself that have become stuck with old slights, insults and hurts?
- Can you decide to treat yourself with gentleness and kindness as you would your best friend?

You may, of course, choose to be closed and defensive; to catch up on gossip, do a bit of character assassination, pass on the latest rumour or pay somebody back for something they did yesterday, last week or even ten years ago; to follow your plans single-mindedly, regardless of what comes your way; to retaliate and react, missing opportunities for growth; to react with suspicion, negativity and lack of trust; to be stubborn and refuse to open up to new concepts; to hold people on the hook with bitterness and resentment that keep both of you in negativity and pain. The choice is yours. Your intention is powerful and will be realized – so be careful to ensure that you spend a moment looking honestly at what it is. A bit like being careful what you pray for because you might get it!

Setting my intention goes something like this:

In all my transactions today, I intend to come from a place of love within me, to a place of love within others; from a place of honesty in me to a place of honesty within others; from my integrity to the integrity of others; from a place of openness to a place of openness as I respect the rights of all living things. I intend to be gentle, kind and forgiving. I intend to be aware of the wonders of the universe and to greet them all with gratitude and awe. I intend to welcome whatever flows into my life to teach me today, and to listen to the conversation that the universe is trying to have with me. I intend to be inspired, to have joy in both work and play, to be grateful for all that I have in my life and for every opportunity I'm given. I intend to use my intuition and all my other spiritual gifts in all transactions today and to help wherever I can, even if that help means standing still and doing nothing, or letting go of someone I love. I intend that there shall be peace and harmony and that wherever I can make restitution, I shall have the courage and willingness to do so. I intend to live my humanity and divinity simultaneously today and to move further along my path to enlightenment. I rededicate my life to love, to peace, to harmony, to healing, to teaching, to my spiritual growth and the spiritual growth of others.

What do you intend in embarking on a new phase of the journey of your soul?

Take a moment now and set your powerful intention, then read on . . .

1 WHAT IT MEANS TO BE HUMAN

The most exciting breakthrough of the twenty-first century will occur not because of technology but because of the expanding concept of what it means to be human.

John Naisbitt, *Megatrends*, 2000

This is a book about the endless journey of the soul – that spiral of evolution from our inception billions of years ago to that moment long from now when we will once again reunite with whatever we know as the Source – the Beloved, God, the Divine, the Force, the Cosmic Creator, the Cosmic Oversoul, the Great Spirit, Jehovah or Allah. We shall deal with our entry into the physical world in Chapter 2; here we address the material and non-material world, the soul and evidence of its survival, spirit and the transcendent experience. Being human is a temporary chosen condition, whilst our essence, our soul, continues forever. But let's begin at the beginning.

THE BEGINNING

In the beginning there was only the Source, which wished to experience the material world. Out of itself, It created a myriad of souls which were released into the cosmos. Those fledgling souls experienced the universe, learned and developed, and returned to the soul planes, perhaps briefly, perhaps for hundreds of years, before venturing out once more in order to evolve further. Each of us is one of those souls, still journeying, still on our evolutionary path. We have ascended through various life forms to humanity, and we are still growing, still striving towards our goal of enlightenment.

Our journey, then, is a rich learning ground in which we exist simultaneously in a physical and non-physical reality as physical and non-physical beings. Our link with the Divine is ever present since we remain part of It, but we can strengthen and expand our connection by our intention and desire to establish contact and make our spirituality a major part of our lives. In doing so we are richly rewarded since our whole reality changes, as we shall see.

So in our quest to examine ourselves, our spirituality and our journey, let us first of all look at the earthly life – what is sometimes called the mundane phase.

THE EARTHLY LIFE – THE MUNDANE PHASE

We are very complex bioenergetic beings. The 'me' that is writing this lives mostly inside my physical body that in turn lives in the physical world. Maintained by millions of chemical reactions every minute, my physical body is the temporary home of my soul. Although my body is an amazing creation, it is nevertheless limited in space, time and function, my five senses constantly reporting impressions of the physical world in which I live. That physical world consists of other physical bodies, both animal and human, the plant and mineral kingdoms, the planet earth and other planets and stars, and all the material things – a world that we can see, hear, touch, taste or smell. The material world, including our physical bodies, consists of atoms, molecules and subatomic particles vibrating at varying frequencies. But much of our real life goes on in the non-physical world – that which is 'inside' us, or at least that is where we perceive it to be – but also that which is around us. Our 'inner' world is in fact the function of the part of our body which extends around us – our aura or human energy field – and is not 'inside' at all, and beyond that there is what we may call the universal energy field, in which everything else exists. Once we begin to acknowledge that there is more to us and the world than the physical reality we have created, we begin to expand in terms of what we expect to perceive. That expanded expectation immediately opens up new possibilities and what was once inaccessible to us starts to be integrated into our awareness. You would not be reading this had you not already started to increase your awareness to take in more of the reality which is our world.

We began in cosmic harmony with a knowledge of cosmic law and cosmic love. Most of us have quite naturally diverged from that blissful state as we have become involved with our emotions and desires and with the process of being human. We have forgotten that we are primarily spiritual beings and that it is to the higher realms that we truly belong. Earthly life is an initiation, a time of chosen challenges, each giving us the opportunity to learn and grow, preparing us for the time when we are ready to return to eternal peace, perfect harmony and cosmic union with God. The human path we have chosen is not always easy. In fact M. Scott Peck begins his acclaimed *The Road Less Travelled* (Simon and Schuster, 1978) with the words 'Life is difficult'. Well, not always, or not consistently, I hope. If life is consistently difficult, either we're ignoring the lessons that present themselves, disregarding the signs while defiantly or stubbornly refusing to make better choices, or perhaps we have chosen a steep learning curve this time. Scott Peck and I, in our capacity as psychiatrists, have probably seen many people who have courageously chosen a hard path, some of them heroically opting to process more than their fair share of the negativity and karma of the world so that the rest of us may be spared from doing so (see page 311).

The universe, our spiritual guides and the angels, often living among us in disguise, help us with signs and synchronicities to find our way, while none the less constantly respecting our free will. The choice of how we develop is ours, but everything we need to do so is available to us. And, like in any good film, every single thought, word, action, nuance and emotion is significant; every loose end is tied up in the final scene. *Nothing* is irrelevant.

It's possible to complete all the tasks we have opted for. Nothing is beyond us. We've been given amazing resources – wonderful people all around us to support, love and sometimes challenge us by showing us aspects of ourselves we would otherwise avoid; teachers and mentors who are just like us but perhaps a little further along the path; models of love, service and beauty we can emulate; a fantastic array of other living creatures to teach us, give us pleasure, love and care for; discarnate beings – angels, guides and others (we'll talk more of them later); and a vast and wonderful universe as our school and playground. Our inner wisdom and intuition will guide us if we let it. And of course there is the Spirit. We're very well provided for.

THE NON-PHYSICAL WORLD

We have only to switch on the light to be aware of the non-material universal energy field (UEF) – the universal soup in which we live and which is sometimes referred to simply as the field. These non-material but very real light waves have been harnessed for our use. Radio and television give us further proof of this. Then there are X-rays and microwaves, all existing in the same space and time frame as us, all rarely interfering with each other. We tend to accept these because in them we have tangible proof in the form of equipment that converts the invisible to something we can readily perceive.

What we may find more difficult to accept is that there are planes of consciousness, called the soul planes, from which we came and to which we shall return. These planes exist simultaneously and have been described as a series of bands of ever-rarefied density existing like concentric circles around the earth and reaching out into space. We shall talk more of them in Part II. As we learn to tap into the UEF, we find at our disposal a great web of help and reference, rather like a spiritual Internet, that we can use to guide us if we feel a bit lost. In this way the whole universe appears more rich and exciting. There is also a non-physical part of our bodies that most people cannot see – the energetic body or aura – which extends around our physical body and within which is the chakra system which penetrates the physical and connects at the central power channel which runs up our spine. You can read about this in more detail in Appendix 1. There are many other entities living in harmony with us that are also invisible to most of us. Although our physical bodies are miraculous creations, most of the really important work goes on in the non-physical reality. We can now isolate chemical compounds, neuropeptides, that signify thoughts and emotions, but the vibrations that stimulate such chemical changes are non-physical. There is no physical substance to intuition, love, hatred, or any of the other emotions we feel constantly. When we have a hunch, feel comfortable around one person and uncomfortable around another, feel touched by some world event, or feel a presence, we are functioning in the non-physical world – the world in which our soul exists.

THE HIGHER VIBRATIONAL PLANES

As the energetic vibrational frequency becomes significantly higher, we eventually reach other planes where discarnate beings operate. These beings are around us constantly, coexisting with us and extending their light and love into our reality. Although the frequency of their vibration is generally too high for our physical eyes to perceive, if you pause for a moment, close your eyes and extend an invitation to souls filled with light and love, you may be able to feel them gather around you. You may feel the quality of the silence change and may also be aware of your heart chakra opening in the middle of your chest and in your back too. Your breathing may change a little and you may feel tingling in your hands or at the sites of your other chakras. In fact you may be able to 'see' these beings with your inner vision. You may catch some of this only for a moment, then question whether it was real. It was.

As you develop your consciousness and your awareness increases, you will be more able to feel, communicate with, and perhaps eventually see such beings if you want to. Since they are on a different frequency they rarely speak with us in words, and we need to learn a new symbolic 'language'. The more evolved the soul, the higher the plane it frequents and the higher the intelligence and the purer the love, wisdom and healing it can impart to us.

Both teachers and guides from the soul planes are available to us while we continue to live here on the material plane. Guides are generally helping us in our earthly life, as we achieve more awareness. Teachers are helping us ascend on our spiritual path as we extend ourselves to become all that we can be. We have known our guides and teachers since long before this incarnation and they have already served us in many ways (see Chapter 6). They love us unconditionally with deep compassion, and they will be waiting to greet us when we return to the soul plane. Although the choice is ours, it seems rather foolish not to utilize this wonderful ever-available free resource. We simply need to take time to have a conversation with our guides, as we would with an earthly teacher or a trusted friend. You can silently share your plans and goals with your guides, tell them you feel lost and request to be shown the next step, and ask questions on any topic. Interpreting the response is where we often come unstuck. First of all, we need to be open to receiving a reply – sounds obvious? Well, maybe, but I've had people at workshops who claim they are longing for contact, but are then not open to receiving responses and are quite ambivalent when it comes to the point. We need to be physically, emotionally and spiritually aware and willing to pick up every clue, no matter how small, ludicrous or seemingly irrelevant it may seem. Don't expect that the response will come to you in words. It might be quite different. For example, you bump into a rack of books in a bookshop and a significant book falls on your foot; you or someone else makes a slip of the tongue that, when you think about it, is meaningful; you drop your keys and have difficulty retrieving them, then find that you've found the key to some issue; you forget to post a letter that you thought was important, then find that what you expressed in it needs to be rewritten; someone calls just when you're thinking of a new project and drops a nugget of information into your lap; you think of your new project and instead of pleasure you have a feeling of anxiety that makes you check your plan; you're wondering about your relationship and you find yourself feeling nauseous. None of these is a chance occurrence. They are all giving you guidance. The responsibility to interpret and act on the guidance you receive is yours.

Fairly recently I was sitting happily writing when my computer flagged up that I had a new e-mail. I opened it to find that someone had sent me an unsolicited horoscope reading for the day. Very strange. It said that as a Leo I might be inclined to try to do too much and spread myself too thinly and that the offer I had recently received, while on the face of it exciting and rewarding, didn't have to be accepted. I hadn't received any such offer and deleted the message but held it in my consciousness. Later that day I received a call from New York asking me to do a tour of five major cities in the USA about four months from now and in a specific time frame. My initial reaction was one of delight. I glanced at my diary and found that I could make the time schedule, but that it would give me only days to be home after a major tour and then have to set off again. I remembered the message of the morning and said I needed time to think and would call back. I finally replied saying that although I would have loved to do the tour, I really couldn't because the dates were not suitable for me. The conversation ended and I felt a mixture of sadness and relief. Thirty minutes later I received another call from the same person asking if we could negotiate a different time. I agreed to do it three months later at a time which was perfect for me. Had I not had the message that morning, I might well have simply accepted and pushed myself to do it. But had I done that, it would have been a decision made on the basis of fear that I might lose this fantastic opportunity. So this lesson highlights the soul / person-ality polarity. The choice was wisdom, trust and love versus fear and doubt. The fact that I had received guidance that I didn't need to accept the offer, led me to refuse it. And of course everything worked out perfectly.

On a different note . . .

Many years ago, I was feeling quite stuck with one of my patients who certainly didn't appear to be open to anything other than a strictly orthodox psychiatric approach and whose long-standing depression seemed resistant to any intervention. I was silently asking for some guidance when the message came very clearly that I should offer her a drink of water. Now, this is something that I would not normally do, especially on a cold afternoon in mid-December in London! However, trusting that there must be a reason, I asked her if she would like a glass of water, at which a startled look suddenly appeared on her face, followed by a flood of tears – the first since I had started to see her about three months earlier. It was our greatest breakthrough. She said that she suddenly remembered being in bed at the age of about three and getting up to get a drink of water, only to be smacked firmly by her father and put back to bed where she cried herself to sleep. She said that she had often been thirsty in the night but had never again dared to get up and ask for a drink. In fact she thought that since that time she had never really voiced her needs because she couldn't bear to have them denied. Thus she simply went along with whatever anyone else said while becoming angry and resentful inside. Our therapy had taken leaps forward and went on to be very successful.

VIBRATIONAL FREQUENCY

Thoughts, emotions and intentions are all brought about by changes in vibrational frequency within the energetic body and are often prompted by changes further distant from us in the UEF. Just be around someone who is negative and see what happens to your energy without their speaking a word – the vibrational frequency lowers and so does your energy as the whole atmosphere changes. Their negativity has a powerful effect, drawing away the energy that normally nourishes you and, if you're not careful, taking your personal energy too. Low-frequency emotions such as sadness, despair, anger, resentment and the fear that underlies them all reduces energy, makes us feel lethargic and makes everything feel heavy. Gossiping, complaining, seeing the worst in people, being suspicious and sarcastic are all ways in which we can reduce the frequency. When we remove ourselves from the light of our soul by negative thinking or behaviour, we move into the darkness, which allows negativity to gather into clumps of energy that we call evil. The absence of light can cause us to feel afraid, and the fear causes more low-frequency vibrations and exacerbates the situation even further. In the long term, living under such stress results in physical and/or emotional illness. (If you have someone who is chronically depressed and negative in your sphere, have a look at the wonderful book, *How You Can Survive When They're Depressed.*) Conversely, being sunny, optimistic and unconditionally loving, and having others similarly positive in your locale, can really boost your energy as high-vibrational frequencies are radiated into the atmosphere. Imagine what happens when someone smiles at you, touches your hand or radiates love. We can do a great deal for our health if we choose to create a positive reality by thinking positive thoughts and letting go of any negativity which only serves to damage us and those around us. Letting go of rigidly held ideas and opinions which obviously cause us pain and disharmony is the only wise way forward, while removing ourselves from negativity is a decision to honour ourselves and heal our souls and ultimately the world by improving the quality of light and love that we emit. Would you like to add that to your intention?

THE SOUL

Extending around the physical body are layers of light energy – the auric bodies – that are in constant motion and of a frequency so high that generally they are invisible to most people. We shall discuss them in more detail in Chapter 9.

In fact the auric bodies – usually simply referred to as the aura – are the light of our soul. Within the aura is an intricate system of channels and vortices of energy – the chakra system – which penetrates our physical body and allows us to be nurtured simultaneously by divine energy which enters at the top of the system via the higher chakras, and also by the energy of the earth which enters at the base of the system. All the chakras are essential to our health and well-being, since they ensure the circulation of energy from the UEF, bringing with it masses of information every second.

Julie Soskin in her beautifully channelled book *The Wind of Change* (Barton House, 1990) talks of the soul being our unique energy, each with its own light. Larry Dossey has defined the soul as some aspect of the psyche that is not subject to the limitations of space and time, and which may precede birth and survives death. Many have sought to describe this indescribable wonder. And me? Well, perhaps I shall try to do so by just giving you my perception of my own soul.

My soul is the purest essence of me, immortal, unique, immeasurable and capable of anything. It's the highest part that is still individually and uniquely me, and it gives my life richness, depth and meaning. From my heart which is at its very core, it connects me to the earth with joy, and lifts me to the heavens in ecstasy, soothing me and bringing me the utmost peace as it renders me simultaneously human and divine. It is my wisdom, my awareness, my courage, my devotion, my potential and all the gifts to which I aspire and also the memories of all that I have achieved in love, clarity and clear consciousness. When I'm in touch with it, it gently takes my breath away, leaves me in awe as I feed from it, exact every bit of meaning from it, wondering at the magic of the moment. It prompts me to live my life in gratitude and to encourage others, rejoicing in their happiness and success. It has travelled through a constant spiral of development and transformation since the beginning of time. It has lived in many forms, from the amorphous to the structured, and for thousands of years now it has been clothed in human bodies. It will continue on its journey until I finally reach enlightenment.

However, being aware of my soul is easy in the joyous things. What's sometimes harder is to remain in contact when it's painful and difficult, and when I seem to have lost my way or when I'm hurt, angry, sad and disappointed, when relationships go wrong and I feel betrayed. To be willing to listen even when I feel afraid to hear, and to allow myself to be dragged back out of the darkness into the light. And also to allow my soul lovingly and compassionately to recognize the souls of others even in their sadness, loss, frustration and anguish, and in behaviour which is neither attractive nor pleasant as they try to make sense of their suffering. This is my soul also.

IS OUR SOUL TRULY IMMORTAL?

That the soul is immortal is not a new belief. The scriptures talk of eternal life, referring to the immortality of the soul, not the body. As early as the fourth century BC Pythagoras wrote of the soul being separate from the body and that it would be finally reunited with God. Ancient cultures throughout the world have believed that the soul would be released from the body after death, and indeed from South America to Europe, Egypt to Greece, Africa to Australia, burial places have been found where there is evidence of rituals designed to help the soul leave or to prepare for its return.

If you're looking for substantial evidence of survival, there's a lot of it. If you're looking for indisputable proof, there may be none. But if you can listen with your soul you will have a deep and sure *knowing* of what is. Let that be both your guide and your 'proof'. But if you're still stumbling in the pain, grieving for loved ones, afraid of dying, fearful for one who has died, or just being healthily sceptical, then the evidence can be comforting, and an essential part of healing. Be patient and loving with yourself wherever on that scale you find yourself.

Most people who have lost a loved one may feel a presence – a sense of their departed being with them – at some time, usually fairly soon after their passing. It might be that suddenly quite powerfully they're in your mind, or you feel the hairs on the back of your neck tingle, smell their particular scent, hear a tune, suddenly need to turn round and look behind you, feel a warmth around your shoulders – or whatever. Something tells you that the person who has died is actually here in some form. Some people actually physically see their loved one as an apparition, though this is less common. Sometimes they come in 'dreams', though anyone who has had such an experience knows that this was no ordinary dream. If you have experienced any of these phenomena, please don't dismiss them as imagination. Those who love us and have departed will often try to comfort us, to let us know that they are here and that they have survived. Talking to them when you feel their presence can be a great comfort to you both. We'll look at this again in Chapter 5.

SO WHAT EVIDENCE IS THERE FOR THE SOUL'S SURVIVAL?

Here we're going to deal with four sources of information:

- Past-life work
- Near-death experiences

- Mediumship and channelling
- Instrumental Transcommunication

PAST-LIFE WORK

For me, the whole point of past-life work is to help people move on, to heal old wounds that still prevent them from enjoying their lives and fulfilling their potential. I have not researched my findings, which are purely anecdotal, though some of my patients have gone on to verify information later. The following is a typical experience.

Mary came to see me having had a whole series of difficult relationships. She'd also had a lot of 'treatment' that had left her feeling that she would never be able to lead a happy and normal life. A bright and effective young woman, and valued most of the time at work, she'd been urged to come to see me by her employer who was fast running out of options since occasionally Mary's behaviour was totally unacceptable.

Mary said that when she was without a boyfriend for a while, though she felt lonely, she was quite stable. But when a new man was on the scene, within a few weeks she slipped into a pattern of behaviour which she hated but seemed powerless to change. Each relationship began with high hopes and apparently good prospects, but very soon she would become possessive, then suspicious. Nights were initially spent on the phone with lots of seductive sexual talk which initially seemed to flatter and amuse the new conquest but eventually became a nuisance, and Mary would begin to detect the all-too-familiar nightmare of rejection. She would then escalate her behaviour in an attempt to seduce him further and cling on to what she had created, but only succeed in alienating him further. She would then call at ridiculous hours demanding attention, interrogating him about where he'd been and with whom, and trying to trick him with childish games. Although she understood very well that it was her behaviour that drove men away and that being distracted and lacking concentration at work was getting her into trouble, she was incapacitated by anxiety if she contemplated letting go of the need to control the man in her life. Mary's life appeared to have been stable with good parents who'd been married for nearly forty years. She had an elder brother with whom she had a good relationship, though he too was irritated with her behaviour and could see why the men she pestered wanted to run away. She had a good circle of supportive friends who were nevertheless also exasperated by her behaviour, and she was bright and loved her job.

At her very first consultation she was so anxious that her words came tumbling out in a torrent that was difficult to understand, and I suggested that she might like just to breathe with me for a few moments and relax a little so that we could talk about what was really going on. Within a very brief period, her exhaustion and the calm atmosphere of the consulting room prompted her to relax and within moments she had a cataleptic flutter of her eyelids indicating that she was going into a mild hypnotic trance. I asked her what was happening, and I have paraphrased her response, which was in the present tense.

She said she was a young married woman in Germany in the 1860s and that she adored her husband and their three children. Her only sadness was that as a merchant her husband had to spend so much time travelling away from home. One day while she and her husband were out together with their children, a man approached them very pleasantly, obviously recognizing her husband, though calling him by a different name. Her husband had acted strangely, telling the man he must be mistaken, and had hurried his family away, leaving the stranger gazing after them in amazement. Some months later she had seen this man in a shop and he had approached her, asking her name and what relationship she had with the man he had seen with her in the market square. She gave her name and said that the man must be mistaken in having thought he recognized her husband. He assured her that he had not, and that though he did not wish to cause her any distress, he knew her husband quite well – and also his wife and children who lived some miles away in the town he had recently left.

Over the next few months Mary did everything she could to prevent her husband from travelling, feigning illness, becoming sexually seductive and trying to please him in every way. When he was away she was miserable and constantly anxious for his return. She could no longer enjoy her home or her children, lost weight and became ill, harassing her husband with questions about his travelling and his work and becoming increasingly suspicious.

Unable to deal with the situation any longer, she finally went to look for the stranger who told her where her husband was said to live with another wife while he was away from home. She decided to go there while her mother cared for the children. In my room she became anxious and hyperventilated as she reported what she found. A young woman not unlike herself but heavily pregnant sat in the garden watching her two small children at play. Mary hid and waited and could hardly bear the pain when, a while later, her husband arrived and, scooping up the children, hugged them and carried the younger one into the house. Crying in my chair now, she described what followed as she finally summoned up the courage to go and knock at the door. Her husband opened it and blanched as he saw her. She fainted – and in that moment Mary sat upright in her chair, wide awake.

She looked at me open-mouthed, her mascara staining her face as tears continued to course down her cheeks.

'Was that real?' she asked. And before I had time to answer, she said, 'It was. I know it was!' Over the next few weeks in four more sessions we pieced together the rest of the story and had a look at how it related to Mary's current behaviour. She was once again trying to deal with her worst nightmare of being betrayed and abandoned, while her fierce control, clinging and manipulation forced the very thing she feared most. Healing of the feelings of abandonment and betrayal by her former husband, and also of the guilt and shame about her abandonment and betrayal of her children by ending that life by suicide helped her to forgive the past and those involved in it and allow herself to begin again in the present.

Mary's story is typical of many, some of which I shall share as we proceed. No one witnessing the cathartic nature of the session, the dramatic improvement in her current behaviour or her sense of relief could deny the reality that this was a past life in which the essence of Mary, her soul, had lived and died albeit in another body.

Many people either planning or stumbling spontaneously into past-life work initially do not believe that they have ever lived before. Sometimes, however, symptoms and behaviour patterns which have dogged people for years and which refuse to respond to any form of intervention suddenly disappear when they are viewed from this perspective. As we shall see in Chapter 9, most of the population of the world today believes in reincarnation – that is, that the soul survives death and is born again with another physical body. If we have indeed lived before in another body and find ourselves alive again in this one, we have strong evidence that our soul survived previously, and the likelihood is that it will survive again after this lifetime. That means that our departed loved ones have also survived.

BUT IF IT'S RESEARCH EVIDENCE YOU NEED . . .

There are many people who have dedicated their lives to researching such phenomena. Dr Brian Weiss, a fellow psychiatrist, has done thousands of past-life regressions and has published several books about his work which make fascinating reading. (Some are in the bibliography.) Dr Ian Stevenson, a psychiatrist at the University of Virginia, has spent the greater part of his professional life researching past-life memories of children, using strict scientific criteria. His research has taken him all over the world where he has interviewed over 3,000 children and their families plus, where possible, the family the child claims to have belonged to in a previous human lifetime. His results are outstanding and would leave most people in no doubt as to the fact that these children have lived before, died before and survive to tell the tale. In many cases they can recall the time of their most recent previous life, describe the mode of their death, family members and the home and surroundings in which they lived. Occasionally they have been found to speak the language of another culture and may in some cases also exhibit customs that are foreign to their current family but most definitely a part of the culture they claim to have belonged to. Many of these children are very young – four years or younger – and could not possibly have gleaned the information from any physical source. Usually the life to which they refer is very recent – reincarnation appears to have occurred within ten years or so – and ended in violent death. Dr Stevenson has also recorded birthmarks borne by these children commensurate with the fatal injuries they describe. Some of these children exhibit behaviour that would correspond with a period of continuous development, for example sexual behaviour appropriate to an adult but not to a child. Most of them (like me) start to be aware of a past life at a very early age. Often they then stop talking about it and appear to forget it till much later, picking up the strands again in adulthood.

Perhaps one of the most compelling studies is that of Helen Wambach in the 1970s. Following a spontaneous past-life experience of her own, she set off to research the phenomenon, regressing over 1,000 people, usually in groups. She asked various questions, the answers to which could be verified in many cases, such as details of clothing worn, food eaten, etc. at the time of the previous life studied. Wambach was able to find out a good deal about the death experience and also about birth and the soul phase in her study and we shall come back to some of that in Chapter 9.

CRITICISMS AND THEORIES ABOUT PAST-LIFE WORK

Much criticism has been levelled at past-life therapy, some claiming that the 'memories' are not memories at all, but a mixture of current life data, stored geographical and historical information and fantasy woven together, any gaps being filled in so that the whole makes sense rather in the way that someone suffering dementia might confabulate. Those who pose this theory believe that we are born with no memory and that any memory we do have must therefore have come from this lifetime. This is called cryptoamnesia. Another theory is that we can dip into the collective unconscious theorized by Carl Jung and tap into some experience which is not necessarily our own. There is also the possibility of a time slip, where suddenly we find ourselves very vividly in a different time and can observe what is happening. Rosemary Altea (*Proud Spirit*, Eagle Brook Morrow, 1997) claims that she believes in survival after death and also in reincarnation though not in past lives. She is very scathing of those who do claim past-life experience, theorizing that they are in fact allowing their body to be used by some other soul who needs to re-enact their death experience in order to come to terms with it. None of these theories accounts for the emotional content, and the person's subjective knowing that what they are experiencing is their own, that there is a sense of personal involvement.

Also there is always profound meaning, which makes sense of current life issues. The emotional content of a past-life regression has to be experienced to be believed, despite the fact that afterwards the therapist is often asked the question, as in Mary's case, as to whether the experience was real or did the client make it all up. Another criticism levelled at past-life therapy is that 'Every woman thinks she was Cleopatra'! In fact one organizer of metaphysical workshops refuses to deal with any past-life therapist, including me, because of that very thing. Ah well!

In my practice, having conducted hundreds of past-life regressions, often with people who are celebrities in this life, I have only twice come across someone famous (never Cleopatra!) in the past life. Interestingly, one very humble lady who had previously lived as a famous aristocrat in England in the twelfth century, had such a sense of shock at what she discovered that for a while she refused to say what she had seen despite the fact that she was aware that I already knew. In the other instance the client was a child who could not quite name the person he had been in his past life, though I could.

NEAR-DEATH EXPERIENCES

Perhaps the near-death experience (NDE) has given us more information than any other about the process of 'dying'. Oddly named, this term refers to the phenomenon of being pronounced clinically dead, with absence of any vital signs, and then returning to life either spontaneously or after resuscitation. We shall discuss it further in Chapter 6. Partly due to medical advancement and improved methods of resuscitation, more people than ever before are able to make that journey back from what previously would have been absolute physical death, their soul having survived. They are able to report quite amazing things, such as the procedure in the room or at the site of an accident where they suffered apparently fatal trauma, or what was happening in other geographical areas that they could not possibly have physically witnessed. Not everyone who has been resuscitated speaks of an NDE – some come back with nothing but a blank in their memory for the time that was lost. The vast majority of those who do have an NDE, however, have found the experience a positive one (reports vary but appear to be around 85 per cent), and even those for whom it may have been frightening mostly report that life changed radically and positively after the experience. Those who have had such an experience describe it in remarkably similar terms and thousands of accounts have resulted in a picture emerging which may vary somewhat but has common elements. I mention it here because it has given us so much information and very strong evidence that the soul continues to live independent of the dying body, and this in itself has brought hope to many who are dying or who have lost a loved one.

NEAR-DEATH EXPERIENCES ARE NOT NEW

In ancient Egypt each new king was thought to be a direct reincarnation of the god Osiris. This was tested by sealing the initiate god-king in a sarcophagus until, starved of oxygen, he had a near-death experience. This ritual was carried out in the Great Pyramid by a group of priests and pharaohs and was known as the cult of Osiris. When the lid of the sarcophagus was opened after about eight minutes, the person was revived by the rush of air and then described what had happened to him. These descriptions, recorded in the *Egyptian Book of the Dead*, are similar to those described after near-death experience today. The *Aztec Song of the Dead* is a poetic version of near-death experience recorded by initiates in the Aztec civilization. In the sixth century Pope Gregory the Great collected records of near-death experiences as proof of life after death.

MEDIUMSHIP AND CHANNELLING

A medium is someone who has the capacity to receive and transmit messages from the souls of those who have made their transition fairly recently – usually within the last fifty years or so. Some mediums are extremely gifted, though sometimes of course the message gets lost or distorted in the interpretation. Some are clairvoyant (they see clearly without a physical stimulus) and can see the souls of the departed, while others are clairaudient (they hear clearly without a physical stimulus) and can hear them. Some receive messages in words, and others in symbols. Some report a stream of *knowing* with no actual sound or vision, but an increased awareness, while others use all modalities. When I practise mediumship, which I don't do very often, I receive fully formed messages in which I have a definite impression of the tone of voice, the mood and the power of the message, sometimes with a considerable amount of humour. The soul will often change course during the reading, giving messages of love and comfort, suggesting that loved ones look for a particular object or remember an incident that only they shared. Then sometimes the mood will change and a message comes through from the soul now in the mantle of a powerful ancient being rather than the personality the family remembers. When this happens I'm aware that the departed one had some very special work to do, both here and in the soul plane, and that those who are left here are somehow to carry on that work. Often this happens in the case of young people who have made their transition. The souls of children and adolescents will often deliver extremely powerful messages, perhaps about how they came to teach medicine as the result of the illness from which they passed, and what they want their parents to do now. Sometimes they bring messages for named medical practitioners who have worked with them and who have got to know them well. Almost always they bring their parents messages of comfort about their earthly work having been complete and having only come for a brief time. But always there is evidence of survival.

The message can only be as good as the conduit by which it is perceived and transmitted. Sometimes there is distortion in the reception and sometimes the soul one hopes will come and give a message simply doesn't appear. Occasionally people come along expecting to have something like a telephone conversation with the person who has passed, but it's not usually like that.

Channelling is somewhat different. In clearing our chakras from base to crown, we can open a channel through which we can ask to receive information, wisdom, call it what you will, from sources other than those who have recently passed on. In channelling we usually ask for the highest wisdom, the highest healers, the highest teachers or the highest masters to use us as a conduit, and the information that we receive is often not of a personal nature but more to do with global issues, the universe, humanity or other galaxies. There are some very famous channels such as Sanaya Roman and Duane Packer whose channelled books, *Spiritual Growth, Living with Joy* (Sanaya Roman only) and *Opening to Channel* are among the most beautiful, loving and easy-to-read channelled works. Many others, such as the late Jane Roberts, who channelled Seth, and Ruth White, who channels Gildas, have added greatly to the wisdom and knowledge we have about the universe. More recently there is Glenda Green who channelled *Love without End* and of course Neale Donald Walsch with *Conversations with God*, Books 1,2 and 3. Though the last two move us away somewhat from evidence of survival, this discussion would not be complete without mentioning them.

CHOOSING A MEDIUM, CLAIRVOYANT OR CHANNEL

None of these skills should be used as a party game! If you do need some help and would like to seek the advice of a medium, clairvoyant or channel, choose carefully. As with most things, personal recommendation is probably best. It is best to go to see someone like this when you're feeling physically and emotionally well if possible, rather than at times of great distress and trauma, though I'm aware that it is often when we are most vulnerable, for instance after a loved one has made their transition or when we feel in inner turmoil, that we look for quick answers and comforting messages. However, this is part of a developmental process and you need to be well enough to be present and discerning.

Here are some pointers you might like to keep in mind:

- The experience should be pleasant, empowering, energizing and inspiring.
- You should feel comfortable with this person and equal to him or her.
- There should be no insistence that you follow some particular direction or change in any way – although advice may be given, it should leave plenty of room for personal choice.
- The atmosphere should be warm, compassionate and understanding.

- There should be no criticism of you, implied or otherwise.
- If there is a lot of jargon, as a rough rule of thumb there's probably a lot of ego too, and for me that's always suspect.
- Showmanship is unnecessary – this is a therapeutic service, not a pantomime!
- Asking questions is fine, though sometimes you'll be asked to wait till the end of the session to do so rather than break the communication in full flow.
- Dates and times are usually so approximate that many prefer not to give any.
- People who are inspired to do the best of this work have also done their own inner work and are therefore well grounded, loving and creative. Despite their heavy workload they are usually organized and finely tuned.
- Good mediums will rarely if ever intrude upon anyone by launching into readings that are uninvited. (I was appalled one evening while at a dinner party in a restaurant when a woman got up from the table and started to wander around behind everyone giving them 'healing' and 'readings' – this between the main course and the dessert! Not for me, I'm afraid. Although I may be being judgmental here, I think there was more ego than healing going on.)
- Ideally a medium will give you what you need to stimulate your own intuitive process rather than proving their capabilities by providing you with every detail.

There are some fascinating incidents where otherwise very ordinary people channel information from the souls of those who have passed away. People from all walks of life visit mediums and channels and receive comforting personal information from their departed loved ones. Sometimes what is channelled is for a wider audience. I have chosen just a couple to report here.

In the 1930s, a medium, Eileen Garrett, channelled information from the captain of a British airship which had crashed the previous day and in which the captain and crew had been killed. The information she reported was to prove correct in every detail and enabled technological difficulties in the design of the airship to be corrected. In the 1960s, in England, Rosemary Brown, an ordinary woman with no prior musical training, began to write wonderful music. She reported having had a 'dream' when she was small in which a man told her that she would be 'visited' by musical masters and would continue to write their music. Years later, she saw a picture of Franz Liszt, recognized him as the man from her childhood dream, went home and without thought or preparation wrote a symphony perfectly in his style! Other musicians followed until Rosemary had written compositions directly channelled from Chopin, Debussy, Rachmaninov, Beethoven, Brahms and Bach. In Chapter 7 we shall be looking at how souls often continue their work in the astral world.

INSTRUMENTAL TRANSCOMMUNICATION (ITC)

In the 1950s, in the USA, Italy and Sweden, voices were recorded on audiotape which appeared to come from nowhere. Some years later, video recordings were made. In the mid-1980s, pioneers Friedrich Jurgenson, a film producer in Sweden, and Konstantin Raudive, a Latvian psychologist living in Germany, using a variety of equipment including computers, video recorders, radio receivers and televisions, recorded similar voices and visual images, usually clips of no more than a couple of seconds' duration, purporting to be the voices and images of people who had died. They termed this Instrumental Transcommunication. Collectively known as the Raudive Voices, they included such people as Sir Winston Churchill, Adolf Hitler, President John F. Kennedy and Tolstoy. Initially they were thought to be a hoax, but as time has gone on more and more messages have been received, often giving very convincing information that could only have been known by the person claiming to share it now. Though the voices were strange, with unusual syntax, the messages appeared to be important none the less. After his death, the voice of Raudive himself was recorded by his colleagues. Visual images were usually of photographs which had been taken earlier, and the voices explained that since they now had no visual form, this was the only way to identify themselves. The voices claimed that they had all lived on earth, and that as souls they were still alive, but in a different dimension. They talked of the astral world as the true reality. We shall discuss the astral world further in Part II. More recently, researchers in the USA and Europe have recorded voices the patterns of which have been compared where possible with recordings made when the personalities were alive. In all cases voice patterns were found to be similar. In the late 1980s the Cercle d'Etudes sur la Transcommunication (Study Circle in Transcommunication) was set up to research the phenomenon and in 1988 the Timestream project came into being, following instruction received purportedly from the astral world. This claims to have as its advisers in the astral world Friedrich Jurgenson, Konstantin Raudive, Thomas Edison and the British explorer Sir Richard Burton. In 1995 the International Network for Instrumental Transcommunication was set up and the work continues.

Much of what has been reported has been the subject of criticism and ridicule; the researchers have been accused of setting up an elaborate hoax or being the naive victims of such. However, many of the people involved in this work are dedicated to forwarding our knowledge and as such deserve our respect. Leonardo da Vinci had similar problems! Those of us who are genuinely interested in forging links with the astral world await developments, perhaps with a critical and sceptical eye and with feet well on the ground, but also with the willingness to be open to new and convincing evidence.

Remember, one of the suggestions in setting our intention was that we should simply be open to new truths and possibilities.

SO WHAT ABOUT SPIRIT?

Although 'soul' and 'spirit' are often used synonymously, they are not the same. By tradition, however, the discarnate soul may often be referred to as a spirit, and I may use it in that context myself later. However, Spirit (note the capital S) is what we might also refer to as the oversoul, or what the philosopher Plotinus called the World Soul. It is what we may refer to as God. It is whole, continuous and constant, manifesting everywhere as creation, uniting our souls in shared awareness, vision and experience. It is the purest of awareness, the knowledge, the truth, the collective, the superconscious, the wisdom of the ages and the universal energy which holds us all in unity. It is that from which our souls are derived. It is that to which we shall finally return as fully enlightened souls. It resonates to love.

UNION BETWEEN SOUL AND SPIRIT – THE TRANSCENDENT EXPERIENCE

Although after many journeys of the soul we are finally reunited with Spirit, we can achieve that union temporarily even here on earth. This union is the transcendent experience, as, with our bodies fully grounded in our humanity, we learn to open our crown and reach the Divine. It's the highest and most pure experience of which we're capable while remaining in human form, one of the greatest joys of life which changes our lives forever as it becomes an integral part of our spiritual life. Through transcendence we can glimpse the bliss of heaven, and know the purest love that fills us and surrounds us and radiates from us as we become, even if only for a moment, part of the body of God. In this moment we are whole. Transcendence is an experience that I can only describe as having an orgasm with life. This union is what I call living in love with God. Sometimes it occurs spontaneously and without warning, perhaps when listening to music, reading poetry, walking in a forest or even watching a film that inspires us. Sometimes it happens during meditation, or even at times of illness or crisis. We can also learn to have this experience at will. We only have to breathe, get grounded, be aware of our humanity, then gently but purposefully open our cleared chakras and ascend till we feel ourselves gently bump the supreme superconscious and feel it reach out and embrace us. Suddenly we're home, we flow into the Spirit and become part of it again. Held at the breast of the great consciousness, we're nurtured, loved, cherished, re-energized and eventually released again to return to our humanity where for the moment, by our own choice, we belong.

DRUG-INDUCED TRANSCENDENCE

Drugs such as Ecstasy, LSD and MIAA have been reported to precip-itate transcendental experiences, but once ex-drug users have been taught to transcend, they will invariably report that the experience is different and more satisfying without the use of drugs. Working on our chakras, purifying our aura, living in love and gratitude so that our light shines around us clears the path to transcendence. We need nothing more.

Throughout this book we shall be constantly expanding our understanding of our soul and its quest finally to return home. I hope that you may now see that there is consider-able evidence that the essence of you has survived for centuries and that the likelihood is that you – and your loved ones – will continue to survive long after this earthly life-time.

✿ AFFIRMATION

I am a beloved child of the universe, here for another season. Immortal and invincible, I survive.

✿ MEDITATION

The following meditation will help you feel the connection with your soul, and as you become more able to relax into it, you may be able to have a transcendent experience. Go to the sacred space that you have prepared. Have with you your flowers, a candle and perhaps a crystal and make yourself comfortable in your chair, on your cushion or meditation stool. Have with you all that you will need – some water, your journal and pen – and take the phone off the hook, giving yourself about forty-five minutes of undisturbed time.

Take a deep breath and breathe all the way out and as you do so let your body relax. Let your shoulders fall and your chair take your weight and allow anything negative to flow out through the soles of your feet and your root chakra. Take another deep breath and this time allow white light to pour in through the top of your head, shining down now through every cell of your body, cleansing, healing and balancing as anything you no longer need simply discharges into the earth from the soles of your feet and your root chakra. Relax.

In this moment allow yourself to feel the gentle touch of the unseen forces that are around you, loving you, holding you tenderly. Know that your guardian angel is close by and that you are being gently held. You are a beloved child of the universe and very valuable in the sight of the Sprit of whom you are a part. Though your soul separated to be unique and wander to experience the Earth, in many ways you have never been separated at all. Allow your chakras to open gently now. Your root chakra spinning with ruby-red light down and down into the earth, holding you secure, forever grounded into its loving embrace. Your sacral chakra opening to reveal its orange translucent light spinning and spinning as you feel your inner balance, feel your powerful sexuality and feel your masculine and feminine principles coming together in their eternal cosmic dance. Move your focus to your solar plexus, as it in turn gently opens, spinning its yellow light all around you. Feel your power now and know that you are a great being with unlimited potential, and the will and motivation to become all that you can be. Now let your heart chakra open and allow love and compassion to flow into the space around you, creating more and more love, cherishing you in this moment as your humanity and divinity come into perfect balance. Your throat chakra now opens, spreading its blue light, and you feel your creativity rise. Your communication becomes clearer. You know that if you were to decide to speak right now you would be articulate in truth and integrity. Your brow now opens to show its indigo light clarifying your vision so that you can see your path and visualize your way in the world. And now your crown, opening up shining white as light pours forth from you, higher and higher, up and up until you feel the gentle touch of the source, Spirit. Pause and simply savour the moment as with one healing breath you feel yourself mingle with the Divine. Allow your self to rise gently through your crown, becoming expanded and limitless, at one with the Divine, being held in the gentle embrace of the universe. Know that you are held simultaneously by the earth and the cosmos. With the gentlest of breath now expand further and feel your soul mingling with Spirit. Breathe very gently and allow yourself simply to hold the experience without grasping or control. Just be. When you are ready you may if you wish ask for the highest wisdom, the highest guidance, the highest teacher, guide or master to come to you now. Open your awareness and just be. Know that whether or not you perceive a presence, the masters are there when in reverence we call. If you wish, ask something now — about your previous existence, your survival or the survival of others. Allow yourself time simply to let information, ideas and symbols drop into your open consciousness. Collect them without thought or criticism. Let them simply be there and you will remember them. Let another piece of information or another symbol enter and know that the meaning will be clear later if not now. Just be. Allow yourself as long as you wish without expectation or demand, just remaining open to whatever you are ready for and whatever is ready for you. Know that there will only be loving communication, only gentle messages, nothing harmful or negative can enter. You are primed with love to attract only the most loving and pure of energy.

Just be for as long as you wish and then, when you are ready, send a wave of gratitude. No matter if you feel that little has happened. It surely has. Your guardian angel and other loving beings are gathered around you. Now, with the gentlest of breaths, start to return into your body through your crown chakra and visualize yourself taking up the shape of your body, the limitations of your physical being. Feel yourself totally and comfortably fully inside your body. Feel your chakras again one by one. Adjust so that your chakras are perceived in their rightful place. See the colours around you again. Check once again that you are fully within your body, your root chakra spinning deeply into the earth. Send your attention down through your root chakra and know that you are at one with the planet, human and grounded whilst simultaneously part of the Divine. Now gently close your crown chakra, ensuring that you are fully present here. Now your brow and then your throat. Now your heart, gently, gently. And now your solar plexus, then your sacral chakra, but leave your root chakra open and spinning down into the earth. You are free but simultaneously attached to and supported by the strong robust energy of the earth.

When you are ready and feel fully present, take a long breath and feel your fingers and your toes, then gently open your eyes. Have a stretch and a drink of water, then record everything that happened in your journal.

✪ PRAYER

Let us know that the Divine is always waiting for us, holding out a hand in welcome, all we need to do is raise our vibration and be willing to reach out. Let us reach out with love and compassion in the human world – touching another heart is touching the hand of God. Let us reach out with courage, being willing to defend our values while granting others the peace and freedom to have their own. Let us reach out to help those who have stumbled and pick ourselves up after we ourselves have fallen, and find a better way. Let us reach out by refusing to judge. All is in divine order and in this moment let the unseen forces of the universe hold us in the palm of their hand and never let go.

2   BECOMING HUMAN

Your children are not your children. They are the sons and daughters of the longing of life itself.

Khalil Gibran, *The Prophet*

Now that we know we have survived for eons, we could tap in to our *Journey of the Soul* at any point on the amazing ascending spiral of life, whether here or on the soul plane; a thousand years ago or at this moment. However, in this chapter I have chosen to begin at a point shortly before incarnation, at the preparation for pregnancy and the mystery of how we arrived here – the mystery of birth – so that we can examine the process of becoming a human being. Although our journey is a spiritual one, I wish to address practical issues too – for while we are here being human, with a physical body, emotions and a mind, they deserve consideration, especially since they reflect our soul. In some parts of this chapter I shall appear to be addressing women only, and what's more women who are pregnant or even in labour. Please forgive me for this and adapt if you're the father, a relative or friend, or if you are reading this and are not planning a pregnancy.

Women who are pregnant are at the epicentre of creation and this wondrous time deserves great respect and honour. However, there was a time when women would approach childbirth with terror almost every year of their reproductive life. The maternal death rate was extremely high, mainly due to infection (often spread unwittingly by birth attendants) and haemorrhage, and each pregnancy carried risk, not only for the mother but also for her other children who could be left motherless. Even if the birth was successful, the fact that pregnancy occurred year after year left women exhausted, their immune systems depleted and vulnerable to opportunist infections. There are still areas in the world where mothers are fearful of pregnancy – not only in the so-called Third World countries, but also in the highly developed ones. For instance, in the southern states of America care is not available to all women, and in other places women still die believing that they were cursed to give birth in pain and possibly forfeit their lives in the process.

In the 1960s, when I had both of my children, the technocratic age had not reached its peak. Nevertheless, some of the most sacred moments of my life and those of my children were lost amidst a flurry of commands, drips, machinery, bright lights and people talking over me as though I didn't exist. During the birth of my son, the obligatory and recurrent interference with this most natural process was at best disempowering, as I was told what to do with my body, its natural instincts being overruled until someone else decided what was appropriate. Almost four years later, when I birthed my daughter, things were slightly different, but again after a long and arduous labour, I was so medicated at the moment of delivery that I had to struggle up through layers of hazy consciousness to reach her before she was whisked off to be sanitized and dumped in a cold metal basin to be weighed. Only when she was dressed and wrapped in a blanket did I have her to hold, and I remember trying to get through layers of cloth to look at her and touch her skin, to be told in no uncertain terms that it would be my fault if she caught cold! The spirituality of the moment was lost – if ever it had been acknowledged – to everyone but my baby and me.

Imagine my joy when twenty years later in London I met two wonderful young spiritual midwives who had stepped out of the stranglehold of their training and were supervising water births in the homes of women who chose to take back the power of giving birth. They talked with such respect of the women they worked with, and of the honour and privilege of witnessing the love between the mother and her partner as they held each other, danced, breathed, laughed and cried through the hours of labour. Both were fully involved on every level. The partner would help to keep the water temperature stable, do back-rubbing and neck-massaging, hold hands on the contracting uterus and feed light snacks and cool drinks. And at the moment of delivery, these beautiful midwives would simply watch and wait, ready to take charge if necessary, but trusting that in the soft and gentle atmosphere, with low light and sometimes soft music and candles, this powerful and amazing being – a woman labouring to birth her child – instinctively knew the way. The holiness of the moment was never missed.

Deborah Jackson, in her beautiful book *With Child* (Chronicle Books, 1999) points out that birth and mothering have been reduced by medical science to a series of chemical reactions and physical cues to which the mother is simply expected to respond. However, in many parts of the world the tradition of birthing is still practised according to time-honoured ancient matriarchal wisdom, with women who have borne children taking care of other women in childbirth. Since at the time when birth became a medical event, only men were allowed to study and practise medicine, men took over as the attendants to birthing women.

Midwives, often the natural healers, were no longer able to practise legally, although many of them continued to do so, albeit surreptitiously, by popular demand. Along with the medicalization of birth came much of the equipment we now associate with the modern delivery room. But sadly, the gentleness and sanctity of the birth process is often now lost.

Thankfully we are in the midst of a revolution, and women are taking back their power, both those who are birthing and the women who are called to help them – the midwives. There *is* a place for medical care, of course. Although infant mortality rates are nothing to be proud of even now, medical care has done much to reduce them. Maternal mortality has been greatly reduced too. But, as is often the case in medicine, we seem to have gone too far and lost the plot! Our aim needs to be to help mothers to give birth safely, not to take over the whole procedure and treat the mother as though she were merely the convenient container from which the child is to be extricated. On a soul level, women know how to have babies, although of course it's good to have someone who can skilfully and lovingly care for them stand by to help if need be.

Let's look at what happens through pregnancy and birth.

PREPARATION FOR PREGNANCY

Although our emotions, attitudes, nutritional status, customs and beliefs are always reflected in our state of health, this is never more so than in pregnancy. It would be ideal if all prospective parents could spend some time sorting out their own health and the personal aspects of the relationship into which the baby is to be born. This includes dealing with issues of their own birth and childhood, and unresolved feelings about any earlier pregnancy. Dealing with our own birth issues either by regression, hypnosis, psychotherapy or psychodrama is a very good preparation for pregnancy for both parents! Any old traumas, expectations and fears can be gently released and replaced with positive expectations and affirmations to prepare the way for a good outcome this time. Ideally the mother needs to be well and happy so that there can be an uninterrupted flow of energy and love that will facilitate the amazing physical, emotional and spiritual changes that are to happen during the pregnancy. While actively building another human body inside her, she needs to be able to give attention to herself and the growing child, and not have the flow blocked by anything negative. Preconceptual care can ensure that both you and your partner are in good health, physically, emotionally and spiritually before you conceive, and primes you as you prepare the home that your baby will inhabit for the first nine months of its life.

It is not unusual to be carrying painful memories of one pregnancy and to dump these on the new child. May had a longstanding problem with which to deal at the start of her second pregnancy.

May was a beautiful woman of forty-two who was three months pregnant, her first child having been born almost ten years before. May had been determined that she would never have another child since the birth of her daughter, Beth, had left them both so traumatized. She became my patient initially within six months of Beth's birth, when she was depressed and angry, awaiting a perineal repair, and feeling cheated out of what should have been a wonderful experience. She had a list of things that had gone wrong: she had not been attended by the midwife she had got to know well during her pregnancy; her own doctor who had been in favour of a home birth was on holiday, and his locum was most unhappy that a thirty-two-year-old primagravida (a woman with a first pregnancy) was to be delivered at home; May had wanted to have little, if any, medication, but had been quite roughly informed that having an intravenous line open was a safety precaution and that should her labour not progress quickly enough she would be given Pitocin to help the uterus contract. Her husband was with her throughout, but she had also wanted her mother present. She was told that one companion was enough and that she could choose either her husband or her mother. She'd had a rough forceps delivery while effectively tied to a bed, when instinctively she wanted to walk about and squat to deliver the baby. She had hoped to cut the cord herself but someone else did it. She asked that the baby be with her at all times, but Beth was taken out of sight for examination and brought back bathed and blanketed, despite the fact that May had asked to massage in Beth's vernix (the white creamy substance on the baby's skin). Although she breast-fed Beth, she became aware, quite by chance, that the nurses would sometimes give the baby glucose drinks, expressly against May's wishes. The huge episiotomy had not healed well and she and her husband had not been able to make love since Beth's birth because of the continuing pain. The list was endless. No wonder she was angry!

Very sensibly she had come to me early in this pregnancy to deal with the feeling of anger, fear and powerlessness that had resurfaced. She wanted to be as sure as she could that she would have much more control this time and not feel like a bystander at the birth of her second baby. Interestingly, there were also issues about her own birth that had recently arisen, and she needed to deal with these too. Ideally these might have been better dealt with before she became pregnant, but it's never too late.

By the time of the delivery, May was feeling much more in control, having healed her old wounds and had the opportunity to discuss her fears with her new consultant. The birth was natural and required little intervention and she was delighted to feel that she had truly laboured to produce her child and was able to breast-feed.

It has been shown that the experience of our birth has a great effect on our emotional and psychological development, and there can be long-term benefit for ourselves and our children in healing any scarring and integrating our experience. Since giving birth is potentially one of the most amazing, fulfilling and spiritual moments of your life, it's worth investing some time in preparation. This includes taking time to talk to your doctor about what you can expect, making decisions about the kind of birth you'd like, where you would like to have it and with whom (see later) and policy on drugs and intervention.

UNPLANNED AND UNWANTED PREGNANCIES

Slightly less than half of all pregnancies in the Western world are unplanned; the majority are due to failure or lack of contraception. Almost half of all American women have had an abortion before the age of forty-five. Although many women may feel unready for pregnancy, that the time is not right, or that they are unprepared physically, emotionally and spiritually, often these unplanned pregnancies can have the most wonderful outcomes provided concerns are addressed while there is time. It's been said that there is no such thing as an unwanted baby. Many women who are unable to bear their own children have been chosen by the reincarnating soul to be adoptive parents. There is a poignant moment in the film *The Glenn Miller Story* (RCA, 1953) where, having accepted that his wife is unable to bear children, Glenn Miller says that there are two children out there somewhere who are nevertheless theirs. Adopted children have chosen to bring gifts to two sets of parents and the lives of the adoptive family can be transformed by this wondrous blessing. However, for many women the consequences of having a child are simply too much to contemplate, and termination becomes their choice. In the last fifty years we have moved from the back-street abortion with its serious complications and high death rate, to termination almost on demand. The debate concerning the rights of the mother and those of the unborn child has raged unabated for many years. Approximately half of the women choosing abortion feel nothing but relief afterwards. However, the other half may pay highly in terms of sadness, guilt and regret. A small percentage of those women who feel that abortion is akin to murder still choose it in preference to what they perceive will be the dire consequences of having a child. It's often these women who suffer for years in a variety of ways – whether they're unable to relax and enjoy sex, or to conceive, or to feel worthy of the continuing love of their partner. Sadly, many relationships between loving partners who for some reason have had to make the decision to abort their child, flounder on the rocks of guilt. In the end, however, it is worth remembering that the choice was not only that of the mother and father but also of the soul of the child. If there has been agreement on a soul level between the mother and the child that this baby will not be carried to term, then the decision is already made. Neither abortion nor miscarriage harms the soul, which may return to incarnate within the body of another child of its chosen parents. It's part of the learning process for all. If you're still carrying some pain about a past abortion, and if you're having difficulty in conceiving, see the meditation on page 51 which will help you to contact the soul of your child, clear the loss, and allow you to forgive yourself so that you can get on with your life.

PROBLEMS WITH CONCEPTION

In *Total Wellbeing* (Hodder & Stoughton, 1999) Dr Hilary Jones and I dealt with this issue at length, and perhaps you would like to refer to that book. Most women get pregnant relatively easily, but for some it can take quite a while, often somewhere between six months and two years. Probably one in six couples in the UK have trouble conceiving, and women over thirty-five who have not become pregnant after six months of trying might like to take some advice. Having the natural desire to have a child and being unable to conceive is both painful and frustrating, leaving many women devoid of the joy of making love just because it feels good, a crowning of the love between them and their partners. Instead, sex becomes the outcome of a great deal of strategic planning, with only the desired goal of conception in mind. Be aware that there are many blessings in every moment, and if for some reason you are not to mother a child in this lifetime, and if mothering is important to you, perhaps there is a child somewhere who has chosen you as an adoptive mother. Perhaps the last thing you want to hear is to relax! But it is an old well-told truth that often conception occurs when the woman has finally accepted that she is not going to get pregnant. There is more chance of that happening when you start to live a more balanced, fulfilled and creative life. However, even if in this lifetime you are not to give birth to a child, remain aware of your inner creativity and power. Women are at the very root of the creative process, and whether or not we have children, as women, we're still creating a new world in every moment.

NESTING

It's not only birds and animals that experience the nesting instinct! Many women will recall having a burst of energy shortly before or even during labour, when they feel compelled to clean the house and tidy cupboards. For most prospective parents, preparing the baby's room is part of the nesting process. Sometimes problems with conceiving can also be due to the mother's need to feel that the nest is ready. There's an old saying, 'New house, new baby' – and certainly some of us will remember subconsciously delaying conception until we were in the home that felt right. I'm not suggesting that you can solve your problems by going out and buying a new home, but you could certainly test the hypothesis by creating a new atmosphere in the one you have. Could you change the energy by moving furniture, placing things differently, playing music, lighting candles and burning incense? Is the atmosphere conducive to welcoming a new soul? Do you need to change the way you treat your home, get rid of clutter and make it feel secure? Do you need to plant a garden? Is there a space you can make sacred and go there sometimes and talk to the hovering soul of your baby – even before you get pregnant? Follow your intuition and you'll always be right.

CLEARING OLD BUSINESS – CONTACTING THE SOUL OF A PREVIOUSLY LOST CHILD

Whether you've lost a child through stillbirth, abortion, perinatal death, cot death, childhood disease or trauma, there are often lingering feelings of sadness and guilt, anger and fear, and a sense of unworthiness about having another child. These can get in the way of you feeling empowered to conceive or give birth, even years later. Sometimes it's even difficult to have a loving relationship.

Beatrice had had a child at the age of fourteen. In many ways naïve and innocent, she had not acknowledged the pregnancy until she was five months pregnant. Her boyfriend then attracted the attention of the police, and her strongly religious family sent her away to a convent to have the baby, who was to be adopted immediately. In the event, the baby was stillborn. The reaction of both the nurses and the family was that it was a blessing that the child had died, and Beatrice was quickly sent home where the incident was never again mentioned though she was banned from seeing the equally young father of the child. Beatrice found herself isolated, alone and filled with both guilt and grief for which there appeared to be neither outlet nor remedy. She had immersed herself in work and had little social life, still living at home with her parents, caring for them and assuming that she would never marry. Now, twenty-five years later, a kind and loving man with whom she had worked for some years had fallen in love with her, but Beatrice felt constantly unworthy and fearful of his suggestion that they start to think of marriage and having a family.

In the course of her treatment we decided to have a ritual during which she would contact the soul of her child, forgive herself and let go of the pain she'd carried all these years. Once this was finally released, Beatrice's whole life changed, and at last she was able to learn to love herself enough to feel worthy of being loved.

Lee had similar difficulties.

At twenty-eight Lee had been a very happy young mother, in love with her husband and ecstatic to have a little girl, Elizabeth, who everyone commented was very special. Lee could hardly contain her pain while relating to me how Elizabeth had been playing in the garden one minute and the next Lee had heard the screech of brakes and screams. She described being almost suspended in time as she watched from outside herself as her body ran out into the road and picked up the body of her dying child, and heard herself scream from somewhere apparently in the distance. Elizabeth did not recover, and neither had Lee. Over the next three years she had been depressed and angry – angry with herself and angry with God. But the worst thing was the guilt that had eventually destroyed everything. She was unable to allow any intimacy between herself and her husband Ron, who, despite his pain and shock, was endlessly supportive and loving. Eventually however, Lee's projected guilt drove them apart, and with much sadness on both sides the marriage ended, although they continued to be supportive friends. She had never forgiven herself for not supervising the child better. Now some years later Ron was happily remarried with another daughter, and Lee was in a relationship with Tim, a loving man who wanted to marry her and have a family. Despite a healthy sexual relationship and lack of contraception, Lee had not become pregnant, and since she was now forty both she and Tim had undergone investigations, but no physical cause for the secondary infertility had been found. Lee had never completed the business with Elizabeth's soul. We decided upon a ceremony to help her to finally let go of her feelings about Elizabeth, and she contacted Ron and asked him if he would join us in my consulting room. As always, he was supportive and eager to help.

Within a few months of completing the ritual (see later) Lee was pregnant and she and Tim finally began living together. Even though she was still not ready for marriage, her broken vows to Ron still weighing heavily on her mind, Lee was on the way to a happier and healthier life and to being a mother again.

Having a ritual either alone, with your partner, or with a loving and supportive friend or therapist, can often clear the way to release you from the past. If you have any similar old business, perhaps you'd like to try the following meditation to finally release yourself.

❂ MEDITATION TO CONTACT AND RELEASE THE SOUL OF A PREVIOUS CHILD

Choose a place where you will be comfortable — either your sacred space, or, if you prefer to keep that very private and want to do this meditation with a witness, choose somewhere where you will not be disturbed, where you can have some candles, some flowers and, if you have a photograph – even a scan – of your child, that too. If you have no photograph, sometimes having some other object that symbolizes the child is helpful – a toy, an item of clothing, a blanket or something that is special to you from that time. It might be an idea to have some tissues too! Take the phone off the hook. If you've chosen to be with someone else, make sure that they are in line with your own spirituality and that they understand the sacredness of this process. You may want to hold their hands.

Now . . . take a deep breath, close your eyes, and allow yourself to relax. Let your shoulders fall and the earth take your weight. Let anything negative simply flow out of the soles of your feet and your root chakra, and relax. Take another deep breath, and this time allow light energy to enter in through the top of your head and shine through every cell and every atom of every cell of your body, cleansing, healing and balancing, bringing everything into harmony. Relax. Know that what you're about to do is for your higher good and the higher good of all, and that the process you're about to enter into is one of pure love.

Take another deep breath and extend the light into your aura, and feel yourself come into alignment with the universe. Relax and simply allow yourself to be. Take as long as you wish simply to breathe. Adjust any part of your physical body so that you're comfortable. Then, with another breath, imagine that you are gently leaving your body to go to a beautiful place where you and the soul of your child can meet. For instance, it might be a forest glade, a garden, or a place in the clouds. Gently allow yourself to go there now, and adopt a position that is comfortable for you. With love, create a place that is welcoming. Breathe gently as you take in the splendour and sacredness of this moment. Allow yourself to feel whatever you feel, as you absorb the love and beauty that surround you. Take as long as you wish, to feel ready for the next step.

And when you feel at ease, send out a message to the soul of your child inviting it to come to meet you. Pause, and hold the space in love, and when you're ready, allow the soul of your child to appear now. Visualize the soul if you can, but if not, don't worry. Your calling will be answered. Allow yourself to feel. You will become aware that whatever has happened in the intervening time, the deep and wonderful connection there has always been between your soul and that of your child, remains just as it always was. You may perceive your child as older, a young man or young woman now, or perhaps exactly as he or she was. Enjoy the connection. Know that there is neither sadness nor shame, fear nor guilt, anger nor resentment, but only love flowing between you. Feel the connection with your heart.

Now silently tell the soul of your child anything that you want to say – about how you feel, how it felt for you to lose him, how it has been over the years, how much you've always loved him. Allow yourself to take time to share anything that you've needed to say over the years, but without anxiety about forgetting anything – you can always come back here again if you wish. Take as long as you want, and when you feel you've finished, pause. Listen now, and absorb the communication from the soul of the child. This might come to you as words, thoughts, insights, feelings, symbols, or simply as a flow of love that soothes your heart. Feel the connection and understand that this has never faded and never will. Know that this soul chose you as an earthly parent – the perfect parent – and has been with you forever, guarding you, guiding you, wanting only your higher good. The soul has never been parted from you. The soul continues to live. Allow your inner conversation to proceed until it feels complete, then with love and gratitude, gently but finally let go. Allow the vision of the soul to recede, and send another wave of gratitude up as high as you can.

Allow yourself as much time as you need, then, when you're ready, gently make your way back from this place and once more find yourself fully in your human body. Take a deep breath and make sure that you're well grounded. Be fully aware of your physical presence. Feel your fingers and your toes, and when you're fully aware in a place behind your closed eyes, gently open them and be fully present. If you are with someone and hugging feels appropriate, do it now!

Have a drink of water and, if you want to, discuss your experience with your companion or write in your journal. Take some time before you return to your normal daily activities.

PREGNANCY

If you're pregnant and were never before able to see your body as a temple, now's the time to do so! Your body has always been a temple to your soul (a cliché but true!), but during pregnancy it's the holy place wherein you are building a new human body. Everything that happens to you will be happening to your baby also. Its blood supply and nerve supply is the same as yours, therefore if you want to be gentle with your baby, you have to be gentle with yourself. Toxic substances such as cigarette smoke and alcohol will affect your baby too. Anything that is causing you fear, pain, tension, or to feel less than wonderful about yourself, could do with healing now. This is a time for connecting to your innate creativity and spirituality, a time of great power and also of surrender. Although you can do much to make this process as wonderful as possible, there is another soul with some power here too – that of your baby. Also your body, made for the creation of children, has a great power of its own, and knows how to complete the journey already begun. Long before we started to understand the medical process of pregnancy, millions of women had babies, and their bodies, just like yours, knew what to do. But as always, the more we understand the better.

Although we are told that most of the changes in our

bodies during pregnancy are due to hormonal shifts, and to some extent that's true, many of them are due, at least in part, to the changing vibrational frequency as the soul of the mother and the incoming soul work together in partnership to prepare for entry at the time of birth. The soul needs to reduce its vibrational frequency while at the same time, that of the mother (particularly her uterus) need to be increased. Many of the physiological changes and symptoms of pregnancy, from dizziness to morning sickness, have a spiritual basis. Most of these symptoms require no intervention, but should you feel that you do need some relief, perhaps you would like to have a look at *Total Wellbeing* where you'll find some suggestions for an integrated approach to your difficulties. Learn truly to listen to your body, your emotions and your soul and see what's right for you. It will be right for your baby also.

Some months ago I met a beautiful young woman in Australia, who was seven months pregnant with her first child. To me, she demonstrated the ideal of motherhood. She and her husband were obviously very much in love and thrilled about having their first child. She said that from the first days of the pregnancy she had had a strong desire for the colour orange (interestingly, the colour of the sacral chakra which governs sexuality, inner masculine/feminine balance and also the female reproductive organs including the uterus). She felt that it had special significance for her and her baby. She tied a beautiful orange ribbon around her waist, lit orange candles and wore an orange scarf. It was obvious that she was having a constant dialogue with both her body and her baby. She would find positions that were particularly comfortable for her – on the floor, on her knees, draped across her husband's legs – and she would readjust regularly as she listened to the signs from within her. She placed her hands on her swollen belly when we were singing songs, and she and her husband placed both their hands on the baby when we were meditating or praying. The baby was included in everything. Eventually, when I was back in Texas, I received a joyous e-mail to say that the baby had been born, birthed naturally and without medication or intervention, in the same atmosphere of love and acceptance in which he had been conceived and cradled throughout the pregnancy.

This increased awareness that most mothers can feel if they pause to notice, is incredible. Even women who have never thought in spiritual terms find themselves able to see the mystical significance in what otherwise seems mundane. Sometimes, like May, they also find that old issues surface to be dealt with once and for all. It is never too late gently to explore and release them. This openness that pregnant women feel needs to be handled with love and sensitivity, since on the other side of the coin there is increased vulnerability. Harsh words, cruel gestures, negative comments and insensitivity can make their mark all the more intensely on the pregnant psyche, and of course on the unborn child too. Although pregnant women do not need to be wrapped in cotton-wool or shielded and protected from life, they need to be respected and supported by loving people around them.

COMMUNICATION WITH THE UNBORN CHILD

Some women know from the moment of conception that they're pregnant and the bonding process begins right then. Others start to bond as soon as the pregnancy is confirmed. Others may not feel bonded until well into the pregnancy, or even after the birth. Nowadays the practice of scanning and giving the parents a photograph of the baby in the womb, and of being able to know the baby's sex if you wish and start choosing names, all add to the deepening attachment, as you can already physically see your baby as a person. But on a soul level, bonding has been there ever since the time when, before you incarnated, you agreed to come together. (If you feel that you have never bonded with your baby, or with your mother, see Chapter 9). The soul that is to incarnate into your child is often hovering around you for years.

Some years ago I ran a group for women who were either pregnant or trying to get pregnant, and those members of the group who had attended during their pregnancy and had now delivered their babies often joined us. It was an astounding experience. These women were able to share their insights and deal with any old and lingering fears and doubts they might have, while each one also took time to talk to the baby in her womb, sing to it, play it music and just be still, reflecting upon the wonder of it all. We would meditate and visualize together, affirming safe and rewarding, spiritually fulfilling deliveries. Not only were these women richly rewarded by a deepening bond, but almost invariably the children were radiant beings who were bright yet placid. Although we had no fathers in the group – perhaps a mistake – don't forget to include your partner in this wonderful experience. The sooner he can bond also, the more mutually supportive the two of you will be when the child is born. This is a miraculous time, and if you allow yourself to relax and tune in to your body (and your baby) you'll find that even if this is your first baby, you have a wisdom about childbirth that is ancient.

SOME IDEAS . . .

- Why not get all the women you know to affirm with you during your pregnancy?

- Why not organize an e-mail group of pregnant women who can tune in to each other at some time each day and visualize their power?

- Why not agree a time each day to light candles, focus on yourself and your baby along with all the other pregnant women you know?

- How about forming a group to discuss the true spiritual nature of your journey?

- How about singing together? Singing relaxes your body, opens your throat and allows your creativity to flow, and when in labour, helps your cervix to open.

- How about getting creative with some rituals of your own since we have given up many of them in the West?

- Have a look at the chapter on the relationship with yourself in *Affairs of the Heart* and reassess your ability to love yourself even more specially now.

- How about a pregnancy journal that you can present to your child perhaps when she herself is pregnant, or he himself is becoming a father?

- How about writing letters to your unborn child that you can give him or her later?

- How about setting aside a special time each week when you and your partner can talk about the changes that the new baby will bring to your lives?

FROM THE BABY'S POINT OF VIEW . . .

The baby is growing in an ever more restricted area and is captive to your moods and hormonal changes. Already it feels your love or your rejection. Its world is warm, wet and bathed in soft and peaceful light. It hears your heart beat constantly and also your voice which it will recognize immediately after birth (see the beautiful quotation in Chapter 9). In fact there's evidence from regressions that the baby can often see both the inside and the outside of the womb. This may be because, although full incarnation does not take place till the moment of birth, the soul may be in and out of the child's body during the pregnancy. We shall discuss this more fully in Chapter 9.

WHO SHOULD BE THERE APART FROM YOU AND YOUR BABY?

Something for you to decide well ahead of time is who you are going to honour by inviting them to be with you and your baby during your labour and delivery. Perhaps you could meditate on it, use your intuition or call for inner guidance, since this is a very important issue. You are in charge. Perhaps you could discuss your spiritual beliefs with the people you choose ahead of time, so that no one brings into this sacred space and time any thoughts, fears or undisclosed feelings that are not in line with yours. And that includes the doctor and the midwife! During labour you will be very focused on yourself and the baby, and while this is an amazingly powerful time for you, you can also be quite vulnerable as you surrender to the process. So those people you choose should be able to love and support you, physically, emotionally and spiritually, without you having to worry about their needs. People who are willing to massage your back, rub your feet, give you water, light your candles (this will not be possible in a hospital room or anywhere where there is an oxygen supply), sing with you, pray with you or even dance with you, and if necessary protect your rights for you, are good choices. Usually women would like to have their partner with them, whether or not this is the father of the baby. Another woman – perhaps your mother, your sister or a close friend – can bring a different perspective, and if she has had a good experience having children herself, so much the better. Only you can decide whether or not you want your other children present. Some women do, and others know that they would be so concerned about their children's needs that they would lose the focus on what is essential now. At the moment when your baby is finally born and incarnates, only those whom you choose to have the privilege of witnessing your miracle should be there.

LABOUR

Many years ago, shortly after I qualified as a doctor and before I had the courage to stand up as a medical practitioner and say that I was also a spiritual healer, I did a six-month gynaecology and obstetrics placement in a hospital in the north-east of England. When I was on call, rather than going off the ward when it wasn't busy, I would spend time talking to the women in labour. With my hand on their abdomen I would feel for their contractions and sometimes sit for an hour or more, channelling healing to both mother and baby while labour progressed. After a few weeks, the consultant asked to see me in his office. He asked me what I was doing with these women. Fairly sternly he said that he had been observing me, and he felt that something was going on. He had noted that those women with whom I sat needed less, if any, medication, had easier deliveries, happier, healthier babies and fewer complications. We talked briefly about healing, in which he didn't believe; however, he said that he was aware of something happening that he hadn't seen before. As I left he smiled, and with a wink suggested that I continue doing whatever it was that I was doing, but just did not tell him about it! He started to call me 'Dottore Sympatico', and we laughed about it many times.

All that was happening was that these women felt empowered, and therefore relaxed into the process, as almost all women can, and their bodies did the rest. The process of labour is perhaps the most powerful demonstration of what our bodies are capable of. And although female animals of all species deliver their babies, there is something amazingly wonderful about a woman labouring to bring her child into the world, as anyone who has had the privilege of watching will testify. She is now in total alignment with the universe, and the soul of a new human being is hovering by her side, waiting to enter her child. Isn't that awesome? The souls of many other beings are also watching and offering help. In fact unseen forces of the universe are gathered to observe this transformation and rejoice. This is the time for which you have prepared. This is the time when you become your wonderful womanly best. No matter who is with you, you and only you are to perform this miracle. A few moments spent between contractions realigning with your soul if necessary will reap great rewards. If the father of the child is with you, hold each other's hands and breathe together. Hold each other's eyes, and together align yourselves with your hearts and souls and affirm that you are holding a safe and wonderful place for the entry of the awaiting soul who chose you as its perfect parents in this lifetime. Send thoughts of welcome, and dedicate this labour to a safe and joyous incarnation. Ride the waves of the contractions, relaxing and resting between them, knowing that your body is working to deliver your child. Be with your baby too, remembering that he is on this journey also, and send loving thoughts and welcome to him as he finally begins to make his entry into the world.

CAESAREAN SECTION

If for some reason you are unable to deliver your baby naturally, please don't feel either guilty or cheated. Try to keep focused on the fact that there are greater forces at work here, and that the timing and the birth will be exactly as they should be. All is in divine order. You and your baby have made an ancient and spiritual pact to be at this place and time together, and all will work out just as it is meant to. If the choice is Caesarean, then that is part of your baby's pre-birth plan, and something that the two of you agreed long ago. It sets a different stage for both of you and is part of the unique story of your relationship. Women who have been abused, who have difficulties with relaxing into their own sexuality, or who are in fear or holding repressed anger, may have difficulty in simply surrendering to the process of labour and may then require some assistance. Dealing with old feelings and trauma before you get pregnant (see page 43) can help to alleviate this.

PRE-BIRTH

In the delightful *Benjaya's Gifts* (M'haletta and Carmella B'Hahn, Hazelwood Press, 1996), there is a message from the unborn child to his mother, asking that she help him remain conscious of who he really is. And certainly for a brief time after birth we do remain conscious of who we are. As we shall see, there are many children born now who do remain conscious and maybe that is the sign of greater change. However, generally if we were to remember the powerful and amazing souls that we are, many of the lessons of this lifetime would be in vain. That we forget is therefore part of the natural process of the earthly life. Much later on the human path, we start once more to remember. However, we do come into this world with love, security and knowledge of who we are. You only have to look into the eyes of the newborn to see the wisdom there. Sometimes babies will actually communicate to you who they are, for at this time they remember.

Many of us have pre-birth memories. Some people have been able to describe verifiable events that took place while they were *in utero*, and have recall of things that were said and the physical setting in which these occurred. The memory of previous lifetimes is not at all unusual. Some of us have memories of our birth too. You may think this fanciful. No matter. The following is a transcript of part of one of my own regressions in which I talked of my memory of birth.

I am free . . . unconfined, unrestrained . . . and so full of joy . . . floating and drifting. I am shining, radiant and filled with love . . . It is so joyful and peaceful . . . I seem to be ancient . . . I know that I am ancient. Oh . . . but I've done some things that were painful for other people . . . that's why I have to go back. I betrayed . . . I was cruel . . . I want to learn . . . There are deeds I need to complete. There are pledges to keep. There are souls whose paths are inter-twined with mine . . . Oh and there are beloved souls . . . There is such love . . . Such love . . . Such beauty . . . Such endless compassion and love . . . We are almost ready. My chosen parents I know well. We have loved forever. We have played many parts together . . . They have prepared for me and all is now ready. It is time. They are waiting for me. My body is prepared . . . It is time . . . it is time . . . My parents are waiting to receive me. I know I will soon forget who I really am. My body is being pushed. My mother is in pain but she loves me . . . my head feels pressure . . . I know again the feeling of pain . . . It has happened before . . . It is time . . . My body is ready . . . My body is almost born

. . . I relinquish my freedom . . . I am about to be born again . . . I am ready . . . Oh . . . I am here.

The baby has been making the journey from that warm, wet, safe place with gentle light and sweet, comforting sounds out into a world where it is noisy and bright and cold. It has been squashed and pushed and sometimes pulled by various parts of its anatomy down a narrow passage during which time its lungs are stimulated to take its first breath. Sometimes it has been lifted out into very strange surroundings during Caesarean section. Ideally it will be welcomed very gently and lovingly, with the softness of its mother's voice and the warmth of the touch of her skin, but sadly this is often not the case. This holy moment is often marred by noise and light and rough handling – the first thing that many people will remember is being struck and made to cry.

THE MOMENT OF INCARNATION – THE ENTRY OF THE SOUL

At the moment of incarnation the final lowering of the soul's vibrational frequency occurs so that the soul can enter the physical body, just as easily as the soul leaves at the moment of the transition we have called death. In this single sacred moment, incarnation takes place. We shall talk of this again in Chapter 9. If the birth has been a natural one, both mother and baby are awake and aware, and the child presents himself as a brand-new human being. This is a period of immense bonding, calm and awe. Skin-to-skin contact is essential. It's natural and beneficial for the mother to touch, caress, massage and explore the child she has created, while the child responds. In *Gentle Birth Choices,* Barbara Harper suggests that fathers should be encouraged to take off their shirts so that they too can have close contact with the baby, and during this time forge lifelong bonds. The joy of the woman holding her child to her breast within a few moments of birth, and the baby instinctively searching for and finding it, is awesome. Already the baby recognizes his mother's voice and can focus just enough to see the distance from her nipple to her eyes. This soul, free only moments ago, is communicating in the only ways now available to him – with his eyes, his voice and movement – as he begins to adjust to the restriction of his tiny body. The familiar presence of his mother is essential, and if she is not there, and he cannot feel her touch, hear her voice, recognize her smell and fix on to her eyes, he may become alarmed. This is your time with your child, essential to both of you. Enjoy the magic of it, savour the wonder. It will be with you for the rest of your life, and with your child always too.

RELUCTANCE TO INCARNATE

The changing of vibrations during pregnancy must be complete so that the vibrational frequencies of mother, baby and soul are balanced at the moment of birth. However, despite the fact that the child's body and the mother's have been well prepared, sometimes at the last moment there is non-entry of the soul. The result is stillbirth. Although this must appear the most cruel of lessons, a lesson it is none the less. If part of the parents' curriculum is to learn the pain and the grief of producing a dead baby, then the soul will not enter. This is yet another ancient agreement between our soul and theirs. However, it is not unusual for the same soul later to enter a child prepared by the same parents, or at least by the same mother. The same can happen with miscarriage. Where for some reason the physical form is not perfect, the soul may withdraw and the foetus will abort, and again the soul may await another opportunity to come. If part of the learning process for both parents and child is that the child should have some disability, then the presence of such disability will be perfect for the child, and will be part of the preparation for incarnation as we shall see in Chapter 9. Everything is in divine order, and the soul will enter only when everything is perfect for it to do so. In the case of stillbirth, it is important that the mother and father should be able to spend time with the baby and to touch and feel its body, so that their grieving may be completed and cleared. Naming the child and having some ceremony to acknowledge the child's existence are essential to healing.

Sometimes a soul incarnates despite its reluctance. This is often so in the case of a multiple birth where one soul accompanies the other in order to help it incarnate. Where there has been reluctance, the child often has difficulty grounding (see Appendix 3), and may be restless, a feature which can continue into adult life. These children often prefer not to have their feet on the ground, sitting with their legs drawn up under them or up off the ground. In later life a variety of conditions manifest due to the dis-ease of the soul about being present on the planet. Addictions, depression, suicidal intent, negativity, cynicism and a tendency to opt out of life and never fully appreciate its joys are other indications of reluctance to incarnate. Sometimes the cause of the reluctance is a very rapid and poorly planned incarnation after a traumatic death where the soul feels lost and fails to ascend into the light to rest, recuperate and consolidate before choosing to return. (We shall discuss this phenomenon in later chapters.) Often the energy of such people is low and they feel constantly sluggish and below par, often reporting recurrent feelings of sadness and depression for much of their lives. Healing past life wounds and giving encouragement to incarnate fully can help greatly.

Occasionally after a particularly traumatic birth, there is only partial incarnation, whereby the soul may remain partly out of the body for years. Physically, chronic problems particularly with the lower limbs can be the result. The restless soul may also have difficulty in remaining fully incarnated and will dissociate from time to time. Wherever there are root chakra problems (see Appendix 2) it is worth examining to see if the soul is fully present. We shall deal with soul loss, which is a different phenomenon, in Chapter 4.

FORGIVENESS AND RELEASE DURING PREGNANCY OR BEFORE

If you find this difficult at the moment, don't worry. Maybe you could come back to it after reading the following chapters and see how it feels then.

Just as your child will choose the perfect mother and father, you did that also. If there were or are difficulties between you and your parents, and things you're finding hard to forgive (even if your parent is no longer in physical form here), you might like to take a moment, with as much peace and love as you can muster, to look at what you know of your mother and her life. What was it about her that made your soul choose her as your biological mother? What unique gifts did she bring to you? What did you gain from being her child? (Sometimes we can only see this in terms of coping skills.) Can you thank your mother for these gifts and forgive her what until this point you may have blamed her for?

Then look at all that you know of your father and his life. What was it about him that made your soul choose him as your father? What unique gifts did he give you? If there was abuse, perhaps it made you stronger, gave you compassion for others in pain, gave you insight into the difficulties of others. Can you thank him for

---

these gifts and forgive him for what till this point you may have blamed him for?

What did you learn from them jointly as parents? What was it all preparing you for? Although some of their gifts may have been painful, nothing was wasted. All was essential to the growth of your soul.

Take a deep breath and forgive and let go as much as you can and let there be a wave of love and gratitude between you now.

If you suffered abuse during your childhood, make sure you have some chakra healing before you yourself become a parent if you can. You've had a hard enough time without trying to deal with this pain reawakening while you're pregnant.

✿ AFFIRMATION

I open to the wondrous creation of life. My body is able to do the work for which it was created. My baby and I take this journey together to an awesome spiritual delivery and incarnation.

✿ MEDITATION DURING PREGNANCY

If you are pregnant you can do this meditation at any time, alone with your unborn child. Or you can choose to do it with the father of the child or your partner. If you have a friend who is pregnant you may choose to do it together. In preparing your safe place for use during your pregnancy, please note that some oils are not suitable for use at this time. These include: basil, calamus, cedarwood, clary sage, hyssop, jasmine, juniper, marjoram, mugwort, myrrh, pennyroyal, rosemary, sage, thyme and wintergreen. You might also like to bear in mind that for centuries, malachite has been known as the crystal to choose to safeguard pregnancy, and since it's also good for your heart chakra, it might be something that you could have with you now.

As usual, go to your safe place and take all you need with you – your journal and pen, some water, flowers or a plant and cushions to support you in whatever position you feel most comfortable. You might find that if you are advanced in your pregnancy, a reclining chair with support for your feet or lots of cushions on the floor may be best. Don't worry if your back is not erect.

Now take the phone off the hook and ensure that you will have about forty-five minutes of uninterrupted time. Close your eyes and take a deep breath. Feel your lungs fill with refreshing air and know that at the same time, your baby will have a good supply of oxygen too. Send a loving thought to the baby as you take another deep breath, visualizing it entering into all of your cells, nurturing them and passing into your baby also. Smile at your baby as you breathe again. Now with the next breath allow yourself to relax and breathe out anything you no longer need through the soles of your feet and your root chakra, knowing that the Earth that supports you will take it and detoxify it. And now another breath, once again visualizing it cleansing, healing and balancing both you and your baby. Feel the harmony between you both as you breathe in unison. Smile again as you visualize your baby warmly suspended in your womb. Know that as you smile there will be a release of nurturing endorphins to both you and your baby. Then allow yourself once again just to sink down into yourself and relax. All is well. Breathe love in and breathe out anything you no longer need till you reach a point where you are both inhaling and exhaling love. Relax.

Gently scan your body and if it feels at all uncomfortable adjust your position now, then relax.

Focus now on your child and let your heart open with unconditional love and set your intention that this will be a healing and loving experience for you both. If it seems appropriate, widen your focus now to take in the father of the child since the two of you are the chosen parents, whether or not you are together, no matter what the physical reality might be now. Know that the choice of the soul of the child has been fulfilled in having the two of you as parents.

Take your focus down to your abdomen, into your uterus and to the beating heart of your child. Breathe and feel the connection from your heart to the heart of your baby. Visualize the bond of love passing between your hearts and with compassion, widen your focus to include the soul of the child hovering close to you. Allow shafts of light and love to flow from the soul to you and from you to the soul as you bid welcome. Feel also the loving presences of guides, teachers and angels around you in this sacred moment and allow gratitude and welcome to flow to all that are here for the higher good of you and your baby.

Feel the love and warmth and cherishing of those who hold you secure in this moment. Be aware now of the physical reality – the physical connection between you and your child; your blood supply is his blood supply; your nerve supply is his nerve supply; your calm is his calm; your rest is his rest; your food is his food; your air is his air; your loving care for yourself is your loving care for him. Make a commitment to nurture, cherish and take care of yourself so that you do the same for him. Feel your abdomen with your hands and allow light to flow out through your palms and touch your child. Send waves of love to him. Feel his gentle response. Enjoy.

Now focus on yourself. Be aware that of all the souls in the universe, this child's soul has chosen you as the perfect mother for its physical form. And the chosen father is the perfect father. You can give this child exactly what his soul needs to launch him into this chosen life. All is in divine order. All is perfect. You and only you can give him the unique qualities he desires from his mother. Feel the honour of being chosen for this role. Feel the privilege of bearing this child. Whatever may happen to him in his lifetime, you and only you have this moment with him in this unique relationship. Open your heart even further and allow conscious love and gratitude to flow from your heart to the heart of the child. Pause and in this moment allow any message to flow between you now – send and receive any significant communication. Just allow any loving message to enter your consciousness without active thought. Receive without censoring. Allow yourself to know the loving message from the soul of your child.

Stay like this for as long as you wish, and when you feel ready, send a wave of gratitude for this time with your child.

Set your intention once again – that the rest of this pregnancy will be exactly as it is meant to be, that your delivery too will be exactly as your soul and the soul of the child have agreed, that you are an active and willing partner in this wonderful mystery of birth. Now take a long deep breath and once again be aware of nurturing your child with oxygen and visualize every cell and every atom of every cell cleansing, healing and balancing. And again, see the sparkling clarity spreading from you to your child as you begin to become more aware of your physical surroundings and of your physical presence. Gently move your fingers and toes and start to become more aware, bringing your focus now to a place behind your closed eyes. Take your time, and when you are ready, gently open your eyes.

Take a while to be quiet, gently stretching. Have a glass of water and move about a little before recording whatever you wish in your journal and then gently getting on with your day.

✹ MEDITATION DURING LABOUR AND BIRTH

You are now reaching the holy moment of the incarnation of the child you have so lovingly welcomed to grow inside your body. Your body knows what it has to do now to birth your child, and whatever happens it will be right, so you have no need to worry. It will be exactly as your soul and that of your baby have planned.

So, between contractions now, breathe and relax. Allow yourself to be aware of the awe of this time and of your sacred task in delivering this child so that its soul may finally enter. Breathe now and allow light and love to pour into you and your baby. Relax knowing that every contraction now will bring your baby closer and closer to the moment you have both been working for. Focus on your baby so that both of you can rest between contractions . . .

And then as the wave begins ride with it, ride it knowing that your are labouring in the way that women have always done, your body taking over, your uterus working now. Ride the wave. Feel your baby. Send him love. Ride and allow yourself to be lifted out of the pain . . . as the crescendo comes now know that you and your baby have moved forward . . . breathe . . . feel the light . . . feel the love . . . Know that you are honoured, held and protected in this moment . . . breathe and let the wave gently subside again and breathe . . . Send love to your baby, knowing that you are both journeying together. Send love to the soul waiting now, preparing to enter. Breathe. Accept all the love and gentle attention that are your right . . . Move to be as comfortable as you can and gently communicate with your body and your child. Take time to relax and prepare for the next wave.

✪ PRAYER

Let the love of the Creator surround me always as I acknowledge myself to be at the centre of creation. Let the process to which I surrender deliver me and my child safely as we tread this spiritual path together. Whatever the lessons that my child and I have agreed to, I welcome with love for the higher good of us both.

3   LIVING THE HUMAN PATH

Life is the rose's hope while yet unblown:
The reading of a never ending tale;
The light uplifting of a maiden's veil;
A schoolboy riding the springy branches of an elm . . .

John Keats

Now we are here, on the human path. From a place of peace and harmony on the soul plane, we have reincarnated once more to an unstable, ever-moving existence trapped in a limited, heavy, physical body. We know our mission, though we may not be consciously aware of it, and we now set out to achieve as much as we can in this lifetime. While evolving and developing our consciousness, we are also presented with opportunities to resolve our karma and come to a joyous inner place where at last we are at peace. The many relationships we have chosen are important to the process. Gradually we begin to rediscover who we are, so that finally, we may come to the point where we can live contentedly the joyous adventure of being simultaneously human and divine. Whatever our individual agenda holds, there are stages through which we all pass and we shall discuss some of them here. There are obstacles which we shall encounter too, and we shall discuss some of those in Chapter 4. We may have many lifetimes in which to complete our developmental tasks which include:

- Understanding the laws of the universe and living by them
- Developing our consciousness
- Resolving our karma
- Realizing our mission
- Rediscovering who we are and living a joyously spiritual life
- Becoming enlightened and finally returning to reunite with the Divine

That's all!

In every incarnation we give ourselves new challenges to help us experience from every polarity – poverty and abundance; love and indifference; grief and joy; nurture and abandonment etc. Often we repeat the same lesson many times until we finally utter a joyous 'Aha!' and, understanding, raise our awareness, free at last. The choice of tasks for this particular lifetime, and how to accomplish them, is entirely up to us. Sometimes we choose many painful tasks, sometimes a few easy ones. Often, in retrospect, we may regret our choices. However, everything we chose was of benefit to our soul, and also impinges upon the lives of those with whom we had contact, aiding their growth too, whether or not any of us could acknowledge that at the time. In order to gain maximum benefit from the new challenges we have set for ourselves, in childhood we forget who we are, and, to some extent, the lessons we have already learned. As we develop spiritually and bring our tasks closer to completion we radiate love, peace and light to the world around us. So let's begin . . .

UNDERSTANDING AND LIVING BY THE PRINCIPLES OF THE UNIVERSE

These principles form a basis for living wisely, peacefully and consciously, respecting all life and encourage us to grow in spiritual wisdom. Basically they state that:

- the basic component of the universe is energy, which may be in physical or non-physical form, and which is in harmonious balance. *(Do you want to choose to align with the harmony of the universe and feel at peace, or resist its flow and experience discomfort and chaos?)*
- the infinite intelligence, which we may call God, exists in all energy, and is an expression of unconditional love. *(If you choose to view this Divinity as loving, benevolent and supportive, it colours everything in your life positively. You will become unconditionally loving too. Conversely, if you view it as punitive and judgmental, that is how you also become.)*
- we are all united in this never-ending loving energy, and therefore what we do to one we do to all. *(Everything in the universe, being part of the infinite whole, is interconnected – and that includes us and everyone else no matter what colour, race or creed.)*
- we are perfect as we are in this moment, and as long as we remain connected to the Source we are able to see all as perfect. *(When we disconnect we become discontented and we fail to see the beauty in ourselves and everything around us.)*
- we create our own circumstances by what we think and the way we act and we have free will to create our lives in any way we wish. *(What a responsibility! No one to blame but ourselves for the mess we get into!)*
- we can access the divine intelligence by being silent,

observing our feelings and listening to our intuition. *(How often do you take time just to be silent and listen?)*

- everything around us is a reflection of ourselves and we attract into our lives people and situations that will help us grow by mirroring what we need to see in ourselves. *(Do you like what you have attracted or would you like to change yourself so that you attract nicer people?)*

- everything is in divine order and is neither good nor bad but simply something more to help us learn. Thus everything is perfect in its own way. *(No point in worrying – all is as it should be and in any case, worry is an insult to God!)*

- our relationship with others reflects our relationship with ourselves *(Aha! Are you having trouble in your relationships? Look within!)*

- just as everything is perfect, everything has meaning and purpose. When we find our true purpose we feel inspired, energetic and at one with the whole universe. *(Are you feeling worn out, fed up or lacking energy? Are you out of line with your universal purpose?)*

- when we are in alignment with the universe and allowing ourselves to follow the natural flow of energy, we feel free, aware, light and flowing with love. *(A bit like some of the previous principles – are you as light and flowing with love as you could be?)*

- it is our natural state to live in an abundance of energy, whether physical, emotional or spiritual. Therefore prosperity in all its forms – in love, work, finance, health and joy – are ours by right. Where there is a block to abundance there is a block in the flow of energy. *(Are you as prosperous as you could be? If not, what is blocking the flow?)*

- living in a state of gratitude and charity makes way for a permanent flow of energy which may be manifest in any or all of its forms. *(Are you grateful for all you have? Do you show it? Say it?)*

- we are constantly and simultaneously teaching and learning, giving and receiving. The more we become aware of this, the more likely we are to remain in a state of gratitude and abundance. *(Are you grateful for all the teaching you get – even from those people with whom you're having difficulties or whom you haven't been able to forgive yet?)*

- any attempt to control by attachment will block our flow of energy and that healthy detachment actually bonds others to us in love. *(Are you able to allow those you love to have freedom to be who they are, even if that means you might lose them? Is it good for you or the one you 'love' to be bound by control?)*

- that upon which we focus expands, and therefore ideally we need to focus on love, peace, joy and the finer aspects of all those with whom we come into contact. *(Do you focus on the things that irritate you rather than those that give you pleasure?)*

- doing what we love helps us express who we really are to the world and in doing so helps raise the vibration of the planet. *(There's that responsibility again – that I can change the whole world doing what I love and radiating happiness and love because of it. The reverse is also true!)*

- the universe will handle the minutiae of our lives if we stay in the moment and simply be who we are. *(We can't change the past and the future will never arrive. We only have this moment. Enjoy it!)*

- we will find around us what we ourselves express – smiles beget smiles; laughter begets laughter; love begets love; peace begets peace. *(Similarly criticism begets criticism; envy begets envy; anger begets anger, etc., etc.)*

DEVELOPMENT OF CONSCIOUSNESS

As we have evolved over billions of years, since we were fledgling souls with no real form, we have lived in wondrous places and on barren landscapes, and through a myriad of experiences we have grown, finally taking on a human form. During the course of each human lifetime, we have ample opportunity to raise our vibration and develop our consciousness to the level at which we realize that we are all one, that unconditional love is the only way forward and that we have spiritual gifts which can transform not only our own lives but also the whole world. Every moment gives us new choices. However, we don't live our lives in isolation. We have to contend with the choices and behaviour of others, planetary movements and world events and how these impact upon us.

Nevertheless, how we choose to respond is up to us – the consequences are part of our training. We can choose a path of harmony, or to be drawn into negativity and become affected by it. Sometimes when we think that we have got to the point of inner peace we are once again faced with chaos, testing our resolve. In my own experience, often at the times when it appears that life has finally become level and peaceful, a new situation arises – always of my own making of course – to which sadly I may not always react with the unconditionally loving, harmonious response I would prefer. This is the 'back to the drawing board' time when the universe has shown us where we still need to pay attention and do some work. As we evolve we finally come to loving detachment where we have little expectation of outcome, trusting that the universe will always get it right in a way that we could neither plan nor predict, though that's no excuse for complacency. Until we learn to live in harmony and balance, aligning ourselves with the forces of the universe, we're unable to find that inner peace which is essential for our final ascent to enlightenment.

So what do we mean by consciousness?

In the past we assumed that consciousness was a function of the brain – and indeed it is linked with our neurophysiology. However, over recent years it's become obvious that it neither originates nor is produced there, but exists within every cell and also within the whole energetic body. Memories, once thought to be localized, are now known to be spread throughout the whole cellular network and beyond. In fact what has emerged, not only for consciousness but also for the whole universe, is a holographic model, where every fraction of the system contains the whole, taking us beyond both Newtonian and quantum physics. That means it's possible to access all universal knowledge, in whatever historical time frame or space reality, at any time. We can access the angelic realms or even the centre of the earth should we wish to do so. All we need to do is induce an altered state of consciousness, for instance by means of hypnosis, meditation, listening to music, chanting or breath work. As we develop and unravel the ancient mysteries, this becomes a fairly simple process.

Consciousness, then, exists everywhere, and is not limited by the confines of a human body. Experiments show that even when cells are removed, for example with a swab from the inside of our cheek, they continue to respond in unison with the rest of our body. And near-death experiences (NDEs) and out-of-body experiences, discussed elsewhere, show that consciousness can exist outside of the body. And of course consciousness is not the monopoly of human beings. Everything in the universe has consciousness.

Breaking down consciousness into easy bites makes it more palatable, so let's look at what we mean by conscious, subconscious and superconscious.

The Conscious

Although our conscious knows nothing and has no memory, it acts like a scanner that never rests, constantly scrutinizing every aspect of our inner and outer world, constantly collecting all the facts and impressions that filter continuously through our senses and our chakras. It then scoops up previously filed information from the subconscious and helps reorganize it all so that we understand it better. If we now have absolute clarity on some topic, it will be filed in the superconscious, but if not, it's all stored in the subconscious once more until something else happens which allows us to unlock the wisdom within it.

Let's have a look at the following example to see how it all works together.

Someone tells me something about a planetary alignment. I listen with interest but don't know very much about the subject, and after the conversation ends, my conscious files the information in my subconscious. Later I'm in the waiting room at the dentist and pick up a magazine and read an article about astrology. While reading it, my conscious collects more new information and makes associations with what I heard in the previous conversation. Now it makes more sense. However, I still don't know a great deal about it, but it certainly has my interest, and once more I 'forget' about it – my conscious refiles it all in my subconscious. A couple of weeks later, I'm having difficulty with my office equipment – faxes don't go through, my printer doesn't work, I lose some of the text from my computer, and then the phone rings. I bemoan the situation to my friend, who laughs and tells me not to worry because Mercury is in retrograde motion and everyone's communication systems are affected! Now it has my full attention! My conscious scoops up the associated information I've gleaned in the last few weeks, and in putting it all together, I start to see its relevance to my life. It's possible that my conscious might file it away again in my subconscious, but the likelihood is that I will now actively search out more information to add to what I already have in order to understand the situation fully and learn how I can use it all to my advantage. This is the conscious at work, then – collecting, filing, making associations and refiling.

The Subconscious

What we have already experienced, whether in this lifetime or others, but haven't yet completely processed, is stored in our subconscious. Also here is ancient information, for instance about the planet and so-called racial memory, which enables us to remember how to do things that those before us have learned. Language, how to talk and behaviour that is common to all of us is stored here. Some of this may be individual memory from past lives, but much is collective. It's one of our tasks to understand our subconscious experience, and we have set the stage perfectly to allow us to do that. However, much of what is stored in the subconscious holds anguish, loss, guilt or shame, both from this life and lives past, and usually we avoid contact with it as much as possible since we're afraid of the pain. We repress the memory of it and try to pretend it isn't there until we can do so no longer. Unless we actively work on it, there it remains. However, as we develop, the veil separating conscious from subconscious thins, and the contents of the subconscious become more accessible to us. We can more easily make insightful associations between what is happening in our conscious world and what is still unprocessed in the subconscious. We may process some of it in our dreams, but often our development prods us to start to take a look, and also things start to happen in our lives that help it to surface. Sometimes this can be quite disconcerting. We may have been working on ourselves and feel that we have a better understanding, are making good choices and living according to our integrity, when something happens which knocks us off our feet and leaves us reeling in self-doubt. But all that has happened is that, now we're ready for it, we're being presented with a new opportunity to process some of that old stuff and finally let it go. Life becomes a rich detective story as we constantly look for every clue to greater understanding.

Since I've worked on myself for a long time, I can hook things up very easily now. Sometimes someone will say or do something and suddenly, a current flashes through my mind, body and aura, spreading out in all directions, making a myriad of associations. Things that people said or did years ago are suddenly back in my conscious in full technicolour. A bit disconcerting for those around us who hoped we'd forgotten! Often these are things I thought I had already processed, but the emotional component that comes up with them tells me this isn't so. It feels quite different when I simply remember something that has been dealt with, since there is no emotion attached. Now here's the good part! I then have the option to process them actively once and for all, or to swallow them down once again, knowing that I will have to return to them some time in the future. The benefits of allowing ourselves to follow the associations (and the pain) are enormous.

Recently, for instance, someone accosted me with some pretty controlling behaviour. Suddenly I had a flood of associations with my childhood, and in particular with the fact that my father was strict and authoritarian. Then I leaped to other events that I had not yet dealt with, most of them revolving around my sister Pam. As a child I was always a 'good' girl, obeying the rules and not testing the boundaries. However, when Pam courageously began to push the limits, I became angry, not with her but with myself, because I didn't have the courage to do the same. When I saw her get into trouble for challenging the rules, I was always so sad and fearful for her, because I really loved her and admired the courage she demonstrated. She was my hero. She was like a female knight who was strong enough, wise enough and willing enough to push the limits and stand up for her rights (and mine!), even though she knew the price would be high in terms of discipline. Pam in fact carried the burden for both of us, pushing the rules so that we both benefited. I daresay she was pretty angry with me because I didn't pull my weight, as it were, but still benefited from all she had fought for and gained. Suddenly I could process so much that had been dormant for fifty years or more. In soul terms, that was our agreement. She, beloved soul of many lifetimes, came ahead, paved the way for me and taught me great things. Together we have worked out so many lessons in different guises in different lifetimes. Although our human relationship this time has often been strained because of the unfairness she suffered, she has continued to be my hero throughout, and my love for her, in this life and beyond, has never faltered. So I thank the person who pushed me with that controlling behaviour and prompted me to pull all this from my subconscious and finally file it where it belongs.

Here we have seen the conscious and the subconscious working together and eventually processing data which can then be filed in the superconscious.

The Superconscious

This is the collective wisdom of the ages, enlightened teaching, awareness and everything that has been fully processed and from which we have received insight – all crystal-clear and available to each of us. When we access the superconscious we have our greatest sense of connection; find our higher purpose; feel perfectly coordinated; know rather than understand – *knowing* being of the soul and *understanding* being of the mind; and have absolute certainty that divine order reigns. Here we are fully alert, alive and able to flow spontaneously with the universe, and from here, any of us can channel information.

However, each of us also has a responsibility to contribute to the superconscious for the benefit of all humankind. In choosing what to deal with in this lifetime, we opt to process some issue so that the wisdom and learning will then be available for others. Some of the topics we may choose may be wonderful and delightful to experience, but others are not. There's a moving piece in Khalil Gibran's *The Prophet* where he refers to some going ahead and failing to remove the stumbling-stones, leaving those coming after to fall also. But in life, have you noticed how many have actually chosen to stumble to make us aware of where we too could fall? They demonstrate for us the way *not* to go. I don't need to murder in this lifetime. There are others who are highlighting that particular stumbling-stone for you and me. Nor do I need to die of hunger – there are ancient wise souls who have come for a brief period to live in suffering and die of hunger, their faces on millions of televisions throughout the world, to highlight for all of us that we need to share what we have with others. Also some opt, for the benefit of the whole universe, to process something about abuse – either as victim or perpetrator. Painful though the subject is, for their own growth and also out of love for the whole universe, they choose to learn, process and then make the information available to the rest of us so that we don't need to experience abuse personally – we know it's a terrible thing without having to go there ourselves. One would think that there's already sufficient wisdom on the subject of abuse for us to need no more. However, this is patently not so, since it still happens. Many of my wonderful patients are courageously processing for the rest of us lessons about violence, abuse, neglect, crime, victimization, rape and murder, so that eventually we shall reach a point where we'll have so much data that we shall all know that it's wrong and that we can find a better way of living in harmony with each other. So, rather than sitting in judgment upon those who appear to be causing themselves and everyone else difficulties, perhaps we could choose to understand and have compassion and even gratitude rather than judgment. They go there for all of us.

We can access the superconscious in meditation and in transcendence. The more we work with our spirituality, the easier it becomes to move between the conscious, the subconscious and the superconscious.

ATTAINING UNITY CONSCIOUSNESS

There are three main levels of consciousness through which we ascend as we expand our awareness, increasing as we go our capacity to forgive, allowing ourselves and others freedom to heal.

Individual Consciousness

This is where we begin – believing that we are individuals and that what we do affects no one but ourselves. Usually we grow beyond this quite quickly, but sometimes we remain locked into that individual perspective, seeing everything only from our point of view, feeling like victims of others' aggression and holding grudges and resentments.

Sometimes very bright, intelligent people are unable to see how their behaviour affects others. For example, those who drink or take drugs and behave in a sociopathic manner are often oblivious to the devastating effect it has on all who care for them. They see their partners deteriorate in pain, and fail to make the association even when it's spelled out for them. In extreme cases there is what is known as psychopathic personality disorder, where there is no development of conscience and cold disregard for the feelings of others. All of these people have some degree of root chakra dysfunction, probably due to difficulties they suffered before the age of five when the root chakra was in the process of activation and development, and they are stuck in individual consciousness. Sadly, they often need to lose all that they profess to love in order to do the work that will help them painfully climb to the next level of consciousness.

Group Consciousness

As we develop our second (sacral) and third (solar plexus) chakras, we come to see ourselves as part of a group, be it a family, school class or community, and recognize that our actions affect and are affected by those around us. As adults we can see that although each of us is unique, acting according to our emotional state and our personal circumstances, nevertheless we are all part of an intertwined and integrated system, our actions impinging upon others in ways that we previously failed to recognize. We can also start to see that sometimes we have been the 'victim' and at others the 'aggressor', and that we may have hurt others quite unintentionally, as others have hurt us too.

Eli's father died during the war. His mother tried to cope with bringing up her children alone, but this wasn't easy, and none of them got the attention they would have liked. There was no time for helping with homework or encouraging education, and Eli was unable to achieve his potential academically. In his teens he was angry and resentful about his lost opportunities, jealous of those around him who had a father to support them and watch them play football, and eventually he found an outlet for his frustration by trying to right the balance by taking for himself those things of which he had felt deprived. By his twenties, Eli was known to the authorities as someone who was often involved in petty crime, and he already had been deprived of his liberty on more than one occasion. He was now a police target when there was local crime, and his anger, frustration and sense of injustice escalated even further. His girlfriend became pregnant, and although he felt unready to be a father and had no model of fatherhood of his own, he was thrust into a situation where he had to provide for a woman and a child. He knew no other way of doing so than that which he had practised since his teens. Very soon Eli was in prison again, and his girlfriend was left trying to support a child alone. Her frustration and sense of loss because of her own abusive childhood led her to feel unable to cope, and sometimes her frustration, sadness and pain would erupt in anger. She resorted to the only thing she knew and she began to try to control the child by smacking him. The child is now suffering abuse, and is growing up feeling angry and ready to take on the world with violence and to extract from it everything he feels it owes him.

This is a simplified but nevertheless common chain of events. Everyone in this scenario has acted to the best of their ability. In three generations, no one set out to cause harm. Each did what they could in the light of their emotional state, the information they had and their personal circumstances. With whom are we to be angry? Whom do we have a right to judge? Whom are we unable to forgive? The father who died? The mother who couldn't give her children the time they deserved? The youth who knew no better than to try to deal with his loss and lack of guidance by getting into trouble? The child/woman who felt lost and eventually couldn't contain her pain and lost control? The abused child who exacts a price from the world with which he is angry?

The hurt that we have caused each other has been part of our helping each other to grow. Although we all need love, it's often pain that stimulates change. So at the level of group consciousness, we can start to view others with compassion, empathy and love. Forgiveness becomes easier when we can see that those who have hurt us may have done so without malice, but simply while trying to sort out their own feelings and their own life events.

Unity, Universal, Christ or Buddha Consciousness

The development of our soul eventually raises us to the level of unity consciousness, where we recognize that though we are all unique and separate souls, we are unified in one Spirit with one consciousness, and are recognized as individuals only by the love we radiate. And since we are all joined, what I do to you I ultimately do to me and to everyone and everything in the universe. I cannot hurt one person without ultimately hurting another. If I do harm to someone I dislike, I do the same harm to those whom I love. Destructive thoughts, words and vibrations, aggression, fear and violence harm everyone – ourselves and those we love as well as those upon whom we focus our anger or hatred. And similarly, if we radiate love into the world we can touch everyone. The smile I smile at my child teaches him to smile at others. The love I show my patients spreads out and yields fruit in distant places and times.

And since we are all connected and have all been part of each other's development for as long as there has been life, forgiveness become redundant – there is simply nothing to forgive, just things to be grateful for. Revenge becomes anathema, harming ourselves as much as the other person, whereas tolerance, kindness, peace and harmonious thoughts and actions benefit us all. Just spending a few moments sending out loving thoughts helps neutralize some of the harmful vibrations which are forever reverberating round the universe. Sadly, as a whole, we, the human race are generally operating at a level below unity consciousness, otherwise we could not consider the retributive 'justice' in the death penalty or in some other forms of punishment meted out in various parts of the world. There is good news! Even if for the greater part of an earthly lifetime we have been stuck in individual or group consciousness, at the moment of what we call death there is the ascent to unity consciousness. Finally we see and feel the all-embracing, all-encompassing love which flows into us and holds us, but of which we are also part.

NURTURING OUR SOUL

Our soul, like everything else, thrives when nurtured, and time and effort spent nourishing it will be richly rewarded in easing our journey and facilitating a rise in consciousness. Our soul thrives on inner peace, quiet and gratitude. It responds to love, music, poetry and the spoken word, truth, integrity, beauty, wisdom and all the finer gifts. It delights in joy and harmony, play, laughter and charm. It enjoys just being, and loves being loving. It loves humanity, service and life. It wants us to expand our boundaries, to burst out of the structure our minds have created, to take risks, rise to challenges, have fun and become our magnificent selves. It rejoices when we spend time with people we love and who love us, and when we do what we do out of love. It is strengthened by processing our pain, or helping others process theirs. A positive attitude cheers it and forgiveness empowers it. It is bruised by aggression, discordant noise, disharmony, dishonesty, violence and abuse. It is saddened by self-destructive behaviour and by longing, which causes us to miss the beauty of now.

So the choice is ours, whether we treasure and nurture our soul and smooth our way to enlightenment, or harm it and hinder our own progress. We can choose softness and gentleness, kindness and love, or harshness and aggression, meanness and revenge. We can choose silence, meditation and peace, or argument, criticism and sarcasm. We can choose walks in the forest, music and harmony, or smoke-filled noisy places with aggressive voices, alcohol and drugs (though there are angels there also!). We can learn to use our intuition, becoming aware of every single gift of the universe, hearing its nuances and seeing its signs, or ride roughshod over it, trampling its tenderness. But when we're struggling in pain, it often feels as though we have no choice at all. Don't worry – it's natural to rise and fall with our emotions, moods and relationships and to have cycles of building and destruction. It's all part of our development as we learn inner balance. You can make a new choice again in every moment.

Developing our soul is synonymous with developing our whole energy body, and in particular the chakra system, which reflects our every attribute – physical, emotional, intellectual and spiritual. (There is a brief verbal sketch of the energy system in Appendix 1.)

DOES WORKING ON YOUR SOUL SHORTEN YOUR LIFE?

On the face of it this sounds like a ridiculous question, but it is one that was posed to me in good faith. If our task is to refine our awareness and come to full consciousness, then does working on our soul mean that we complete the work and get ready to leave sooner?

There are wise and ancient souls who come only for a brief period with little to learn and much to teach, but for the rest of us, working on our souls doesn't shorten our lives – it gives us longer to be happy, to teach and mentor, to find peace and of course to continue to learn. The learning never stops, even through the moment of departure, transition, or what we have known as death. Doing our soul work makes life a passionate adventure, every moment a sublime and exciting clue as to the next move, the next gift, and the next piece of the vast jigsaw. As we use our intuition to decipher the language of the universe, we're able to move forward gracefully, negotiate the choreography of this vast theatre and begin to dance with life. The more we do this, the more we explore the further reaches of our soul and prepare ourselves for our reunion with Spirit.

Now we've looked at the development of consciousness, let's move on to our next task of resolving karma. So first let's see what we understand by karma.

KARMA

Karma usually gets a bad press but, very simply, karma is the rule of cause and effect, a balancing of the books, and a merciful teacher that allows us freedom to do whatever we wish, but gently shows us the consequences of our actions, rather in the way a loving parent might, who knows that there is neither growth nor real love in colluding with their children. I believe it was Stephen Levine who asked: what could be more exquisite than a teacher able to help us remove the obstructions to the natural brilliancy of the soul? Although it might appear that karma is not in effect in some people's lives, and that they 'get away with murder', it always is, even though it might take a lifetime or two finally to resolve and push the lesson home. As we have seen, unity consciousness shows us that what we do to others we ultimately do to everyone, including ourselves. With that understanding comes the realization that we have absolute responsibility for where we find ourselves, though we may be balancing in the present something that happened a long time ago – even in another lifetime. Sometimes we're called to compensate others for what we did to them in previous lifetimes, and occasionally we may come together again and again as we explore a particular aspect of life together until we finally understand. Wherever there is something that is recurrent and that we don't understand, it's worth thinking of a possible past-life connection with karma that we need to resolve. This is not always the case, however. Have a look at Evelyn's story.

Hilary and Evelyn were sisters who had always had a difficult relationship. Though Evelyn remembered times when they were very young when she felt they were fairly close, it had been a battlefield of a relationship for most of their lives. They had had periods of time when they had tried to get close, Evelyn usually being the one to make the overtures and bridge the gap, but there had also been several periods of years when they had had no contact whatsoever. Evelyn, now in her fifties, was once more trying to make sense of just what had happened, since the mere thought of her sister filled her with sadness and reduced her to tears – the anger having long since gone. Despite the work she had done on herself, this was one area with which she still could not seem to come to terms. The current cold war had been in existence for four years. Evelyn said that she had always loved her sister, but that she recognized that she must have done things that hurt Hilary. She knew that occasionally she could be clumsy in the way she expressed herself and immediately regret that yet another misunderstanding had arisen. But the main issue that she remembered was that at various times during their lives up until she was about thirty and Hilary thirty-four, Hilary would take her things. Hilary being older and more powerful, in their younger days this took the form of bullying as she would take toys, books, records or clothes and refuse to return them. Later it would be more subtle and yet more destructive. Evelyn would be looking for some treasured possession and find it missing, only to find it hidden elsewhere later. Very occasionally her possessions would disappear altogether. Pocket money was another nightmare as Hilary would spend hers, then raid Evelyn's moneybox. Apart from this, Hilary seemed to be constantly angry with her sister, and uncharacteristically, Evelyn would tiptoe around Hilary, trying not to ruffle her feathers.

The whole issue had such a past life flavour that I asked her if she would be willing to have a regression and see what we could find.

Evelyn found herself in nineteenth-century London, a quite wealthy man, married with six children. She described the house, its furnishings indicating prosperity, and the clothes he wore as being well tailored. However, on describing his children Evelyn was visibly shocked to find them very poorly dressed, living upstairs in quite sparse surroundings with a nanny whose duty it obviously was to keep the children out of sight and earshot of the parents. The main surprise came when she immediately recognized the youngest of the children as her sister Hilary. Of all the children, this child appeared the most neglected and sad. We scrolled through time to any key event that was particularly relevant, and Evelyn found herself three years later at the bedside of the child who was dying of tuberculosis. The child's mother, Evelyn's wife in that lifetime, was crying, while Evelyn stood by watching and waiting for the inevitable, apparently unmoved by the experience.

Although we went on to deal with her own death experience in that life, that is not relevant here. As soon as she was fully back in the moment, properly grounded and able to discuss what had happened, the tears began to flow. For the first time she was having insight into what had gone wrong in her relationship with Hilary. She had been a neglectful, mean father, who had provided the bare minimum for his children, and had hardly valued them or their lives at all. Now, in this lifetime, Hilary had the upper hand and was balancing karma. We then looked at how best to deal with the situation, and Evelyn felt that Hilary would not be open to this as an explanation for their difficulties. We decided upon a ceremony where Evelyn could connect with the soul of Hilary, and from soul to soul, communicate her sadness, sorrow and regret and ask for forgiveness. Evelyn was more than ready to wipe the slate clean of resentment and anger about Hilary's behaviour in the past. Rather than feeling guilt-stricken abut what she had found, Evelyn was ecstatic. To finally understand was worth so much, and perhaps at last she could have a mutually loving relationship with her sister. Although that took some time and some careful handling on Evelyn's part, it did eventually happen and certainly to date there has been no more difficulty between them.

There are ways in which we can neutralize our karma, so to speak, by doing good works, being charitable, being loving and honest and living with integrity.

REALIZING OUR MISSION

Each of us has an individual mission or purpose (see also Chapter 9), the fulfilment of which is not only our life's work, but also our gift to the whole of the universe and to God. It is our responsibility to find and fulfil it – a duty to ourselves and the universe. Everything that your soul has experienced in all lifetimes thus far – in relationships, in work, in play, in love, in sorrow and in joy – has been moving you inexorably towards the fulfilment of this purpose – your destiny, your vocation, your individual and unique mission, your *raison d'être*. This is at the point where our physical, emotional, spiritual and intellectual gifts and our intention all come into perfect balance, and our will is perfectly aligned with that of the Divine. We feel bright and aware and our potential is unlimited as we pour our love into the world. Whether we are healing the sick, helping people grieve, making the perfect cardboard box, making music or taking care of the environment by carting away the rubbish, we are doing what we came to do. There is always an element of service. Whether you are to entertain, to protect, to govern, to heal, to invent, to nurture, make laws, or whatever, when you move finally into the sphere which allows you to express your vocation, the universe will move all obstacles and your progress will be not only unimpeded but impelled. Achieving our life's purpose demands that we are generous, honest, moral, sober and willing to be aware of the synchronicities that the universe sends to show us our way. As we develop our consciousness and nurture our soul, we are led to our purpose by what gives us joy and a feeling of such passion and excitement that we simply must fulfil it. This is what I feel when I have a new client to see for healing or psychotherapy, a workshop to teach, a conference to address or a new book to write. I cannot imagine not doing it. It feeds me, energizes me, thrills me, enlivens me, strengthens and stretches me. It is my life. This is what your purpose feels like. If you haven't found yours yet, don't worry, you will. Our throat chakra, which governs creativity, communication, truth and integrity, eventually helps us put all of that out into the world in the form of our vocation. It also demands that we follow the signs that the universe gives us and call upon readily available help from the non-material world (see Chapter 4). Listening is part of communication and so is asking for help. (Do you remember our intention to listen to the conversation the universe is trying to have with us?) Once truly on our path, insight and wisdom simply flow and we feel a joy in our hearts that sustains us through whatever trials might befall us. As a rule of thumb, if what you do makes you feel good about yourself, you're looking in the right place.

REDISCOVERING WHO WE ARE AND LIVING A JOYOUSLY SPIRITUAL LIFE

Sir Winston Churchill stated that the empires of the future would be empires of the mind. I beg to disagree, however. The empires of the future are the empires of the soul. Though as children most of us forget who we really are, as we develop and begin to realize our spiritual gifts, usually in our fifties or sixties or sometimes before, we start to remember. We begin to see ourselves as the spiritual beings we have always been and life becomes easier as we begin to trust more in the great universal pattern of life and in divine order. We find ourselves being calmer, worrying less about outcomes and being less ruffled by perceived insults and injuries. We begin to recognize those around us as the souls we have known and loved forever and come to a point where we acknowledge simultaneously our humanity and divinity. At last we live our purpose and find inner peace. Life now becomes a joyous and passionate adventure, every moment holding new excitement, our awe and humility growing side by side, moment by moment, as we once again develop child-like wonder at the amazing beauty that constantly surrounds us. There may still be essential challenges, as we shall see in the next chapter, but our attitude to them has changed to one of not only openness and acceptance, but even delight at the opportunity to test our skills and expand.

But spiritual gifts and experience can be misinterpreted if we're not careful. Much of the phenomenology I was taught as a young psychiatrist I saw as spiritual and mystical rather than psychotic. (However, I do believe that psychosis probably exists – though perhaps only because we have not yet found a better way of understanding it and therefore label it to pretend we do.) Some of the experiences that I had as a child and have continued to have to some degree throughout my adult life are what some would label psychotic – seeing things that are not present in the physical reality, feeling things with my hands that some would say do not exist, hearing voices of people who have 'died' and being able to receive messages without any verbal stimulation. Much of this would be claimed to be hallucinatory or delusional, and for this very reason I did not talk about my experiences for many years. This in fact very normal state of utilizing more of ourselves than we previously could has been called the paranormal, since it remains beyond the scope of average human experience. Learning to tap into the superconscious to find wisdom, and learning to increase our conscious awareness so that sounds and sights that were not previously available to us now are, is quite normal for the developed soul. These are the things that I consider to be precious spiritual gifts for which I give thanks every day.

Many people spontaneously begin a period of rapid development in midlife. However, for some this occurs at a much younger age, often precipitated by some life event that opens us to the possibility of something greater than that which we have thus far perceived as normal experience. Several factors, including our experience thus far in this lifetime, past-life experience and the development of our soul, are relevant in the spontaneous development of expanded awareness. Though there is often a global development, one gift may feel more natural and powerful that the others. For instance, though I'm clairvoyant, can view remotely (sometimes!), channel, view auras and chakras, intuitively diagnose, do space clearing and read most of the synchronicities that the universe sends me (I think!), my main gift is healing. However, I have a wonderful friend who is a medium and channel and is clairvoyant, and intuition just pours from her, but she has no feeling (so she claims) for healing. And someone else who has no desire to do healing with individuals may, for example, do amazing work with teams to help improve their productivity and well-being.

Some people feel that they have none of these gifts, but that is never true. They may not yet have developed, and it may be a decision for this lifetime not to develop them at all. However, we are all spiritual beings and have innate spiritual gifts. The more willing we are to develop our soul, the more of these gifts we realize and the more joyful life becomes. That is not to say that there are not ups and downs, but even with those, life becomes a passionate adventure. One of the blessings for me in psychiatry has been that many of the people who have found their way to my consulting room have been just ready to launch into their active spiritual life. The gifts, which may develop spontaneously as we clarify our chakras, are exciting and wonderful even in their raw presentation. However, just as an aptitude for playing the piano is amplified by lessons with a tutor, so spiritual gifts can be honed by training too. A word of caution here! Most people I see are eager to get to the higher gifts but are not so keen to deal first with the work of their lower chakras. Yet it's there that we need to begin doing the necessary work to ensure you're well grounded and happy with your humanity before you attempt to float off in your divinity. Living a joyously spiritual life requires that our humanity and divinity are well balanced, and that means we have the humility to keep it that way.

Some of the gifts you could expect to be able to develop naturally or with training are healing, mediumship, clairvoyance, channelling, precognition, remote viewing and out of body experiences. I haven't managed the latter yet, but it's on my list!!

A few words about intuition . . .

INTUITION

This is that innate skill that allows us eventually to perceive every single word, deed and happening, no matter how small, as significant and containing secret information locked within it. The treasure is encoded, so that we can interpret it and enrich our lives, or ignore the whole concept as some fanciful pipe dream. If you are willing to suspend judgment and test out the hypothesis that everything means something, pretty soon your life will change dramatically. Not only will you have greatly entertaining times working out what things signify, but also life becomes so easy, since we are directed by an endless stream of fascinating clues about where we are, where we're going, what we need to do and with whom, etc. It's like speaking a new language as you engage in dialogue with the universe. Just imagine spending a few moments asking for help on some issue and then knowing that everything from that moment on will be part of the answer. It really can be as easy as that. Though it might take a little while to develop your intuition to the point that you can always trust it, when you do, it will never fail you. The only possible error is in the interpretation.

But a word of caution – in starting to work on your intuition you give an invitation to your subconscious to deal with all it holds and move you to a higher level. However, that means that for a while you may feel you are in more chaos as the subconscious obliges and gives you lots to work on. If you can simply hold steady

---

and remember that everything, even this, has an important message, you will soon emerge viewing life in a totally different, more exciting and enriching way.

LEARNING FROM THOSE WITH WHOM WE INCARNATE

All of life is a relationship – or many relationships. I have a relationship with you even though we may never have met. I have a relationship with the trees around my house and the animals on my ranch. I have relationships with my friends and family, of course, but also with those I have never met and probably never shall. But of course some come directly into my life, drawn to each other as we are so that we can simultaneously teach each other and learn from each other. These people mirror for me aspects of myself I may like and admire and need to nurture, or that I dislike and resist and need to bring to the light to heal. Simultaneously we offer each other signposts about our spiritual growth. We have chosen not only to be incarnated with our family of origin and those with whom we have direct contact, but with a whole generation – many of whom, as we'll see later, we will have reincarnated with before as a large soul group.

Some people come into your life for only hours or even a moment, and leave their mark on your life forever as you do on theirs. I can think of people who came to see me for a single session and taught me something new, brought me something to reflect on, pointed out something in my practice that needed attention. Perhaps they were too hurt or angry to stay and showed me a new aspect of heartache. The people I sit next to on a flight have prompted some of my greatest insights. What about you? What was the person who crashed into your car really teaching you? Something about awareness? Or anger? Or forgiveness? And the person who was rude to you in the supermarket – was he prompting you to look at the times when you're irritable with others? And the person with whom you 'fell in love' and who then broke your heart? What were you learning about real love? The woman who smacked her child and horrified you – was she asking you to look at your own capability for violence? Was she going there so that you could learn from her and not have to experience that yourself? Or to remind you that you have already been there, though maybe not in this life-time?

Our relationship with each and every one of these people is important, those we meet briefly as well as those who never personally make it into our lives. How do we feel about someone on the other side of the world who is having a difficult time right now? Does it matter to you that women are being tortured in many parts of the world? That children are dying in Africa or that an old lady down the road never has a visitor? Why are these things happening now in your lifetime? Certainly you are to learn from it, and perhaps also to be one of those who are to do something about it.

Recently a group of people was instrumental in my life even though I was with them for maybe only an hour. I was travelling by train to a workshop in Scotland. The journey had been peaceful and I was happily thinking about the workshop and tuning in to the wonderful people who were coming, and thinking expectantly about the venue, a beautiful old house which I hadn't previously visited.

Suddenly I was surrounded by noise and chaos.

A family had boarded the train, and though there was no one else but me in the long carriage, they all sat very close to me. The adult couple, presumably the parents, were obviously in disharmony, a situation that the four children exploited to their utmost. The man tried to concentrate on a tabloid, but was continuously interrupted by the eldest daughter – possibly fourteen years old – who made angry, rude and vaguely sexual comments to him, while suggestively licking a lollipop and verbally inviting him to watch, which he occasionally did momentarily before burying his face again in the newspaper. The mother glanced at them occasionally, but for most of the time gazed out of the window, a look of despair on her face. Two younger daughters, one of about ten and already sporting several home-applied tattoos, and the other of perhaps eight, argued in loud and often profane language, while standing on the seats and flicking pieces of torn paper at each other. The youngest, a boy, tugged at his mother and father, neither of whom paid him any attention except occasionally to shout at him to leave them alone. The atmosphere around them was tight and heavy, as though they were in a smoky bubble, and although they were close to me, the vibrations were somehow contained between them and I could see flashes of energy jumping between them, and dense, heavy bonds holding them together.

I wondered just what pacts these family members had made with each other on coming together on this occasion. It appeared that the whole family had come to learn different aspects of abuse, for here in the openness of a railway carriage there were displayed several faces of an abusive situation in which they were all involved whether as perpetrator, victim, witness or passive accomplice. And why did they choose to board the train then and sit within three feet of me? What had they come to teach me? Perhaps they were angels! Certainly they were great teachers. I felt sad but privileged to witness their pain and have felt waves of gratitude for them ever since.

Then there are those who do come more intimately into

our lives bearing gifts – some of which feel wonderful, and others that sometimes we would have preferred, consciously at least, not to have received. But often the happy and peaceful times can make us complacent, and we may then subconsciously choose pain or conflict since they are great teachers. That is not to suggest that we should court pain in order to grow, but more to accept that it is bearing a gift in the form of a lesson we need to learn.

SOULMATES AND KARMIC CONNECTIONS

These give us some of our greatest lessons, of course, and we shall be dealing with them at length in Chapter 7. Soulmates are those with whom we have lived many life-times in many guises – some of them feeling wonderful and others testing us to the limit as they prompt us to grow. They may have turned up as partners, parents, children, very close friends – or even enemies! Since we have lived many lifetimes, we have had more than one soulmate and we may meet more than one of them in this lifetime – or perhaps none at all. They don't always reincarnate with us. Though meeting a soulmate can be a wondrous thing, filling us with instant recognition, knowing, longing and deep connection, it may not lead to a relationship that is either peaceful or with us for the rest of our lives – though of course in many cases it does and, having come together, couples live happily ever after. But our soulmate may have come to help us grow by testing us, pressing our buttons and challenging us as only a soulmate can. And indeed that initial emotion on recognition may be one of fear, anger or revulsion, depending upon what we chose to teach each other in the last lifetime together. We may have unfinished business and be loving and mutually supportive, or there may be animosity and conflict between us. Whatever, the experience will always be one of great learning, even if the learning is about how to separate!

Valerie, a woman in her fifties, a Reiki practitioner doing wonderful work, came along to see me feeling sad and depressed. Her relationship with her partner of ten years was in tatters, her mood was low and her sleep disturbed. She was feeling guilty that she could no longer hold with her partner, whose behaviour she found unacceptable, the warm, loving and patient stance that she had with her clients. She was constantly beating herself up with guilt and shame, feeling that she should have known better, coped better and had better judgement than to have allowed herself to get into this situation. Much of her shame was born of her integrity, and her self-disgust with her own behaviour which now included verbal and sometimes physical violence. If she was as spiritually advanced as she had hoped, how could she find herself in this mess? How in her private life could she deal so poorly with what she would cope with admirably in her professional life?

Valerie had obviously learned a great deal from her partner. He was testing her in areas that she had not yet explored and she had never dealt with such a situation at such close quarters. She was exploring her shadow self, that part of her which thus far she had denied – the part that could retaliate, even with violence, that would self-protect with rage, and she was also learning much about her clients and their partners and the suffering she had only previously imagined. Her partner was a great teacher, an old soulmate whom she had recognized immediately they met, and who had agreed to help her experience these things in this lifetime. It was partly this knowing that had kept her in the relationship so long when everything else told her to get out before they both got severely hurt.

What was necessary now was for her to assess firstly whether she felt she had learned what she needed to know, since only then would the lesson be complete and the situation change, and secondly whether the relationship was strong enough to survive. Sometimes when the lesson is over the whole situation can recover, but sometimes the final part of the lesson is extricating oneself from it and having the courage to leave. Only Valerie knew which choice she needed to make now.

Valerie's attitude to the situation indicated her humility, as, despite her shame she was able to ask what she was learning and take responsibility for her part. Sometimes the more we grow, the more we uncover other areas that need our attention so that we can process more of our unfinished business and become purer souls. We shall be discussing this in more detail later.

All of us, like Valerie and her partner, have made pacts and contracts with souls with whom we have incarnated many times to learn and teach simultaneously and help each other resolve karma.

A person with whom we have a karmic connection, who has been a companion at some time, may feel like a soul-mate at first, but usually, although the relationship begins with much passion, a feeling of familiarity and connection accompanied by what seems to be love, the flame dies quite quickly and we suddenly 'wake up' wondering just what we could have seen in this person. The interests, standards, values and ethics we thought we shared turn out to have been nothing but a honeymoon fantasy. Sadly, it might then take us a long time to extract ourselves from this relationship, the purpose of which has been to complete business that we left finished at some other time.

What we are all hoping for, I suppose, is that wonderful lifelong relationship which leaves us feeling in love most of the time and fills us with wonder and joy. Sometimes there are memories, clues and flashbacks which make the ongoing relationship over lifetimes exquisitely wonderful and filled with amazement.

Let me tell you a true story – perhaps the kind we should all like to experience.

In the 1970s a spiritual woman I know had a past life regression in which she found herself in America in the seventeenth century. She was a Native American man and the village in which he lived had just been sacked by settlers. Most of the people were dead and he found himself rocking on his knees, chanting and holding leaves and herbs on a dreadful wound in his dying wife's right thigh. In the same regression, she visited another life. She was in Paris in the eighteenth century preparing to be married. She was wearing a very distinctive dress and her maid was dressing her hair with pearl beads. She recognized the man she was to marry as the wife of the other life. Both these lifetimes were filled with deep and passionate love for the other person, and after the session her heart was full of great joy that at some time she had experienced such a wondrous love.

In the 1980s, by a strange set of circumstances, she met someone who she would never have thought would have come into her sphere. Even before they met, she found herself having strange emotions about him that she didn't understand. When they finally met, she instantly recognized him as her soulmate, though neither of them was free to be together at that time. A year or so passed and they met again, and this time there was an instant and undeniable connection. What's more, they were both now free. Within a very short period of time they became lovers and she was amazed to find that he had a huge scar on his right thigh – the result of a childhood accident, but in the exact place and of the exact shape she had seen over ten years ago in the regression. Almost immediately they were planning to be together for the rest of their lives. They spent a deeply intimate evening discussing the ceremony they would have. She had thought of something spiritual though fairly traditional. He said he had another idea. He had a picture of her in a particular dress that he could design for her.

He described exactly the dress she had worn for her wedding in Paris. He added that she would look wonderful with pearls in her dark hair . . .

BECOMING ENLIGHTENED – PEACE AND PARADISE

We have all that we need to make our lives paradise, and whatever obstructs our peace is internal, no matter how much we might like to blame others or external events. Acknowledging that everything is in divine order and exactly as it should be can completely change our lives. That doesn't suggest complacency, but humility and acceptance. Learning to change our attitude, to be ever grateful and to come from a place of unconditional love, draws positive loving people towards us and brings us abundance, smooth progress and joy. If we have created a 'negative reality', (read again Clara's story later in this chapter), an inner shift towards positive thoughts and emotions can bring us back to inner peace. This is not only so on an individual level, though as Lee Carroll and Jan Tober, authors of *The Indigo Children* (Hay House, 1999) said, 'Even vast sweeping social change has to start inside the mind and heart of one person at a time'. When the majority of people in any community or country embrace negativity, anger and violence, they manifest this collectively and produce mass conflict or war. Each of us has the responsibility to change our inner reality to one of peace, and in so doing to help the whole universe move towards peace. The choice is ours – peace and paradise or hell. Many of us will not achieve enlightenment in this lifetime. Although we do our best to learn what we came to learn, most of us set up new karmic obligations as we go along, and we shall be back to deal with these in another lifetime, unless we can discharge them in this life with good works and making restitution. It has been said that grace overcomes karma. All of us are aware of some individuals, such as Mother Theresa, who would appear to be at the point of enlightenment on leaving the planet this time. However, enlightenment is an issue between each individual soul and the Divine. No one else is in a position to judge. We will talk more of this later. What each of us can achieve is a step closer to that state of bliss which will allow us finally to return to the higher soul planes which we have called heaven (see Chapter 9) and remain forever reunited with God.

CHOOSING AND CHANGING OUR REALITY

When we're angry or resentful, hurt or feeling abused, it's often difficult to accept that we chose to be where we are. If things have been very painful for you, please just take a deep breath and bear with me for a moment. Invariably we all made the best choices we could in the light of our circumstances, our understanding, the information we had at the time, our emotional state and our level of soul development. The converse is also true. Everyone with whom we have had contact has changed our life and has taught us valuable lessons about ourselves. If you can come to see that nothing – even your pain, sorrow, grief or anger – was wasted, and that there was a purpose to everything, even your suffering, there can be much healing. The thought of your pain being of benefit to someone else's soul might be a bitter pill – but it is so. You were courageous and loving enough to sacrifice your own peace in order to help someone else's growth and your own.

I am loving you as you digest that. Pain moves us forward far more quickly than peace, though please don't think that I'm advocating pain! However, wherever the pain is, that's where we need to pay special attention. Pain, whether due to fear, loss, frustration or anger, shows us where the next bit of repair work needs to be done, where we need to resolve something and move on. So in some ways it's our closest ally. As with anything that needs repair, the damage can just get worse if we delay. When we take courage to face our challenges, the pain almost becomes suspended for a while, as though our work anaesthetizes it a little, even before the issue is resolved. In accepting then taking action, our healing begins.

Have a look at Clara's story. Like Clara, do you need to move from the reality you've created to a better one?

Clara was very depressed and admitted that she had been so since her early adulthood. All her relationships had started well but had deteriorated into disarray, leaving her feeling betrayed and angry. Now in her forties, she had no real friends, was negative and constantly complaining about everyone and everything and used sarcasm and passive aggression as her means of controlling those with whom she came into contact, making it difficult for those around her to maintain their positive outlook. She chose very positive people to be with, but bit by bit became disillusioned as they started to become irritable and physically and emotionally distressed as she mercilessly, though unconsciously, sucked their energy and left them feeling parched and empty. Over the years many people had tried to help her with her depression, but all had failed since Clara was unwilling to let go of her anger and look at more positive ways of thinking and behaving. Underlying her difficulties was the determination that she would not allow her abusive father to get away with what he had done to her. Long since, he had stopped being her abuser, and Clara had taken up where he left off. She uttered one of the saddest comments I have ever heard from one of my patients: 'I have nothing to be grateful for.' What a slap in the face of God!

All that we need in order to change our reality is the earnest desire and intention to do so. But that means letting go of rigidly held beliefs, such as that we can only be happy when we get what we want. Happiness is present either in this moment or not at all. Our stubborn resistance to change what doesn't work, be it a relationship, a career, the place in which we live or the food we eat, keeps us stuck in the pain. Acceptance of what is, seeing what we can change and doing so, can completely change our reality – and that of those around us. Even though there may be things that we cannot change, altering our attitude to them can transform them nevertheless and we can stop wasting any more precious energy on them.

Things we cannot change include everyone else and their behaviour, the weather, the effects of the planets and the past – that includes what happened five minutes ago. Encouraging Clara to think positive thoughts rather than negative ones, to look for the good in people rather than focusing on the bad, to use direct communication rather than the unhealthy and irritating snide comments and sarcasm that were previously her choice, and to learn from but then move on from the past, eventually helped her shift her attitude from one of pessimism to one of child-like spontaneity, gratitude and delight where she could finally see the great gifts of the universe and look forward to a positive future with good friends and a healthy relationship.

Mrs Mary Fasano, a wonderful American woman, knows all about creating our own reality and the power of attitude. Not having had the opportunity to finish school in her younger days, she eventually began high school at seventy-one and graduated with a bachelor's degree at eighty-nine. Talking of her intention to continue with her education, she stated that the world is a final exam that you can never be prepared enough for. 'Knowledge is power and that power of knowledge makes me the most formidable eighty-nine-year-old woman at the bus stop!' she said. What Mrs Fasano knows, and that we would all do well to remember, is that a positive attitude attracts more positive energy around us, and the opposite is also true. She has chosen to create her own strength by the power of her heart, her attitude and her words, and she is indeed a formidable force.

RITUAL AND CELEBRATION

Sadly, much of our ritual and celebration has been lost since many of us no longer attend a particular place of worship or have the ritual of family gatherings or community celebrations. Ritual honours special events, focusing our minds and hearts on the power and sanctity of the moment and bringing together people to celebrate in a way that our ancestors did. In opening to ancient ritual we open to the wisdom of the ages locked in that racial memory of which we spoke on page 81 and draw to ourselves the power of our ancestral and racial line. However, it can be so easy to begin your own rituals that soon attain major significance in your life. Have a special place which is sacred – whether it is the space you have created for your meditation or a corner in your bedroom where you light a candle and some incense in the morning – and get into the habit of blessing your house as you enter and leave, of lighting candles at twilight, of touching your crystals and saying an affirmation. Whatever pleases you. In those moments you will find yourself focusing on the Divine within you and within every aspect of your life. In brief moments you will find that time is suddenly freed of its harness and can suddenly open into a space of peace – even if only for what we might call seconds. Try it. Your whole life will change.

Now that we have looked at the tasks we set for ourselves in every lifetime and understand our consciousness, karma and our spiritual gifts, we might think that life could be all plain sailing. However, as we shall see in the next chapter, we also find ourselves beset with obstacles which present our soul with opportunities to become stronger. Before we move to the challenges, however, we can affirm the joy and power of our lives and meditate on finding and living our vocation.

✪ AFFIRMATION

I acknowledge the power of my soul and celebrate my life. Today I align myself with the unseen forces of the universe and share my intention to create a positive reality for myself and the whole universe.

✪ MEDITATIONS FOR FINDING OUR TRUE PATH

Go to the sacred space that you have prepared. Have with you your flowers, a candle and perhaps a crystal and make yourself comfortable in your chair, on your cushion or meditation stool. Have with you all that you will need – some water, your journal and pen, and take the phone off the hook, giving yourself about forty-five minutes of undisturbed time. Be sure to be careful once you have lit your candle that it is safe while you have your eyes closed in meditation.

Take a deep breath and breathe all the way out and as you do so let your body relax. Let your shoulders fall, your chair take your weight and anything negative flow out through the soles of your feet and your root chakra. Take another deep breath and this time allow white light to pour in through the top of your head, shining down now through every cell of your body, cleansing, healing and balancing as anything you no longer need simply discharges into the earth from the soles of your feet and your root chakra. Relax. Just take a moment now and scan your body.

Note where there may be any discomfort and simply ask what that discomfort signifies. Note where there is any emotional discomfort and name the feelings you observe, then simply let them go. Note where there is any desire or feeling of want, and again simply observe and let it go. Note any lethargy and whether that means that you are resisting the experience you are to have. Note any agitation and restlessness and any doubt or judgment and simply let them go and be at peace in the moment. Allow your whole being to rest in the endless moment of now, knowing that you have all that you need and more and that whatever is right for you will be. Take a deep breath now and as you breathe out, relax once more.

Know that you are here on Earth with a specific mission which includes your own higher good as well as that of others. Know that you are here to be of some service to the world. Your mission is in line with your integrity and inner balance and is harmonious with the forces of the universe. Make a commitment now to clarity of vision and intent, and pledge that you are willing to fulfil your purpose knowing that when we align in this way, transformation takes place and everything magically falls into place. Know that decisiveness is essential now as we open to the higher vision of who we are, cutting off all other possibilities. Look around you now and see that everything is in some way an extension of you – your home, your friends, your environment, your career – all reflect your purpose as manifestations of your attitudes and beliefs. Without judgment now, see what you would like to keep and what you need to let go of. Does your lifestyle reflect your true purpose? Do your spoken and truly felt philosophy and beliefs reflect the person you know yourself to be? Do the people around you support your purpose and energy? Are there those you have drawn around you who in some way have a shared purpose and whose vibrations are synergistic with yours? Are there those who are no longer in line with your purpose and whose energy negates your own? Breathe love and light to them all now and also a flow of gratitude for whatever they have shared with you and given to you to help you see who you are and where your true path lies. Know that when we are in a state of gratitude, we are also in a state of grace. Allow love and light and gratitude to flow from every part of you now as you allow those who are no longer within your purpose to gently detach so that they too can find their true path.

Reorientate again in this moment, this precious moment, in which you are at the point of your power. Here you are, the sum total of all you have ever been. Here you are on the threshold of your purpose as it unfolds. Behind you is all the preparation you have made, all you have learned and experienced in order to be here in this moment. Now, set your intention. Set your intention to fulfil your purpose and to do so with good heart, with all your power, with your dedication and with enthusiasm and gratitude. Intend that whatever and whoever you need to come into your life now to further this purpose is now entering your life and that you welcome them with great love and respect. Intend that whatever wisdom you need now will simply flow through you, and that you will recognize it and act upon it. Intend that you will remain grounded and ordinary despite your extraordinary purpose. Intend that you will be open to the synchronicities that the universe will prepare for you so that you can see your path. Intend that your path will be illuminated with love and light. Add now any other positive intention . . .

Now sense a wave of gratitude for the fact that the universe has registered your intention and be open to receive. You may ask any question now and know that you will receive an answer in some form very soon . . .

Again send a wave of gratitude, and start to prepare for your return to this place and time. Take a deep breath and fill your whole body with oxygen, enlivening your cells and making you feel alert. Begin to be aware of your physical body. Move your fingers and your toes and start to come to a state of full awareness behind your closed eyes. Take your time, and when you feel fully aware, gently open your eyes.

Have a drink of water and stretch, then, when you are ready, record whatever you wish in your journal.

✪ PRAYER

God grant me the serenity to accept the things I cannot change, the courage to change the things I can and the wisdom to know the difference.

4 CHALLENGES ON THE PATH

. . . all things, good and bad, in light and in darkness, walk hand in hand in the simple rhythm of life and death; from flowering to decay, from childhood to old age, in sorrow and in joy.

Mirella Ricciardi, *African Visions*, Cassell, 2000

The challenges we set for ourselves are the greatest stimulants to growth. When we find ourselves in pain, we eventually have to move! In this chapter I've chosen to discuss what I believe to be some of the most important and perhaps frequently misunderstood challenges we may encounter on our human path – this could of course be a whole book in itself, so please forgive the fact that this is a long chapter! As with all challenges, each has a spiritual basis, though this may not be apparent at first sight. And although the topics I've chosen may seem unconnected, they all impede the growth and the smooth journey of our soul, since underlying each of them is separation. Living in unity consciousness – realizing that we're all one and that what we do to others we do to everyone and ultimately ourselves – encourages us to avoid barriers that separate us from others. For wherever we place a barrier or form a group – whether this is based on skin colour, religion, nationality, sex, age, dogma, belief or any other criterion – we simultaneously leave something or someone outside the group, then perceive it as separate from us. The perceived separation gives rise to a feeling of difference between us, a breeding ground for suspicion and hostility, which taken to its conclusion can become racism and, ultimately, ethnic cleansing and war. Finding the spiritual cause for our challenges doesn't necessarily render them easy to deal with; nevertheless, understanding them and being willing to look for a spiritual solution can have remarkable healing potential.

It's wise to note that we need challenges for yet another reason. They tend to limit our tendency to self-destruct. Just note how often, when people appear to be at the point of peace or at the peak of success, they cause chaos which destroys all they've built. It's at the point when we appear to have conquered everything that our potential for self-destruction is at its highest. So it's important for us never to arrive, to become complacent and rest on our laurels. Continuing to grow and taking wise calculated risks stretch us so that we continue to maintain the process of growth. People often ask me why I still keep doing new things rather than rest and enjoy retirement. Apart from the fact that I love what I do and want to continue to do it for as long as I can, I'm also respecting myself and building in the constant challenge I need to stop myself from self-destructing.

So firstly I'd like us to look at a spiritual model of illness, particularly depression, which truly is the dark night of the soul. Then we'll move on to encountering evil and some common behaviour which is much more harmful than we might initially suspect. Finally I'd like to deal with the not uncommon problems of soul loss, soul intrusion and psychic attack.

THE DEVELOPMENT OF ILLNESS

Illness always begins on a spiritual level. However at that

stage we often fail to recognize the signs (for example that we feel bitter and unable to forgive) or even if we do, we choose to ignore them. We're then accosted on the mental or emotional level, but again, we push through the warning signs, think of them perhaps in terms of 'stress', and carry on regardless. Often we even increase our efforts and do more of the same without pausing to interpret what's really going on and what we need to do to change the situation. Eventually symptoms develop on the physical level and at last they have our attention! Sometimes even then, however, we push on until our body shrieks at us and we simply have to stop. Let's have a look at what's happening.

The Cascade Model of Dis-ease

As we said in Chapter 1, every part of us is represented in our energetic body. As detailed in Appendix 1, each of the chakras and auric bodies has a particular function and governs certain aspects of our physical, emotional and spiritual life. Since the whole system consists of finely tuned high-frequency energy, an insult at any level spreads throughout the whole like the ripples caused by dropping a pebble in a pool. Sometimes the effects are felt very quickly and sometimes they manifest only years later.

Let's look at an example. Imagine a man who lost his father when he was ten. At that time his solar plexus chakra was developing, and since it governs among other things power, potential, motivation and drive as well as the digestive tract, we can predict what might happen to him in adulthood. Depending upon his innate temperament, he may become overpowering, angry and aggressive or else feel disempowered and a victim. He may also have difficulties with motivation and ambition and fail to fulfil his potential, or conversely, he may be driven, working too hard and over-achieving. Illnesses are likely to involve digestion – ulcers, irritable bowel syndrome, liver problems or cancer of the colon, for instance. But though the major problem involved the solar plexus, the adjacent chakras are likely to be affected too. The heart chakra may not have developed as well as it might since when it started its development at the age of twelve this man may still have been reeling from the tragedy, and therefore in adulthood he may have problems with commitment, with making lasting loving relationships or showing compassion and empathy. He may also be a candidate for high blood pressure, heart attack or stroke at some time if he isn't careful. Since the sacral chakra (the one below the solar plexus) won't have the flow of energy it requires since the energy is blocked above it, there may also be secondary problems with relating to people, with sensuality, sexuality and his inner masculine/feminine balance, and physically perhaps with the fluid systems, such as the kidneys and bladder. Paying attention to the original trauma, healing it and the energy system, can prevent him from going on to manifest all the physical possibilities set in motion when his father died.

We can trace every trauma at whatever age and predict how it may affect us later, both directly due to its primary effect on the specific chakra and auric body developing at that time, and also indirectly by a kind of harmonic induction throughout the system. Tracing the development of illness in this way also helps us decide what treatment is likely to be effective. For instance, if the problem is one of lack of forgiveness and rage that leads eventually to the person feeling cut off and depressed, antidepressant medication will only mask the problem and allow it to become worse.

Although of course trauma can happen at any time and at any level of development, let's look at the whole system from the top and see the cascade in action. Imagine someone who has experienced a traumatic event so severe that it changes his belief in the fact that there is a Supreme Being (or maybe, because of earlier difficulties or training, he never had such a belief).

At the level of the crown chakra and the causal body he rejects the existence of a divine being and therefore any possibility of a connection. Rather than feeling part of the great universal community connected by Spirit, he probably feels that he is out there fending for himself in isolation. Certainly the notion of being able to draw in divine energy to heal himself and others in all probability seems just crazy.

At the level of the brow chakra and the celestial body the understanding of Divine order and universal blessings is lost and the sense of isolation is increased along with cynicism and perhaps a tendency to ridicule those who do have spiritual beliefs.

At the throat chakra and the etheric template body he may have some difficulties with communication, perhaps finding it difficult to listen, with a tendency to talk at rather than to people. Knowing his purpose in the world is difficult and his cynicism and sarcasm and perhaps the cruel edge to his sense of humour may cause difficulties in relationships, in the work-place and in the community. By now truth and integrity may sometimes be causing him difficulty, and though he may steer clear of legal issues, he may be running a bit close to the edge, with his sense of personal honour less strong and unblemished than it might be. However, being honest enough with himself to acknowledge that might be hard. A bit of fiddling the books, taking the odd thing from work, not paying all his taxes – he tells himself that that's what everyone does. But is it? His spiritual discomfort is now starting to show.

At the level of the heart chakra and the astral body he now has issues around love and compassion, particularly for himself – he doesn't like himself very much. Despite the fact that he tries to hide this, it manifests in relationships which also suffer. He can't bond as well as he might and may be judgmental and critical. Now he feels even more isolated, cut off and alone, and experiences sadness and grief about what's happening in his life – though of course at this point he probably blames everyone else for his misfortune.

At the level of the solar plexus and the mental body he's not coping as well as he knows he could. He has issues with power, sometimes feeling like a victim and sometimes being aggressive. He may not have the courage to be openly aggressive, however, and it's likely that self-assertion isn't his strong point, so he may resort to passive aggression (see later) while punishing those around him with his irritability. His motivation and drive are suffering and he feels neither bright nor efficient. Work isn't going very well. The 'stress' is really showing and those around him aren't getting a good deal – in fact some of them, colleagues, partners, children, feel beaten up much of the time. He's in some considerable disease, but doesn't know how to remedy the problem.

At the level of the sacral chakra and the emotional body his emotions are fragile and he's anxious and depressed from time to time. At times he feels frightened and tearful, but probably won't admit it. His sensuality and sexuality are likely to be suffering and this adds to the lowering of his self-esteem and self-confidence.

At the level of the root chakra and the etheric body he has big problems! By the time the problem has trickled down to this level his very survival is threatened. Not only is he depressed, lonely and lost, but he may start to compensate for his feelings of insecurity and ambivalence about survival by drinking, taking drugs or eating badly, and of course his sleep is disturbed and sometimes he wonders if life's worth living. Of course the results of not eating properly, keeping strange hours and abusing himself generally are catching up on him. The dis-ease he's been suffering on higher levels for a very long time is about to finally manifest as disease.

Now, at the level of the physical body there may initially be just an assortment of vague symptoms. He doesn't feel well, doesn't have a lot of energy and feels jaded. But if he's not yet at the point of full-blown illness, it isn't far away.

Where Are You on this Slippery Slope?

If you look at where you are, perhaps you can't immediately see the steps you've taken. Perhaps it all happened very fast, or perhaps you need to look back years to find the signs. Like the auric bodies themselves, the steps sometimes appear to blend into each other and we can't tell them apart. But they're all there, and if you do have illness right now, you can back-track to see where the problem began. Perhaps it was with something that happened long ago in your childhood, or with a broken marriage (but then why did that happen?), or maybe it even comes from before this lifetime. We'll look at that possibility later. What's important is what you're going to do about it now.

Since the whole problem is a spiritual one, dealing with it in a spiritual manner is of prime importance. First of all, what do you have to lose by looking at it in a different way? I have seen some of the most cynical, unbelieving individuals change their lives completely just by taking a risk that there *might* be something benevolent and wise out there beyond themselves and instantaneously opening to a flow of energy. And like the desert after rain, everything starts to bloom. Doing work on your energy system will affect every aspect of your life, although you need to be realistic. You might be lucky enough to get a quick fix in one session, but it might take a while if your whole system has been out of balance for years. Usually we need to do some work to change every area of our lives so that we grow into a new, healthy way of being.

What Kind of Help Might You Need?

Some interventions are useful at any level – these include healing, Reiki, therapeutic touch, meditation, homeopathy (which works on the vibrational frequency), craniosacral work, massage and of course prayer. Others are more specific. For instance, psychotherapy works best at the brow, throat and heart levels. Colour therapy and visual arts work well at the brow. Sound therapy and music work best at the throat and etheric template level, whereas for the heart chakra work on forgiveness and relationship issues needs attention. Cognitive therapy works at the level of the solar plexus and mental body. Movement and dance as well as activity associated with water (swimming, hydrotherapy, aquaerobics) are ideal for the sacral chakra, and for the root chakra grounding exercises, working with clay or the earth, gardening, walking and outdoor sport and exercise are great. Only at the sacral and root levels is medication or surgery really of value, though of course it may give rapid relief elsewhere. (Please don't stop taking any medication you have been prescribed without consultation with your doctor.) But if, for instance, the depression you suffer is really about feeling isolated from the Divine, antidepressant medication is of little real worth. And if that painful clicking of your jaw (a tempero-mandibular joint problem or TMJ) is really an issue of poor communication and stress caused by not having the courage to speak your truth and act within your integrity, no amount of analgesics, mouth guards or dental work will relieve the problem entirely.

You may feel that I'm suggesting that it's best to begin your work at the higher centres and move down, but as with a tree, we need to nourish and strengthen the roots first and at least ensure survival. After that the leaves will come. Ideally we look after all our chakras every day (see Appendix 1) since an ounce of prevention is worth a ton of cure. However, regardless of what we do, for most of us there are times when nothing seems to work and we're thrust into an inner place that we dread, but one that is essential to our ascent. Let's have a look at depression.

THE GREAT GIFT OF DEPRESSION – DESCENDING INTO THE VOID

However our lives pan out, for most if not all of us there's a time when we sink into emotional (really spiritual) pain, feel that we've lost our way, or can't see the sense of it all any more. Whether this is an existential crisis, a response to life events or a biochemical episode, it's a natural part of life and essential to our spiritual growth that we descend into the void, sometimes more than once, and feel that we're lost with neither map nor compass. There appears to be no way out, no landmarks, no end. The structures we've created to support our lives don't seem to work any more. Those who love us can't really reach us no matter how hard they try. We're on our own. We can wear ourselves out ruminating about a solution, graze our knuckles resisting slipping further into the pain, and exhaust ourselves trying to hold our balance, but nothing stops us finally falling in. It feels awful and whether it lasts for hours, days, weeks or months, it's a time that can lead us to despair and a sense of abandonment and fear that we shall never recover. And in a way it *is* like an abandonment, but of the best kind. Yes, the *best* kind. For here we have nothing but ourselves. The only light to guide us is our own inner light, our connection with the Divine, and so eventually we're forced to use it or perish.

Our Own Personal Wilderness

Here, as we wander in the wilderness, we experience what has been called the dark night of the soul, and believe it or not, it's a great gift. It shows us, here at the tip of the pain, frustration and a sense of loss, where we need to do our spiritual work. The fear of course is that we'll drown in the pain, and that if we do survive, we'll never be the same again. Well, we aren't going to drown, but hopefully we will never be the same again, for if we use this time wisely, we'll come out of it changed forever. For what's available to us now is the resurrection of the soul.

Let me share some of my story with you.

I generally have a sunny disposition and many people think that I could never have been unhappy or depressed, but I'm pleased to say that I have, and sometimes I still have useful, brief bouts of melancholy, which I'll describe later. My heart goes out to anyone suffering depression, but as a fellow sufferer, I can honestly say that it has been one of the greatest gifts of my life.

In 1977 my family — my husband, the children and myself — suffered a series of life events that left us reeling, and we found ourselves leaving my beloved Zambia and back in England with no home, little money and no jobs. Though at the time I coped fairly well, after a few months I found myself sinking into a blackness I hadn't previously known. The quality of the pain changed, and I slipped from sadness and grief into depression. It seemed at the time to be the worst experience of my life and, racked with pain, I thought I couldn't possibly survive. I remember feeling that I'd lost my connection with everything – myself, my children, the people I loved, my ability to be a good doctor, my intellect, my soul, God. I would wake at three in the morning terrified about how I would survive the night, lost and alone, rocking myself while saying a mantra about my children since they were the only thing that kept me from wanting to disappear off the planet. Frightened about how I'd cope with the next day without the sleep I knew would not come; frantic that I might never be able to cope with the children again, and fearful about what would happen to them; thinking that they would never forgive me for having become a bad mother and neglecting them; feeling guilty for being so selfish and weak that I couldn't just shake this off and be myself; wandering about in the night wishing that there was someone awake to whom I could talk; calling the Samaritans just to keep alive a bit longer; still trying to cover up during the day how dreadful I felt, until someone kindly took me aside and said I must have some help.

And of course I did recover, but not only to where I'd been before, for that depression, my dark night of the soul, changed me forever. In 1983 I felt it start to come again, the blackness, the deadness in my soul, the pain of a quality that's so heavy it's almost tangible, and I was determined that if I survived again, I would find a way to deal with it so that I could get the best from it but not have it make a great hole in my life and take me away from my loved ones or my work. I remembered the amazing changes it had brought me before. There had to be a way to have the benefits without the incapacitating pain. I started to work on myself and discover ways of reconnecting with my soul that I've since used with thousands of other people.

Though I never again want to suffer as I did all those years ago, the brief episodes I feel from time to time are extremely valuable. Because my mood is usually bubbly, when I fall, I drop like a stone, and it's a long way from where I usually am down into the bottom of that place. I feel it happen sometimes quite spontaneously (though of course there have always been warning signs that I've somehow missed or ignored), and although I don't like the feeling, I've learned that good things are about to happen if I just handle it well. First of all, there's no point in resisting. My usual strategies don't work for this. Jollying myself along, distracting myself or positive self-talk just don't cut it for this particular melancholy, and the sooner I give myself the space just to fall in, the sooner I'll be out again. I've learned what works for me and now I always use the same procedure.

First of all, I need to be on my own. Then my body needs to be in a particular position – for me that's lying on my right side curled up in the foetal position – and I need to close my eyes and imagine that I'm just slipping into water and it's OK, I'm not going to drown, the river is just going to take me wherever it wants to and then I'll very gently emerge again and I'll neither be exhausted by resistance nor harmed in any way. It might take an hour or two or more, I might fall asleep, or my mind might just wander or seem to do nothing. I rarely cry. I just allow myself to be held by the universe while the inner process proceeds. And that's the key. I see it now as a process. My whole being is telling me that there's something we can't seem to access, something that needs attention. This is the entry point to my pain. Now the inner process will allow what I need to know to emerge as long as I do nothing. For me, that's essential. I do nothing. No cups of tea, walking in the garden, reading a book. Nothing.

Let's look at what's happening here. No matter how we struggle to find a solution, use our logic, get frustrated and gnash our teeth, our linear left-brain thinking just can't find the issue that underlies our pain. We've used every technique we think might work, from getting angry with it to praying about it, but somehow we've still found ourselves in this place. We can do no more. Just hear that. We can do no more. So just stop trying. Accept that whatever you usually do doesn't work in this situation. But that doesn't mean that something else won't. You're being given the gift of a time of great change and development. So just let go and trust that it can happen. You're not going to be in this place forever. You have inner strengths and inner gifts you simply can't access by trying. The good news is that while we're in the void, relaxing our control and taking our left brain out of gear, our more creative right brain gets to work and simply, effortlessly and wonderfully reorganizes data, abolishes old outdated and restrictive structures and comes up with insights and creative solutions that we couldn't have thought of, worked out or planned ourselves. There's no need to feel shame or despair in the void, though people often do, thereby incapacitating themselves further. You didn't do anything wrong. Everything's as it was meant to be, and now you have to survive. Let the universal kaleidoscope turn, and soon all the pieces will fall into a new pattern and all will be well.

Resurrection of the Soul

By allowing yourself space and time, you allow your whole being to shift so that you can emerge changed and with new wisdom, awareness and understanding. And what's more, you'll find that your emotions have shifted too. When we finally come out of the void, we have a kind of resurrection of the soul. We're more aware of the way forward, even if it's only a single step that gets us back on track when we've felt lost. Sometimes it shows us that we need to scrap completely what we've been doing and start again with a different direction. I remember a particular morning as I emerged from that depression in the spring of 1978. I opened the bedroom curtains and looked down at the garden and saw the daffodils. I noted that they were yellow, and was aware that I hadn't been appreciative of colour – one of the joys of my life – for a very long time. I looked up and the sky was blue. I felt tears fill my eyes and I could feel them warming the brims of my eyelids, I was alive again and the world was still there, waiting for me. I went and had a shower and, as I used to do when she was very little, crept into my daughter's bedroom and kissed her cheek, my wet hair falling on her face as I whispered good morning. She looked up at me as though she hadn't seen me for years – or was it that I hadn't seen her? – and said with such deep meaning, 'Hello, Mummy.' I was back. My soul was having its resurrection, and though it felt a bit like a limb that was just coming to life after being slept on awkwardly, floods of pain in with the pleasure, I knew that I had emerged from one of the greatest challenges of my earthly life and had not only survived but benefited. And with the resurrection of my soul came the knowledge that I needed to change my professional life as well as my personal life. I needed to use my experience and my insights in my career. Though service had always been of great importance to me, I needed to change my whole way of being of service.

By the mid-1980s I'd changed my course completely and was a consultant psychiatrist, leaving my first love of surgery behind. Through the pain of depression I'd found my way, and coming into psychiatry was like coming home to where I should always have been. And though I've been an unconventional psychiatrist, combining healing and complementary medicine with orthodox medicine, I found joy in my soul in having the privilege of working with wonderful people who'd also temporarily lost their way, and who honoured me by allowing me to be a fellow traveller in their lives while together we found it again.

KEEPING ONE STEP AHEAD OF THE GAME

I've often likened our progress to ascending a staircase. We climb up on to the tread of the stair and sit there complacent and enjoying the rest. But if we don't move, the universe comes along and provides the stimulus for us to move in the form of a life event, low mood or whatever, and, because it's too painful to stay where we are, we struggle to drag ourselves to the tread of the next stair. We can continue this process for years or get wise! We can learn that if we just keep moving – doing the spiritual work – and stay one step ahead of the game, we don't need any more kicks from the universe. Life will still have its ups and downs for us to learn from, but we can deal with them differently and just keep gently climbing on our path towards inner peace.

Now let's move on to those other behaviours I mentioned. But first, what do you understand by the word evil?

ENCOUNTERING 'EVIL' – BAD OR SIMPLY VERY SAD?

Sometimes there are other issues underlying the development of illness and unhappiness in our lives, and though we're the main players and it's our responsibility to take care of ourselves and keep well – and that includes choosing nice people to be with – sometimes we find ourselves in situations that have somehow crept up on us, and suddenly we wake up in pain. We're part of the equation and have responsibility for playing our part in the game; however, understanding it at least gives us a better chance of making a good choice about what to do now. So let's have a look at some rather insidious but damaging behaviour to which you may be subjected, or to which you may be subjecting others.

Evil is a strong word, and represents a condition which I've often refused to acknowledge, believing that everyone is inherently good. However, at times all of us behave in ways that are damaging to ourselves and those around us. Underlying what we might consider evil is an absence of the immense power of love, leaving a space for negativity to enter. Without our deep connection with the Divine, we become lost and desperate and find ourselves being destructive to ourselves and those around us, being both victim and perpetrator in a game we don't like but can't seem to stop.

But first a word about judgment. It's rare for us to know all about anyone else, no matter how much we *think* we know. And what we *think* we know might be incorrect! Over years of working with people in prisons who might be considered evil by some, I've become more and more aware of the pain they suffer which has caused them to separate, sometimes only very briefly, from their innate goodness. Were this pain brought to public knowledge, compassion and love might well replace judgment and hatred. Sometimes these people are angels walking among us to help us look at our own potential for negativity. However, that said, let's look at what we might perceive as evil and at what we may accept as 'normal' behaviour but which, on closer examination, may come into the same category.

A Definition of Evil

M. Scott Peck in his *People of the Lie* (Rider, 1983) defines evil as that force residing either inside or outside of human beings that seeks to kill life or liveliness. Perhaps, however, an essential element is malevolent intent. Often people involved in destructive, 'evil' behaviour are so hurt and damaged themselves that they're unaware of the devastating effect their behaviour has on others, though granted this isn't always so. Although I prefer to see the cause of 'evil' as absence of love, I do like Scott Peck's reference to 'killing liveliness'. This allows us to look at common behaviour in a different light.

First, let's have a look at something most of us would recognize as evil. Note your reaction to it. Usually it fills us with revulsion, often makes us feel confused or nauseous, and leads us to feel that there's an 'us and them' situation. *We* would not do something like this. Well, we shall see . . .

Some years ago I was treating a woman who was depressed and trapped in a violent and abusive relationship with a man who was quite severely disturbed. He regularly externalized his anguish and fury on his wife and she appeared too frightened to call for real help in the form of the police or the domestic violence team. I'd met him a couple of times and knew he was someone of whom to be wary. He then asked if I would take him on individually as a patient, but to have done so would have been so detrimental to his wife that I refused. He challenged me, saying that he could make me change my mind.

Over the next three days as I stood my ground, he systematically tortured and injured his wife with various implements, then sent her to see me to ask if I'd reconsider my decision. The police became involved and he was arrested and finally committed to prison. This man exemplified for me what we might call evil, his intent malicious and his actions dangerous. He was undoubtedly ill himself, his soul so tormented that his inner light was almost extinguished. He carried with him such negativity that other malevolence was attracted to him and he lived for much of his life in the darkness. Though I feel compassion for him, I know that it would be very unwise for him to be allowed to live among us unless or until he has the willingness to have some major soul shift. However, I also acknowledge that he taught me a great deal and made me have a look at my own potential for evil. Since in unity consciousness we're all one, I need to acknowledge that he was acting out something of which I too am capable on some level. It is not for me to judge him then, but to observe what part of me he could have been mirroring and do my best to change it while sending him light and healing too.

Would we never consider doing something so harmful, or do we just choose different instruments of torture? Do we wound with words and looks rather than material weapons? Yet aren't those just as damaging and don't they inflict just as much (or more) pain? Many battered women will report that in the end they almost manipulate the physical part of the fight because then at least the emotional torture stops – the words hurt more than the fists. And many people who cut or otherwise harm themselves report that the physical pain at least eases the emotional turmoil. Most of us feel the revulsion associated with physical or sexual abuse, but much emotional abuse goes relatively unnoticed.

And how about the following? This is quite different, but does it leave you feeling secure, or threatened by what might happen if you don't agree with certain methods of control? Can you see the malicious intent? Can you see this as evil too?

A middle-aged policeman used to come to Casualty regularly on a Saturday night to have his hands X-rayed. He would proudly announce that he'd 'dealt with' someone who wouldn't now have to take up public time and money in coming to court. He was self-righteous and projected an image of purity, blamelessness and public service. When I eventually pointed out that I didn't agree with his methods, his poorly veiled threats as to what might befall me made me feel nauseous, as I do when I encounter that total absence of love that we call evil.

Is Evil Only a Matter of Degree?

Those who are involved in satanic rituals cause dreadful harm on all levels – spiritually, emotionally, mentally and physically – but are so evidently evil that they need no further mention here. Physical and sexual abuse are also so obvious that I shan't discuss them further. More insidious, and sadly more common, are other forms of abuse, which, according to Scott Peck's definition, could merit the label evil, in that, though they don't destroy the physical body, they kill what he refers to as liveliness. Some of this common behaviour almost passes without notice, and unless we're willing to see it for what it is, it could very easily slide into what we would all have to acknowledge falls into the category of evil. We're not talking of illegality here, but of something much more malevolent – crimes against another's soul. Let's first say that many people who abuse others in this way are functioning at a level of development that leaves them totally unaware of the extent of the damage they cause while acting out their own pain. Some of them *do* know, of course, and many do have malicious intent. Again, on one level they're prompting the 'victim' to grow and meanwhile may be working out karma between them. Some notable dictators have also been called evil. However, one *could* say that some of these are great souls who came to shake us up and prompt us to have the courage to stand up for what's right. Being so openly 'evil', they appeal to the goodness in the rest of us and challenge us to rise up and defend those who are downtrodden. It's unfortunate, however, that many follow them, fearing the consequences of opposition. As long as we don't have courage to stand up for what is right and good, there will need to be people to challenge us with deeds florid enough to prompt us to react.

Take a breath and pause. Bear in mind the part of the definition which says 'killing liveliness', which includes crushing spirit and arresting spontaneity. Then read on . . .

We shall now look at passive aggression and sarcasm, negativity, destructive criticism and undermining, bullying and scapegoating, control and denial, since these underlie greater evils such as dictatorship, racism, torture, slavery, ethnic cleansing, violence and war.

Passive Aggression and Sarcasm

It's been said that passive aggression is more destructive than physical aggression and verbal abuse, yet usually neither a hand nor a voice is raised. Sometimes it's so subtle and insidious that it's hardly perceptible, except for that uneasy feeling we get in the pit of our stomach, knowing that something cruel just happened while not being able to put our finger on it. It can be as subtle as a look, a glance, a grimace or a word. When challenged, the person who is passively aggressive will absolutely deny what just happened, say that they were making a joke and wonder why we aren't laughing, or say that 'it came out wrong', often leaving us feeling rather stupid that we misjudged them and that we're actually the ones who are being unkind and that we need to apologize! However, we begin to feel tortured, harassed, lost and confused as our intuition tells us one thing and the other person (often someone we love) tells us something else with apparent sincerity. In the end we don't know what to trust and we finally submit. Let me give you an example.

Fay is a bright and bouncy woman who has a lot of friends and used to love her life. However, she came along to see me feeling tearful, depressed and anxious and said that she thought she was going mad. Though she loved her husband, lately they could hardly talk to each other without argument. At times she felt confused, lost and frightened and wanted to run away. On one occasion she'd become so agitated that she'd hurt herself and eventually hit him.

When she was away from her husband for any reason, she quickly felt like her old self, was able to laugh and enjoy herself and sleep well. So her problem was obviously specific to the situation at home, or more particularly to being with her husband.

They'd been together for five years, and she reported a wonderful romance, initially a good sex life, and great shared plans. One of the things that had attracted her was his great sense of humour, though over the years she'd found that it had a cruel, sarcastic edge, with its kernel often at someone's expense with a touch of ridicule. Some of the things she had originally seen as part of his boyish charm, such as his mimicking of her and their friends, now seemed distasteful. She was often made uneasy by apparently throwaway comments that she found hurtful, but whenever she mentioned this to him, he either said he was just kidding and asked her if she'd lost her sense of humour, or angrily told her she was sick, paranoid and needed help, then made snide comments almost under his breath as he was walking away from her. She'd become more and more confused by the incongruence between her 'gut feelings' and his denial, and she was now anxious, quiet and with-drawn around him and felt so wounded that she didn't want to be with him in company at all since she spent most of her time with a pain in her chest and a knot in her stomach fearing what might happen next. She'd tried to talk to him about it, but each time the conversation had exploded into a row and now she was afraid to confront him at all.

This is such a classic case of what happens to people who live or work with someone who uses sarcasm and passive aggression as their tools of control. Fay's husband may give the impression of loving and caring for her, but he system-atically tortures her and picks away at her spontaneity till she feels frightened to relax and be herself. The actual damage is immense, and if he were using some weapon other than his cruel mind and tongue, he would have been in prison long before now. Often the other person, in this case Fay, not knowing how to play the passive aggressive game, eventually gets to the point that she loses control and hits out, which of course lends more power to the true aggressor who can now abdicate all responsibility and claim to be the victim. Fay is now seen as the violent one who needs help. Does any of that sound familiar to you? If you see yourself on either side of that equation, please do talk to someone who can help you heal your soul.

Negativity

Depression is a negative state where we can hardly see outside ourselves as we get stuck in a descending spiral, guilt, shame and blame often completing the picture. Sometimes the negativity lingers long after the illness has resolved, born both of fear about ever returning to that dreadful place, and of anger and resentment about the loss of a chunk of our lives. Thankfully for most of us it's relatively fleeting, and we pick ourselves up and climb out of the pit we've dug for ourselves and move on, even if life continues to be a struggle for a while. Sometimes life appears to have given us a raw deal, perhaps because of childhood experiences or losses, and we continue to let these rule our lives, unable to reframe what's happened and see that there's a gift within even the most painful of situations. Where there's sadness, dysfunction or damage to the heart chakra, the mind exploits it and uses fear to interpret the world as threatening, punitive and harsh. Attitude can then mirror this belief and behaviour becomes similarly negative and cynical. Sometimes the behaviour is as subtle as unwillingness to smile or give a social greeting, sometimes more openly bitter, but whatever the means used, the person who employs negativity cuts down the joy and positivity of those with whom they come into contact. (Remember the definition of evil – killing liveliness?) Negativity in the mind of the individual creates a sense of darkness, and where there's no light, love cannot exist either, and it's easy to slip into that sinister place where we become florid with the intent to harm.

Negativity is destructive to us and wears down our loved ones. Sadly, some people make a career out of it, splashing it around on everyone they meet while sucking others' energy and undermining who they are. Though this may not be intentional, it's nevertheless damaging to those in their vicinity. When many people in a location or culture become negative, their thoughts and behaviour *en masse* can create the disturbance we call evil. It's this energetic disturbance that accounts for the changes in behaviour of someone who is generally positive when they are around someone who wallows in negativity and passive aggressive behaviour. As the particles in the atmosphere are intensified by fear, both individuals are drawn into destructive forces and violence, whether physical, emotional or spiritual, and as each then continues to reflect the other, the spiral gains force, increasing the harm to all those involved. Often the only salvation is to remove oneself from the battlefield of negativity and regain some solid ground where healing can take place.

It has to be said that some people carry more than their fair share of the negativity of the world so that the rest of us don't need to, drawing to themselves even more negativity until they're nothing but a shell filled with anger and hatred, gathering around them others who are similarly affected. Once negativity has coalesced and crystallized into a great malevolent force which can harm us, no one would doubt that it has entered the realms of evil, but long before that point, imagine what happens to the spirit of the person who lifts the telephone again and again with a smile on her lips and love in her voice to have herself cut down by the negativity of the other; who tries again and again to do something – *anything* – to please but never succeeds; who never receives even a smile of recognition: who keeps going out of love and compassion, but receives nothing but more negativity. Eventually she gets to the point where she hardly dares say that it's a nice day, or to laugh out loud or show any enjoyment. Has this person's liveliness been killed? Are you doing this to anyone? Is anyone doing this to you? What are you gaining from being a partner in such an abusive situation? Whichever side of this equation you find yourself on, your heart needs some care and attention. This is a malady of the soul that can be remedied if you want it to be.

Just as positivity and love can bring healing into our lives, ward off illness and keep us well, negativity can cause such disturbance in our hearts and cells that our physical body is rendered vulnerable and our soul light dulled. We actually become physically ill. Making a single step to offer love or service, no matter how lost we feel, daring to have positive thoughts and having faith in some force beyond us, gives us power to survive. We can start to send the spiral in the opposite direction and pull ourselves out of the hole in which we're drowning. Remembering that every single thing in our lives has purpose and contributes to our growth can help us to extract the potential from every moment and move on.

Destructive Criticism

As Scott Peck points out, we can break a child without hurting a hair on its head. But that doesn't only apply to children. Sometimes we criticize our partners till we break them. Their self-confidence undermined, they no longer know who they really are and what they're capable of. No matter what the hidden cause is, the results are the same.

Kieran had been a sad little boy, the younger of two children of a bitter and angry mother and a father who was ineffective and unable to protect his children from the onslaught of her rage. A sensitive child, Kieran had suffered more than his sister as his mother had vented her hatred of men on her developing son. He grew into a good-looking young man who, with little thought for anyone else's finer feelings, left a string of broken hearts behind him as he played off one woman against another, revelling in the new-found sense of power this gave him. At thirty he surprised everyone by deciding to marry Ros with whom he'd had several brief flings. Within a few months Kieran was carrying on business as usual, quite openly having affairs with little thought to the pain he was obviously inflicting on Ros. What was more subtle and damaging to Ros, however, was his consistent criticism as he projected his own failings on to her. He complained about everything – her cooking and the way she ironed his shirts, how she dressed and what she said. On the rare occasion when she drove with him in the car it was a nightmare. Sometimes when he did acknowledge that she looked good, he would then accuse her of fancying someone.

One would question just why any woman would allow this to happen to her. However, many women (and some men too) will recognize at least parts of their story – being with an overpowering partner who causes an ugly scene if crossed and slowly but surely eats away at our confidence until, totally undermined, we submit to keep the peace. Has Ros's liveliness been killed here? What if Kieran does this to his secretary too, and to colleagues? Or if we do it to a whole people, another nation – criticizing until they lose their spontaneous way of life and no longer know who they are?

Do you criticize and destroy? Do you allow anyone else to do this to you? If you answer yes to either question, it's time to look at what's happening to your soul. Why is it acceptable either to abandon yourself to someone else's cruelty, or to be cruel in order to relieve your own pain or rage?

Bullying and Scapegoating

Bullying and scapegoating occur in families, in schools and communities and may seem to some to be just part of life and not too much to get worried about. In many dysfunctional families one child may play the part of the scapegoat, providing everyone else with a diversion for their attention so that they don't have to look at the real issues. It becomes easy to blame the child who's behaving badly, getting into trouble, truanting, stealing, drinking or using drugs. The rest of the family is let off the hook. Bullying is often an extension of scapegoating. Older children often bully others physically or emotionally, and though parents may scold, usually the full extent of the abuse goes unnoticed, one child's life being made hell by another, and usually with the added threat that the behaviour will escalate if the bullied child dares to tell its parents. We're all aware of some of the tragic consequences of bullying in schools. Outside of families, we often find that the scapegoat comes from a family of another race or religion, or who chose a different lifestyle, or who are sick or live in poverty. Does turning our eye from scapegoating on a small scale allow us to slide into deeper water and silently condone what then becomes racism, apartheid and ethnic cleansing? At what level do we decide we're dealing with evil?

Control

Control can be quite subtle and insidious or openly aggressive. The underlying message, although most who use control as a weapon would deny it, is a belief that the other person can't live their life, deal with their children, decide what to wear, solve a problem or whatever as well as we can. The more we control, the more we condition people to believe that they're inferior to us, and bit by bit, we render them helpless, obedient automatons who neither think for themselves nor act without permission. And as they founder we feel more and more superior. Sounds awful, doesn't it? It is. Nevertheless this is the game commonly played out in many relationships – parents do it to their children and partners and 'friends' do it to each other. Control strips us of our capacity to be creative and use initiative. Whenever, by whoever – partner, parent or government – we're told how to behave, we're conditioned to believe we are not of our own accord capable of behaving as good, caring, responsible people. And in the straitjacket of control, where we can take no personal responsibility for choosing how to be, sadly we do forget how to behave, proving those in control right. We forget how to drive since we're so used to the person sitting next to us telling us how to do it. We lose our capacity for spontaneous fun and laughter, wit and improvisation since we're afraid to relax and share our inner joy. Control kills our liveliness. What's the difference between someone who controls us within a relationship and someone such as Hitler who broached no opposition to his will? Both are tyrants; it's only a matter of degree. And this same control is what we see in the larger context of colonization, where whole nations, told what to do and how to do it, lose sense of who they are, their traditions, spirituality, language, clothing and customs being lost not only to them but as a precious part of our global heritage.

If you recognize any of this in your life, please pause and take a breath, then ask yourself what right anyone has to control anyone else. What could we learn from our children, our neighbours or other nations if we were willing simply to observe with respect rather than trying to make things happen our way? We may learn a lot and discover things we may like to incorporate into our own lives. Wherever you are in the control game, it's time to have the courage to make changes and honour your unique way to your own destiny and allow others to do the same.

Denial

Denial is a defence that cripples our growth as we refuse to acknowledge the reality about ourselves and others, and the fact that we create the world in which we live. Denial exists where we refuse to take responsibility for our actions, and leads us to blame others while seeing ourselves as blameless, or conversely to blame ourselves for everything. Refusing to see the reality of other people's behaviour, excusing the inexcusable and staying where we continue to be harmed, or colluding with abuse to others, is also denial. The underlying problem is one of fear. We know on a deep level that once we accept the truth, we need to make changes or run the risk of knowingly acting outside our integrity. Though denial is common, for instance in those who drink or abuse drugs and who are unable or unwilling to acknowledge the reality of the damage that they're causing to themselves and those who love them, often their partner is in denial too. Have a look at Russ's story which is a little different.

Russ was in love with Lily. Childhood sweethearts, they had married young and he worked hard to provide a good life for Lily and their two children, Roy and Jade. On looking back, he first became aware that something was wrong when Roy was about six. He came home to find the house in disarray, Roy unusually quiet and Lily not herself. Though she blamed the fact that her period was due, he knew there was something more but ignored it, thinking that whatever it was would blow over. A year or so later, Jade started to wet the bed, and occasionally Russ noticed that she had a dark mark on the tip of her left ear. Somewhere he'd read something about bruises like that being suggestive of the child being struck across the head, but he shook his head to release the thought, feeling guilty for even considering that Lily might have struck her.

Now, two years later, as he was interviewed in Casualty while Jade was being treated for a broken arm, an internal haemorrhage and extensive bruising, Russ wept as he started to put together the signs that he'd seen and recorded but, because of his emotional investment and fear, had denied. His fear and his love for Lily had kept him imprisoned and had contributed to the current situation where Jade was severely harmed and Lily was in a situation where prosecution appeared inevitable and, regardless, she would suffer forever from guilt and shame. He had actually colluded in the abuse of his child and the suffering of his wife also, because of his lack of courage to confront the situation.

There are no such things as mistakes, but sometimes we make decisions that on reflection we regret. That we do so is human and part of our growth. However, taking responsibility for what we've done, to reverse or rectify the harm, is spiritually mature. Similarly, it is important for us to take credit for the good that we do and live with conscious intent.

Getting Out of Destructive Situations

This might be an appropriate place to look at how best to get out of difficult situations in which we're subjected to harmful behaviour. As we've already discussed, intention is a powerful force and precedes the creation of our reality. Once the pain within a relationship exceeds the pleasure, a decision starts to form, even if subconsciously, to leave the relationship. Usually we're aware of this potential outcome on some level for months or even years and give verbal 'warnings' which might be seen as ultimatums but are actually only clear statements of fact. While still desperately trying to hold things together, pouring in more light, more love and more energy to try to stay, we're afraid that we're on a path to termination. Unless there's timely acknowledgement of the danger by both partners, with a determination to address issues, support each other and actively nurture the relationship, the course is set for separation. Having the courage to open and grow rather than close down can transform our reality; however, denial by one or the other or both that our behaviour is causing pain hastens the end, as finally the potential for healthy communication, growth and recovery is lost. At the moment when the inner conflict finally becomes too difficult to bear, and we become de-energized and exhausted, we suddenly decompensate and begin to protect ourselves by withdrawing and becoming less available until eventually there isn't enough to sustain the relationship. Almost simultaneously, though perhaps not yet consciously, we find ourselves becoming available to new energy sources – supportive friends, family and work – as our energy shifts from the soul-destroying relationship to where we can gain some of the nurture, love and protection we so desperately need. Often, after years of misery, the relationship finally founders quite quickly in the end.

Things are easier in work situations, though we need to balance our need for self-preservation with the need for employment. It's worth considering also whether leaving your job constitutes constructive dismissal and whether the universe is giving you indications that your good would be better served elsewhere. Meditate on it, remember your guides and teachers (some of them here and others in the non-physical world) and use them, then make your decision. Rule number one is that you are the most precious thing in your life and your first duty is to take care of yourself.

Now let's look at some other phenomena of which we

might be totally unaware but which can cause us untold difficulties.

SOUL LOSS AND SOUL INTRUSION

Both of these sound a bit alarming, but, as with everything else, when we know what's going on, we can do something about it, rather than continuing to suffer while no one knows the real cause. The following common situations, in which many of us have found ourselves, can leave us open to soul loss and sometimes to soul intrusion too.

- Being in a traumatic situation such as an accident, especially if we're unconscious
- Having surgery, especially when we have general anaesthetic and when an organ is removed or transplanted
- Being in shock and dissociating from our bodies, for example during physical or sexual abuse
- Being incapacitated by fear
- Being in a rage and out of control
- Using drugs and to some extent alcohol, especially if we drink to the point of being unconscious or having blackouts
- Falling in love and 'giving ourselves' to someone
- Holding on to bonds after relationships are over
- Grieving for someone who dies and wishing we could go with them or begging them to stay
- Having a wide open heart chakra (see Appendix 1 and also *Affairs of the Heart*) and being constantly there for everyone because we can't stand their pain
- Spending considerable time with people who are vulnerable, disturbed and needy and feeling desperate to help them

Losing Parts of Ourselves

All these situations weaken our personal boundaries, and, unless we're astute and aware, leave us with little if any protection (see later). At such times we not only risk losing energy, but also parts of our soul may fragment and be lost to us, and what's more, parts of the souls of other people may become attached to us. Over the years, we may have fragmented in many situations and have left parts of ourselves stuck elsewhere, for instance with a person from whom it seems impossible to truly detach even though we're sure that the relationship is over. We then find ourselves feeling tired, listless and drained, suffering burnout, with poor immune function and a variable mood. Soul loss may be diagnosed as Chronic Fatigue Syndrome, exhaustion, nervous debility, depression and a host of other things, and often people will suffer for years without relief, attempts at treatment becoming more and more frustrating and demoralizing. Often health professionals become exasperated as nothing they do appears to work, and the 'patient' becomes more isolated and depressed. If any of that feels familiar to you and if you have been in any of the situations mentioned above, it would be worth having a spiritual assessment. There is also a meditation later that will help you.

Gaining Parts of Other People

Soul intrusion is also underestimated and underdiagnosed. Wherever we have soul loss, we may have soul intrusion also, as we have holes in our aura where soul fragments – or indeed whole souls – can enter. Sometimes we have an attachment or intrusion of part of the soul of someone who is still alive – usually someone to whom we have, or have had, a strong attachment – for example a lover – or someone with whom we may have been in an abusive or traumatic situation. Where the person is still alive, the strong connection remains between us even though this might be the last thing we want. (See Susan's story later.) This may well be the case where people sometimes 'fall in love' with their abusers, for instance the not so infrequent situation where a kidnapped person falls in love with and then sometimes joins allegiance with the kidnapper. And sometimes we pick up whole souls. Not all souls make it to the light after the moment of transition. If for some reason the soul has remained earthbound, it may either wander, remain geographically stuck (see Chapter 6) or attach itself to someone living, eventually becoming incorporated in their energy field. The soul may not even know that it's in the wrong body or attached to some other person's aura.

Usually soul intrusion is not a positive experience for the host. There may be draining of energy or changes in personality or behaviour, although in some cases the foreign soul actually tries to take care of the host. If, for instance, a grieving daughter refuses to let go of her mother and carries her soul, there may be some relief of her grief, and the mother may help her in a variety of ways. In the long term, however, the daughter loses the opportunity to benefit from her grief to become more spiritually mature. Sometimes the situation may become malevolent, and can have a variety of presentations, which may be misdiagnosed as psychiatric illness, which is, of course, unresponsive to usual treatment.

There are several levels of soul intrusion.

In shadowing, the foreign soul may be loosely attached or simply following the host while trying to help. Occasionally it may use the host as a vehicle for its anger. The host may be mildly affected with new and unexplained mood swings, anxieties or phobias.

In oppression, the attached soul has intruded into the aura of the host and overrides the host's natural spiritual function, leaving him confused when he finds himself doing what is instinctively foreign to him.

In obsession, the attached soul has taken up residence within the body of the host and its personality sometimes takes precedence over the personality of the host with marked changes in the host's behaviour.

In possession, which is the worst scenario and thankfully extremely rare, the soul of the host is completely displaced and the person has now become someone completely different.

There are four main techniques by which soul attachment and intrusion occur.

Soul Fragment Transfer

Whenever we feel vulnerable, are ill, shocked or trauma-tized, there's the possibility of losing parts of ourselves and having soul fragments of others attach to us. Often in drug-taking cultures, where people use drugs together in circum-stances which are often negative and filled with clumps of energy which coalesce to form what we might call evil, parts of souls are lost and others become attached. This energy transfer can often cause ongoing problems for many years; even though a person strongly desires to abstain, the attached soul fragments don't respond to his conscious desire. Wherever recurrent relapse is a problem, it's worth checking for soul fragment attachment. This sometimes also underlies the 'personality' disturbance of people who have been abused. They may have either picked up part of their abuser or been so vulnerable that they have been open to entry by the soul of someone who is now disembodied. People with a diagnosis of borderline personality disorder usually have inner conflict which may lead them to behave in a destructive manner, most commonly self-destructive, but sometimes in fact they have soul intrusion. Similarly, in multiple personality disorder there may be a splintered psyche, where each part develops a personality of its own with different behaviour, skills and moods, and all live alongside each other without being able to integrate into a whole, balanced personality. Or it might be that they are constructs to help someone severely disturbed to deal with the world that they otherwise find too confusing to contemplate. But it could also be that there are multiple soul attachments and this is certainly worth looking for. Children with diagnoses such as Asperger's Syndrome, schizophrenia and even Attention Deficit Hyperactivity Disorder (ADHD) also deserve a spiritual assessment. Also, children who are adopted and have difficulties later on may have been more wounded by their early experience than we're at first aware and may carry soul fragments or more. Soul fragment transfer can also happen when we fall in love and during sexual intercourse. I believe that a spiritual assessment should be part of the evaluation of anyone who has suffered rape.

Steve and April's story demonstrates soul fragment transfer.

As a child Steve was physically and sexually abused. He grew up an unhappy teenager and, though he was extremely bright, never achieved his potential academically, and was dogged by low-grade depression, sporadic drinking and heavy smoking. He was negative, cynical and openly ridiculed and criticized those who appeared happy. He found little outlet for his anger except in his drinking which now became more of a problem.

Then April, a strong and lovely young woman, came to work at the same company. There was an immediate attraction and a wonderful honeymoon period followed, exciting and joyous for them both, during which Steve didn't need to drink since he had never felt so loved. April was also very happy. However, by the fourth year of their relationship things had changed considerably. Steve was once again drinking and though between times they had some wonderful days, April found herself feeling ill from time to time, her usual cheery, bouncy enthusiasm for life suddenly disappearing like a burst balloon. Sometimes she felt lost and anxious and she became more and more aware that though she loved Steve deeply, what he called love was not the same thing since it had a punitive, cruel edge and a need to control and interrogate, giving her little freedom to be who she was.

Over the next few months April found herself coming into therapy. She was distressed rather than depressed, and mystified about what was happening to her. She noted that their home felt much better when Steve was away, and though she longed for him to come home, her anxiety began to rise as soon as she knew he was on his way. Trying to talk to him about her feelings simply led to rows in which Steve's manipulative skills dominated and she ended up feeling guilty. Over the next year the relationship continued to deteriorate, while April stopped her therapy, saying that she felt that she could not continue to come along when she knew she wasn't willing to make any radical changes in their relationship.

Then crisis point arrived. I was called to see her one night as she was held in police custody. Her face and body were cut and bruised and at first I thought that Steve must have done this. But not so. He had rarely been openly aggressive, though his endless criticism and questioning had continued, his accusations now including that April must be having an affair since she could no longer respond to his sexual advances. I believed her when she said that this was not the case, but she was certainly more open than she had been to accepting support from friends and family and tried to spend more time where she felt comfortable and valued.

April said that the previous night she had felt something rise inside her that felt unlike herself, and without warning she had started to beat herself up, screaming at herself by name as she struck her head, face and body with her hands and then with anything she could find, while Steve initially watched calmly without saying a word. Only when he appeared to get frightened at the extent of the damage she was inflicting on herself did he try to restrain her, and then, unable to do so, called the police. In the days that followed I talked with Steve who professed a deep and undying love for April. He commented that when she was not with him he felt as though part of his soul was missing and he told me that this was a measure of his love for her. In some ways, his assessment of the situation was accurate. April was indeed carrying part of Steve's soul – the part that he was unwilling to carry or even acknowledge as his own – that part that was enraged by his childhood abuse. The fact that April carried it for him allowed him to use only his tongue as his weapon, while from time to time April acted out the fury in that part of his soul which she carried for him. It was a measure of her deep love for him, and perhaps her naivety, that she was willing to do that, albeit unconsciously.

For April healing came quickly once she let go of the fragment she'd been holding and allowed herself to be who she was – warm and peace-loving and not aggressive. Sadly Steve was unable to take responsibility and deal with his fury and, after they parted, went on to find yet another person to carry it for him – still when last I heard, blaming April that her love for him had been a sham and she had finally betrayed him.

The Soul (or Souls) of Those Who Have Passed On

Sometimes, on abruptly leaving the body, the soul is confused, angry or traumatized and doesn't find its way to the light and the loving guidance available to it in the inter-life. It may then seek a host (the person to whom it becomes attached) who is vulnerable – possibly newborn, abused, shocked, traumatized, grieving, ill or very 'open' while involved in substance abuse. Sometimes there's a conscious or unconscious agreement or request by the host to carry the soul of someone who has made their transition, usually someone the host loved or upon whom they may have been dependent, for example when a relative left behind is dependent and vulnerable and unwilling to let go of the person who has died and holds them back from entering the light. Lesley's case demonstrates this.

Five years ago, Lesley's mother, an angry, embittered woman who had been abandoned by her husband seventeen years before, died after a brief illness. Although Lesley eventually formed a same-sex relationship, she remained enmeshed and interdependent with her mother, always feeling sorry for her and making excuses for her behaviour. Lesley had often told her partner that she didn't know how she would carry on when her mother died and, during the last days, said several times that she would happily take on her mother's pain, and begged her not to die, saying that she would rather die with her. Despite her partner's support, after the death she remained inconsolable. Since that time she'd suffered a rumbling depression and her relationship had deteriorated greatly as her anger and bitterness gradually eroded what had previously been stable and good. Though Lesley was diagnosed with chronic depression and obstructed grief, this was by no means the whole story. Her cries to her mother had not gone unheeded, and she was carrying her mother's soul, which needed to be released in order to go to the light where it could integrate the lessons of the earthly life. Finally getting to the point where she would agree to soul releasement work (see page 155), Lesley was eventually able to let go and have treatment which enabled her to individuate and expand her own personality and horizons.

Needy, Codependent Relationships

When we 'fall in love', our boundaries fall and we happily invite the other into our heart and soul. Even the healthiest of us may at such times leave parts of ourselves with the other. It's even more likely to happen when the two people involved are vulnerable and needy, and disentangling at the end of such relationships is even more difficult, leaving one or both people stuck and sometimes unable to get on with their lives for years afterwards, even when there's been little or no contact for a very long time.

Susan is thirty-one. She had a difficult childhood: her father was an alcoholic and her mother, weak and vulnerable, rarely seemed to have the energy to spend time with Susan or her three younger siblings, or to protect her children from their father's wrath. Susan found herself being the 'mother' of the younger children. Not surprisingly, she had a series of rather difficult relationships before she finally met and quickly married the man she thought was her soulmate, only to find a couple of years later that he was an abusive drinker, and that in some ways she was living a similar life to that of her mother. By the fourth year of marriage, with one child now three, she felt lost, angry, resentful and abused and wanted to release herself from this man she now found herself hating. With a great deal of courage she finally left after a fight during which she was physically beaten and quite seriously hurt. Now, four years later, she still finds herself suddenly getting into rages the like of which she hadn't previously known. Though we could say that she is simply now dealing with her repressed co-dependent rage about both her childhood and the treatment she witnessed at that time, as well as the abuse by her husband and the anger with herself at having allowed herself to get in this position, there may be more to it than that. Though codependent rage is a reality, in Susan's case she is carrying part of her ex-husband that she willingly took on board at the beginning of their relationship and which she then never returned. He is also carrying part of her.

SOUL LOSS AND SOUL INTRUSION IN MENTAL HEALTH CARE PROFESSIONALS

I have no doubt that the depression which dogs many psychiatrists and psychiatric nurses and causes the suicide rate among psychiatrists to be higher than in any other profession, is due in part to the fact that we take on, literally, our patients' pain in the form of soul fragments which we then incorporate into our own aura or physical being. Of course, many of our patients also want to take parts of us with them, and unless we're careful, some of them do! If you work in any capacity with those who are vulnerable and disturbed, regular scanning of your aura and a ritual to give back what is not yours and recall what is (see later) is essential. Ideally do this between seeing individual clients and certainly at the end of every working day.

RELEASING ANY SOUL THAT DOESN'T BELONG TO US

The work to release the attached soul – usually termed spirit releasement therapy – can be taxing, but for those who are willing to embrace it, it can profoundly change their lives for the better. Sometimes we may carry soul fragments for years, even since just after we were born, and usually the attached soul will remain there until it's recognized and encouraged to leave, has the opportunity to attach to someone else, or has resolved its issues and is at last able to go to the light.

This process, which used to be termed exorcism and was seen as a 'driving out' of the attached spirit – quite an aggressive affair – has now taken on a much softer, more compassionate look. The emphasis now is on helping both the host and the attached soul to understand what's happened and on showing that there's a better way for both of them to be. Important first is to assert that the body, including the energetic body, of the host belongs only to the host and needs to be reclaimed. Very often, with the host in an altered state of consciousness due to either hypnosis or meditation, and with the whole working field protected, the attached soul can be addressed respectfully and gently and will usually respond similarly. The responses are often highly illuminating! Most such souls will know exactly who they are and where they came from and will often tell us why they're here, how long they've been here, how they became attached and what they believe their function to be with regard to the host. Sometimes they're quite surprised to be told that they're not in their own body. Some have been residing with a variety of human beings for centuries, moving from one to another, either when the host dies or is traumatized, leaving a way to escape, or when yet another soul comes along to displace them. Although they're some-times angry and don't want to move, sometimes they're quite amenable when they realize that there's a more desirable alternative. When they finally understand this, it's polite to ask them if there is anyone they would like to be summoned to meet them as they finally move to the light. Only rarely is there no one, in which case I ask permission to nominate some high soul to be the guardian who will come to greet the soul who is now finally to return home. Before they leave I ask that the host show gratitude for their having been here and for any help they may feel they have given. If there's reluctance or resistance, I may explain the situa-tion to them again, but finally, very firmly, tell them that they must leave. They invariably do.

GETTING HELP

If you have any reason to believe that you may be suffering from soul loss or attachment, remember that you have the right to ask for a spiritual opinion. This might include situations where:

- you have symptoms that refuse to respond to any form of treatment.
- you feel that part of you is missing.
- you suffer a dramatic change in personality, especially if this is after some traumatic experience or illness.
- you suffer uncontrollable mood swings.
- you feel that your behaviour is 'not you' (though don't use this to excuse bad behaviour – in your integrity you will know!)
- you've suffered serious abuse, physical, emotional or sexual.
- you're suffering flashbacks (visual memories) of something you feel intuitively did NOT happen to you.

Make sure that you find a good therapist or a spiritual psychiatrist who knows how to handle these issues well. In the meantime, use the meditation at the end of this chapter as often as you can, paying particular attention to letting go of what is not yours and welcoming back all that is.

DABBLING . . .

From time to time I hear of people who have recurrent soul attachment and find that they've been dabbling in things they neither understand nor are trained to deal with. For instance, experts who work in the field of soul rescue rarely have soul intrusion because they protect themselves well and know what they're doing. No one

---

but a surgeon would attempt to take out anyone's appendix, but many seem to think that there's nothing to being a psychiatrist and that fiddling with other people's minds is fine! Often I see people with no training doing what amounts to psychic surgery, while others attempt to deal with the most fragile of energy in rescuing souls. Please don't dabble. If it's something that calls you, get adequate training from an expert.

Now to our final topic for this chapter – psychic attack.

PSYCHIC ATTACK

Sometimes without being aware, and sometimes deliberately, others attack us psychically. That means they use their energy to harm us in some way, sometimes to control us and sometimes to take our energy for their own use. The latter has led to the use of the pejorative and inexcusable term, psychic vampire. The person doing the attacking may be someone we know, love, have had a relationship with or have worked with. It might be someone we haven't met, but who somehow feels threatened by us. The first thing to do is always to send light to whoever is doing this and then to get yourself some help. In the meantime, however, there are things you can do to help yourself.

First of all get grounded and protect yourself. You can do this by imagining light all around you. I always used to use white light until I had some telepathic communication with a wonderful Aboriginal elder in Alice Springs who told me that separating out the rays of the spectrum and using all the colours of light simultaneously is better. Then use crystals, which you have cleansed in salt water, sunlight, or simply in an emergency by imagining light pouring through them (energy always follows thought!), and place them around yourself in your living and work space. Haematite is excellent. If you have a haematite necklace or bracelet, keep it clean and wear it.

Next, cleanse your field – that is, your own energy field as well as where you live and work. You can do that simply by imagining light around yourself, though personally I like to do some work on myself in the shower, letting go of anything that isn't mine and washing it down the drain, so to speak, while bringing in light all around me and through me. Remove any clutter from your environment that holds on to stagnant energy.

Surrounding ourselves with love helps, as does getting the person who is doing this to you out of your immediate space, although of course they can continue to attack from a long way away.

Taking care of our own energy, being aware of how we treat others and rededicating our lives to love and the intention to do only good, helps us surmount all the things we've discussed in this chapter. Also remember that, though challenges are essential, as soon as we learn from them we can let them go and return to a state of inner peace. The affirmation, meditation and prayer that follow will help you to return what is not yours, reclaim what is, and come again to peace and the state of liveliness and positive energy that are yours by right.

AFFIRMATION

I live with love and liveliness, enjoying my vitality, my capacity to think, to be spontaneous, to be nurturing and kind. I acknowledge all of who I am and know that I am constantly moving towards the light. I honour the right of others to fulfil their potential and celebrate them in their spiritual growth.

⚙ MEDITATION

Go to your sacred space, taking with you your flowers, candle and perhaps a crystal, some water, your journal and pen, and take the phone off the hook, giving yourself about forty-five minutes of undisturbed time. Make yourself comfortable, and take your time with this meditation.

Take a deep breath and breathe all the way out and as you do so, close your eyes and let your body relax. Let your shoulders fall, your chair take your weight and anything negative flow out through the soles of your feet and your root chakra. Take another deep breath and this time allow white light to pour in through the top of your head, shining down now through every cell and every atom of every cell, cleansing, healing and balancing as anything you no longer need simply discharges into the earth from the soles of your feet and your root chakra. Relax. Now take another deep breath and this time let it flow though your physical body and out into your aura. Feel the peace as you allow the healing energy to flow through you and around you. Know that in this moment you're protected and blessed. Feel the angels gather around you to support you and allow a wave of gratitude to envelop you. Breathe it out as far as you can to touch everything. Know that there's no space between you and the whole universe. Know that you are one with all the wonder and beauty of all time and all space. Take another deep breath and as you breathe out, relax even further.

Allow yourself now to open to connect with the very depths of you. Places to which you rarely go; places that you may perceive as murky and best left alone. You're going to breathe the light of love into them now. There's nothing there that can harm you; nothing that cannot be healed; nothing that need concern you. In this moment you can cleanse and heal it all, and be forever in a place of light. Know that angelic beings are holding and protecting you. You're now finally bringing into the light that part which has been your shadow — that very valuable part of you that has allowed you to understand the pain and depths of others also. Ask for the highest possible guidance, the highest wisdom to guide you safely out of the pain you've suffered and to a place of harmony, where once again you're aligned with the energy of the universe. This is a time of rebirth for you as you let go of the old and emerge into the light. You're about to let go of the old and birth the new, opening to a quantum leap in your spiritual growth. Evoke now the law of grace that supersedes even the laws of karma.

Take another breath now and ask that all may be forgiven. Anything that has been unresolved is going to loosen now and be healed. There's nothing you need to carry with you. Breathe now, and see the bonds that have been holding pain and darkness in your soul becoming loose and dissolving. Breathe again and finally watch those bonds disappear. Now you're going to let go the painful feelings you've also been carrying — any anger, resentment, bitterness, shame, guilt and fear. There's no need to feel them now, simply note that they're there and visualize the bonds that have been holding them and let them loosen. Let them fall away, leaving behind them scars that can now be healed with the light. Take another breath and bring in light and focus it there now. The love and the light can heal everything if you simply allow it. Be aware that anything that was not wholesome is simply falling away, draining out of every cell. Old memories, old feelings — you no longer need them. Let them surface and let them go — draining out of every cell. Let them go and let the space be filled with light.

Now ask that anything that is not yours be released with gratitude, and let it return from whence it came. Take a few moments. Breathe deeply and evenly and will that anything that is not of your soul leaves now and returns either from whence it came or to the light. Allow yourself to feel peace and a sense of cleansing. Pause and take your time.

Now, take another deep breath and ask that anything that is yours be cleansed and healed and return to you from wherever it has been, and welcome it home. Breathe slowly and deeply, feeling a sense of reverence and perhaps a scintillating rush as you become more whole. Let your energy rise and feel a sense of completion. Watch as you are revealed in your magnificence. Take your time.

Breathe again and watch yourself transfigured into your true beauty – a shining being. Behold who you truly are. Watch as you expand beyond your boundaries. See your essence become finer and finer. See your soul. Enjoy. Watch as the angelic beings, guides and masters surround you and allow yourself an inner smile.

Stay as long as you wish. Ask for any guidance and know that whether or not you perceive it now, you will receive it.

And now, when you are ready, send a wave of gratitude out into the farthest reaches of the universe, acknowledging the beauty of all things and their place in your life and your soul's growth. Know that the universe responds with a wave of gratitude for your contribution to the whole world. Acknowledge this with humility.

You are about to make your journey back to this grounded place where for the moment you continue to fulfil your pledge to tread the human path. Allow your light to be once more confined to your aura and bring your consciousness back to your physical being. Acknowledge your humanity and give thanks. Take a deep breath and fill every cell with oxygen, as your body now feels wide awake and alert. Come back to a place behind your closed eyes and be fully aware before, very gently, you open your eyes. Move gently, have a stretch and take a drink of water. Pause a moment before you stand up, and take a short walk around the room before you record everything in your journal.

✷ PRAYER

May the Great Spirit and our guardian angels be with us throughout our earthly journey, as we embrace with love all those who come to travel with us. Let us steer a good course through the deep and turbulent ocean of life and hold steady against the tide of self-righteousness. Let us live in a state of gratitude for the great souls who have been willing to teach us and for all that we experience here. Let us rise as peaceful warriors to the challenges with which we are presented and come finally to a peaceful shore where all will become clear.

5 MAKING THE TRANSITION

Farewell to thee, but not farewell
To all my fondest thoughts of thee:
For in my heart they still shall dwell:
And they shall cheer and comfort me.

Life seems more sweet that thou didst live,
And life more true that thou wert one.
Nothing is lost that thou didst give –
Nothing destroyed that thou hast done.

Anne Brontë

We have dealt with the experience of being human and now we come to the point where we're about to leave the human existence and return to our even more spectacular home – the soul plane. From this temporary sojourn on the planet, we're now to make the transition we call death – that single moment that many fear all of their earthly lives, and about which there's such mystery. Perhaps we can learn to see it as the moment for which we have always been preparing – the moment of going home. In this chapter we're going to look at what we understand by death and some facts about dying in the modern Western world. We'll examine preparations for the journey (our own and others'), pre-death visions which tell us something about the process, and then the moment of transition itself. Lastly, we'll look at various modes of transition, each of which is the final choice of the soul.

With our increased scientific and technological expertise, we're now capable of challenging not only the suffering in life, but also our exit. However, constantly expanding our ability to prolong life may in fact be a misplacement of our limited resources. Well-meaning relatives, and doctors afraid of crossing the boundaries set by their ethics committees, may be determined to sustain life regardless. However, heroic interventions, despite their sense of victory over illness and death, may in fact be both unnecessary and ultimately cruel, with comfort and dignity taking a back seat and personal values and wishes being ignored, while those desperate to keep us alive battle on our behalf against what they see as the worst possible outcome. Often we inflict more suffering while delaying the inevitable by only a few weeks or months, not prolonging life but only the process of dying.

Do we have a moral right to prevent those who are ready for their release from having it? Is it that we ourselves have made an idol of longer life at the expense of quality of life because we are so fearful of the alternative? Unless you have previously directed otherwise, or nominated someone to take decisions for you, however, medical practitioners have little choice but to soldier on to sustain life, often despite its ever-dwindling quality. Disease may well have a natural place in life, and it may be better to accept that since we're all to make the transition at some time, to do so with dignity, timeliness and even delight is neither madness, resignation, failure, nor even an act of courage, but merely reflects a development of consciousness and our readiness for a joyful reunion with the Divine.

WHAT IS DEATH?

We could say that death occurs when our various physio-logical systems can no longer support the life of the phys-ical body, but of course this is only part of the story. Although, if there is considerable pain, the soul may leave slightly before the body dies, what we refer to as death is simply a single moment in the midst of life – a natural moment during which the immortal soul finally departs its mortal, physical vehicle to make the transition between two simultaneously existing worlds – the material and the ephemeral.

For many of us, our understanding of death has been coloured by religious teaching and tradition. For example, in Africa and the Mediterranean countries, death is seen as a natural part of the harmonious pattern of life, its timing perfect according to universal law. Some religions have introduced the concept of hell and purgatory, and with it fear of death and resistance to our natural transition towards God. We have associated death with suffering, the sting of loss, punishment and evil, giving it an almost re-demptive quality. We have sanitized and cosmeticized it rather than honouring it as it is – natural and perfect, with the potential to be the most joyful moment of our lives. Death is neither the punishment for our sins professed by some Christian sects, nor the unnatural state of Hebrew doctrine. In fact, neither resistance nor submission is appro-priate to death. An open embrace may be more fitting, for when we really understand about what is called death we can consciously prepare for our journey home, let go of the tension and tragedy, and simply slip into the next and most natural phase of our spiritual development – and also help our loved ones to do so when their soul chooses the time.

Naturally, we usually view our life from the perspective

of being human. How else would we view it? But if you make a shift in perspective, everything appears different. What if this human part of our existence is simply a field trip? We're here on an educational roller-coaster, learning through the ups and downs of human experience and relationships that which is essential to our ultimate growth. From the joy and light of the soul plane, this earthly life may be considered a place of comparative darkness where we suffer lessons we may not consciously wish to learn at the hands of teachers we don't particularly like. Simultaneously, we ourselves are the teachers, often of unwilling students. We could of course choose to make life here a rich, passionate and bountiful adventure if we make every second count and absorb the multitude of wonders and lessons that the universe serves up to us every day.

So, although we're all part of a very carefully woven divine pattern, this isn't really where we belong. We're only here for a while and then, when we've done all our learning and teaching, giving and receiving, it's time to pack up and go home – to make our transition. Rather than regarding the return journey as sad and awful, we could choose to approach it with joyous anticipation, a sense of completion and celebration, as we prepare to re-emerge on the other side in our true magnificence, and meet once again those we have loved and who have returned home before us.

Before we look at the journey itself, let's take note of some facts, since our views and practices surrounding death have changed considerably in the last century. Many rituals, which prompted grieving to start naturally as the living presented their final love and goodbye to their loved ones and gave them their last materially tangible contact, have been abandoned. For many, the funeral, at which the soul is often present, remains the last time when an energetic tribute can be made in the form of flowers.

SOME FACTS ABOUT MAKING THE TRANSITION . . .

- Approximately 90 per cent of deaths are due to chronic degenerative conditions.
- In a poll taken in the USA in 1997, 87 per cent of the people interviewed said they wanted to die at home. In fact 80 per cent die in some health care facility.
- Even fifty years ago people would die at home with all their relatives around them and leave from home on their last journey to burial. Now, the body often goes direct from hospital, nursing home or hospice to a funeral home and from there directly to the crematorium or cemetery.
- Now, rather than having family and friends perform rituals such as caring for the body, someone is usually paid to do so. What was a community issue has often become a commercial exercise where cosmetic preparation has largely replaced naturalness.
- The older people are, the less afraid they are of dying; surprisingly, women are more fearful of dying than men, perhaps because of their sense of responsibility and concern for who they leave behind.
- Much of the ritual and ceremony around death and funerals has been abandoned, without being replaced by other practices to help loved ones mark this most special of events.
- The natural grieving process has been shortened artificially in the Western world, with expressions of emotion often being frowned upon – those who openly show their grief are still sometimes considered weak and irresponsible.
- The average age at death in the 'developed' world has increased from forty-six in 1900 to seventy-eight at the end of the twentieth century, although in many African

countries it remains less than forty. In Zambia in 2000, the average life expectancy of a man was thirty-seven.

PREPARING FOR THE JOURNEY

Although many embrace their own death willingly, it's a normal part of the process of preparing for death to grieve for our earthly life and also the anticipated loss of those who are coming to the end of theirs. Grieving for the loss of our normal physical function, our mobility and strength, freedom and independence and the expectations we may have had of an earthly future is also understandable. We grieve, too, for our loss of control over life – as if we ever had any! Anger, depression, bargaining with God and surrender are all natural stages in the process of dying. However, at or shortly before the moment of transition, there is a sudden rise to full awareness that there will be survival, and in the end, for most of us, there is peace, even if only in the actual moment of leaving. For many this is accompanied not by resignation, but by willingness and almost a yearning to embark on the journey as we realize that despite the mortality of our body, we can rejoice in the immortality of our soul.

I've often wondered if Khalil Gibran was contemplating his own death when he wrote his wonderful book *The Prophet*. As the ship which is to take the prophet back to his own land is approaching, he teaches the people of Orphales for the last time, and although in the end he reveals his pain about having to leave, he is ready for his journey. This is how I see the process of death. Our whole life is really a preparation for the moment when we leave, even though often we're not consciously aware of this until we are well down the line. Learning more about the transition from this plane back to the soul plane from whence we came can help us to prepare both ourselves and others for what can be a peaceful and even beautiful experience whenever it may occur. If we can start to talk about this great event in our lives as we'd talk of any other, we can usually be granted the great gift of time to say all that we need to say, to enjoy rituals and celebration as well as memories of past pleasures and expectations and wishes for the future.

ATTENDING THE DYING

Whether you are attending a much-loved relative, are a practitioner, work in a hospice or find yourself unexpectedly called to be with someone who is preparing for their transition, hopefully you can help create a peaceful, sacred atmosphere for this unique time. Pause first of all to accept what an honour it is to be chosen to attend the dying even though this can be painful, emotional and hard. The thoughts of the person at the point of transition are important for the gentle release of the soul, and empowering them in the last minutes is a great service. The following practical hints might prove useful. Dealing with the practical can leave us freer to share the emotional and spiritual things that matter most.

- Take care of yourself! Being sensitive to the needs of others, dealing with the grief while being focused on the needs of the dying and switching roles between nurse, hand-holder, counsellor, healer and grieving friend or relative is taxing. Accept support for yourself wherever you can. You have feelings too, and if you have to leave the room and take a breather, just do so without feeling guilty about it. Forgive yourself for being human!
- Pain control is possible and desirable, though many people prefer to have some pain rather than the mental confusion that medication may precipitate. It's been

found that when people are in control of their own medication they tend to use less. Antidepressants may help to keep the dying person emotionally settled but alert.

- Healing, touching and talking are the best antidepressants! Remember that care-givers are more likely to have depressive symptoms than the person who is dying – join a support group if you can and accept as much healing, touching and talking as you can take.

- Food is neither necessary nor desirable at the end, and indeed the anorexia can stimulate the endorphin system and produce a feeling of well-being. Dehydration can have a similar effect.

- Assume that the person can hear everything even if they are no longer speaking and appear to be unconscious. Let the person know you're there and stay close to them, sitting at eye level where possible so that they can get the most out of your presence.

- Allow for silences in the conversation, but be ready to share reminiscences where appropriate. Listen empathically without trying to fix anything, though offering practical help such as contacting other people is fine.

- Allow for anger and grief and don't argue with the person when they say they are dying. Perhaps they need to be able to say goodbye.

- Reading their favourite poetry or prose, listening to music with them and laughing with them can be healing for you both. Express love in any way you can, and don't be afraid to say goodbye.

- The hospice movement is wonderful with its trained and loving professionals and volunteers dedicated to bringing comfort and a beautiful transition emotionally, physically and spiritually.

- Delegate! Delegate! Delegate!

WHAT DO WE TELL THEM?

Someone said, 'Death is like sugar, the element that sweetens life and makes it finite and precious.' The decision whether or not to tell someone that they are dying can sometimes be tricky. But do we have the right not to, thereby depriving the person of the possibility of preparation, and also of doing things that they always wanted to do?

About twenty-five years ago in Africa, my best friend complained that she had been feeling unwell while away travelling, and asked if I would examine her, since she seemed to be putting on weight rather strangely around her abdomen. Some years earlier she had had a small lumpectomy in her left breast, and had been well ever since. However, as I examined her my heart sank. She had a hugely enlarged liver and the most likely diagnosis was cancer, with a primary in her breast despite the fact that the original lump had been benign. Biopsy confirmed the diagnosis and we sat down to talk as two loving friends, but also doctor and patient, about what should happen next. In those days her prognosis was very clear – despite the best of intervention, she probably had about three months to live. At thirty-four this was not happy news, however in her own inimitable style she shed some tears then made a prompt decision.

'I'm going home to Denmark,' she said. 'I'll pick up my mother and we're going to the Grand Canyon. I've always wanted to go there and so has she. Then, if it's OK by you, I'll come back here and you can look after me till it's time.'

That's exactly what she did. Although she stopped off at the Royal Marsden Hospital in London for some treatment and surgery, she came back two months later, having done something that she wanted to do and having said her goodbyes to her family, and spent the last four weeks in her beloved Africa, surrounded by her friends who spent time with her, brought delicacies to the hospital each day and embraced her while she died.

We may not want to do anything as dramatic as going to the Grand Canyon, but to have the opportunity to get our affairs in order, to make peace where we need to, to tell our children what we want them to know – these things are priceless and no one has a right to take that opportunity away from us. Although in the last twenty-five years attitudes to death have certainly changed, and everyone is much more open to talking about it than previously, there's still a tendency to try to shield people from the truth, even when that truth belongs particularly to them. We cannot know exactly how they will deal with it – that's their business. In fact, many people's mental state improves considerably after they're given a terminal diagnosis, as they now find every day precious and live each moment to its full extent, finding beauty and joy where previously they missed it.

OUR ATTITUDE TO OUR OWN DEATH

This appears to vary with age. Kenneth Vaux in his *Will to Live, Will to Die*, Augsburg, 1975, suggests that young children up to the age of three or four see death as going away, which implies that life will continue though in a different place. This may be due to the fact that children of this age, having recently come from the soul plane, still have some understanding and acceptance of it. A little later in childhood, children will often accept death in such a matter-of-fact way that it inspires those around them. By adolescence, when we have begun not only to invest in personal relationships but also to have expectations about the future, there are different emotions about the possibility of these being shattered. In maturity the prospect of death becomes a threat to family stability but in the elderly it often comes as a relief.

It has been noted that adolescents approaching their own death are often treated with great respect and revered almost like pop stars; however, should they recover, the climate changes and it's often difficult for them to reintegrate into their previous culture, ending up depressed and lonely and almost wishing they had died. As modern medicine romps on with its cures, we need to prepare families and friends to deal with those who *don't* die.

PRE-DEATH VISIONS

Pre-death visions, usually consisting of visions of deceased relatives and friends, have been reported by people who are in clear consciousness for hours, or sometimes days, before death. There's usually a sense that these loved ones have come to collect the soul and lovingly welcome it into the soul plane. Though it's been suggested that such visions may be part of a near-death experience, it would appear that in fact, they are a separate phenomenon.

A few days before my mother died, my son Keith, my nephew and I kept vigil with her through the night. I was doing healing with her and there was an air of calm and peace in the room as she drifted in and out of sleep. The men were chatting about childhood memories and I'm sure my mother was enjoying that, rather than the sombre atmosphere there could have been. Suddenly she awoke with her still bright blue eyes clear and she was very alert and strong. She appeared to be looking way into the distance at something the rest of us were not privileged to see. She slowly moved her gaze to each one of us, and finally rested with her eyes fixed on mine. Her face was shining and beautiful as she started to talk about what she had seen and was still seeing. She said that she had been to a land of smiles where there was only love and that that was where she would be going soon. She said that she wasn't afraid because there was only peace and love and light. She was gripping my hand with the strength of a young woman, and certainly looked as though she had shed many of her eighty-nine years. Now, this may seem to be nothing more than the ramblings of an old woman who was dying. Perhaps one would have had to have been there to be convinced that it was not.

Over the next three days until she finally made her transition, she referred to that special night only twice. But on each occasion her skin was glowing and her eyes clear and strong. She knew what she had seen and felt, and she knew where she was going, and wasn't afraid. She said that she had seen 'Him' and that He was shining with light, and that when He had touched her she felt nothing but love and peace. It wasn't possible to ascertain who 'He' was. I'm not sure whether she referred to a Christ-like figure, or to my father, though at the time it felt as though she had interpreted the meeting as one with Christ. She said again and again that there was nothing to fear and that the love and the smiles were more than she could ever have known – this from a woman who had had a great deal of love and smiles in her earthly life.

I was blessed with a similar experience when my father left. The pattern was similar though the ending appeared longer. Some days before he left, my dad took to talking to his deceased brothers at the foot of the bed. He would stare fixedly into a space a few feet away and appear to be listening. He was very attentive, even though he seemed not to hear what was being said in the room even when he was addressed directly.

Occasionally he would turn his glance to mine, a little perplexed, and hold my eyes for a moment as though trying to tell me something without using any words, and then, as though to make sure that I'd got the message, he would give a verbal summary. He told me that two of my uncles were here and that they were waiting for him. He appeared awestruck but nevertheless very present – simply incredulous and almost questioning me as to whether what he was seeing could really be true. Then he talked of his mother and father, and others in the room keeping vigil with him commented that he was delirious. But he held my eyes throughout and we both knew that wasn't so. My father, who'd never been religious, who believed in the balance of nature and care of the earth rather than in God, was having an experience he hadn't expected. He had neither believed nor prepared – at least not openly – for this moment, and was having a rapid development of consciousness in the days leading up to his departure. The look in his eyes and the questioning in his voice were in awe of what he was discovering, and he was trying to give me that teaching as his last gift before making his transition.

I have no doubt that my parents were seeing the souls of their departed loved ones and that my mother had returned from a near-death experience in order to tell us it was real.

FINAL CHOICES AND LAST-MINUTE KARMA

How and when we leave is significant. It's our last earthly act and carries within it the last bit of learning and teaching of this lifetime. The timing is always perfect, and so is the way in which we use our last chance to work out any remaining karma before we make the transition to the soul plane. For those of us who are left, however, there may be questions. Our initial response to hearing of someone's death is often to comment that it's sad and then to assess whether we feel it was timely. Where there's disaster involving many lives, we often judge the situation as 'dreadful', or 'a tragedy'. But in fact all the souls involved have chosen the time and mode of their transition. We shall discuss this again later in Chapter 9.

It was Jacques Cousteau who said, 'Il faut aller voir' – we must go and see for ourselves – and indeed, whatever we may think or feel about death and dying, we shall only know when we go and see for ourselves. However, before then we can make plans and refine our attitude to the inevitable

I used to say that I would choose to go by falling under the number 52 bus, but recently I've changed my mind! The driver would be shocked and people might get hurt, so that won't do – unless the last bit of teaching I have to do is to give them that experience. This morning I was walking out in a thunderstorm and, as always, I was greatly energized by the wonder of the spectacular display. It came to me that a good way to go would be to be struck by lightning and to have my soul move out of my body and up into that wonderful vortex of cosmic energy – powerful and liberating. Kind of like going out with my own firework display! Joking apart, however, no doubt I will make my exit as and when my soul has already secretly planned. As yet I'm only guessing. But if we can look at our exit so lightly and with excitement and joy about going home, then suddenly 'dying' takes on a whole new meaning and we can start to prepare for a wonderful transition. Of course it's different when we're the ones who are left. It feels bad because we can't see or touch our beloved again, and sometimes we have difficulty in perceiving their presence, or do so only fleetingly. We have unresolved feelings, sometimes of guilt and of course a deep sense of loss. But even then, if we can see them having completed something very special here and being ready to graduate, though it's natural for us to grieve, our pain may be less.

Recently I talked with a beautiful woman who was already grieving for the imminent loss of a dear friend. She said that it was so sad since he had so much more to give. He was a philosopher, an author who had just arrived at the point where the world was recognizing him as a major thinker. And now he was struck down with cancer and it seemed so unfair. But was it? Or could it be that this wonderful soul had given what he came to give; had taught others to the point where at last they had realized that his ideas had merit, and that, inspired by his greatness, they could now continue without him? He could now go home, his work complete. He was opting for just two more bits of teaching as he left – about love and about cancer. Those around him who loved him were learning; those who were treating him were learning. Nothing, not a single thing was wasted. Every bit of his life had been of use to those who came into contact with him – for a reason, a season or a lifetime – and his 'death' was no different. He taught and learned in every second of his sojourn on the planet. So have you. So have I. There's no such thing as an untimely death. Everything, including 'death', is in divine order.

Each of us can, like *The Prophet*, continue to teach actively and learn right up until the moment when we have to board our vessel to go home – telling our children and grand-children stories; teaching those around us about love; talking about our experiences so that others may glean a little from our journey, all the while listening for the gems of information we still have to gather to take home with us. It may be that the last lesson I have to teach and learn is about cancer, or dementia or a road traffic accident, and not about lightning after all. But in whatever way I choose, I shall add to the wisdom of the world in some way by my transition, and so will you. We shall go only when the moment is exactly right. And those we leave may weep but will survive and be greater because of our coming and going – just as we are greater for those who have come into our lives, taught us then left.

CHOOSING WHO ELSE SHOULD BE THERE

You may remember that we looked at who should be with you during labour and birth. Now, at the other end of the earthly life, there are choices to be made about who should be present at the moment of transition. The choice of who to die with, if anyone, is ours entirely, and is to some extent based on our own beliefs and the perceived beliefs of others. It's often painful for those who have lovingly cared for someone, often for many months, to find that at the end, they die alone or with someone else. Sometimes we choose to die far away from home and loved ones, in accidents or wars. Though it's a great honour to be present with someone in their last moments on earth, it's no dishonour for those who are not. I believe that sometimes the decision is made to spare loved ones those final moments. Sometimes we choose to go with those with whom we have discussed the journey of death and who we then trust to guide us.

ACHIEVING THE POINT OF PERFECTION AND THE MOMENT OF TRANSITION

So, unless our death is sudden, we've gone through the various stages of grieving for our life, the refusal to believe we're dying, the feelings of isolation and anger, the bargaining with God and the depression as we look back over our life and wish we'd done more with it, and now we've arrived at the point of acceptance that we are to leave soon. The moment of transition is upon us.

My mother and I had discussed 'death' many times and what would happen. She'd talked openly about not being afraid of death, and indeed as time went on and she became less mobile, she talked of welcoming that moment. When it came to the point of her leaving, she suddenly moved her glance from the fixed stare she'd held for some hours to hold my eyes once again as I told her it was all right to go and that she had been a good mother and a good wife and that my sister and I would be fine. She held on to that connection between our eyes and our souls, my arms holding her as she gently withdrew from her body through the crown of her head and her body took its last breath and was still. While I kissed her brow and cried, her soul hovered about me, the roles again reversed — she the mother soothing me, the weeping child.

And my father? Though we never talked of it, I think until the days before his death he'd probably thought that dying was the end of everything, as he'd always assumed it to be as he walked in his beloved fields, hunting for rabbits, and in his work as the local rat catcher. It's interesting that we never discussed my beliefs, but then we really discussed nothing of an esoteric nature. At the point of his leaving, he suddenly shifted his gaze upwards and his face became a picture of wonder as he took his last breaths and moved out of his body. Just like my mother, he comforted me in the next few minutes and then was gone.

As a doctor, I've had the privilege to be with several people in their last moments, and though some have started their final journey from this human life with some trepidation, in all cases they've left in peace. During those last few moments, days or weeks, consciousness develops very fast.

Some years ago I was called in the middle of the night and asked to go to do some healing with an eleven-year-old who was in liver failure and was dying. It was obvious to me as soon as I entered the room that the point of transition was very close, and that what I'd been called to do was to help with the transition of the soul and to do healing with the family rather than to attempt to prolong an earthly life. In fact, the soul of the child was already separated from the body, though his body was still alive. (This is not unusual, though until the body actually dies, there's often a silver thread which continues to attach it to the soul. At the appropriate time this cord appears simply to evaporate and the soul is free.) As the young do, he hovered around his grieving parents and grandparents for some time before leaving, trying to give at least some solace or some sign of survival, and having compassion for the fact that it was easier for him to leave than for them to be left.

The death of young people and children is often seen as a tragedy because it's assumed that they're at the beginning of their life and haven't had time to fulfil their potential or achieve their life's goals. But who is to say that the work of a child is incomplete? They came only for a brief time with little to learn in this lifetime and more to teach. So rather than grieve for their death as a disaster, perhaps we could see them as amazing, wise souls whom we were blessed to know, who opted for a brief visit this time. The compassion, of course, needs to rest with the parents, family and friends.

IF THERE'S TIME . . .

If we're lucky enough to have advance warning that transition is imminent, we can do much by setting the atmosphere of the room to nurture the senses, for example with beautiful sound (I played my mother's treasured musical box to her as she died and recited her favourite poetry), scents such as incense, oils or flowers and colours that will please. Using favourite photographs, cards and paintings to decorate the room and bring in love and warmth can be very healing for everyone. Be imaginative and creative. Even if the person appears to be unconscious, assume that they can hear everything and that, even until the last moments, they will enjoy the love you've shown by making such preparations. There's

---

something very beautiful about arranging flowers or looking at photographs, while giving a commentary on what we're doing, telling of the latest family news and demonstrating our love as someone is preparing to die.

THEORIES ON THE MOMENT OF TRANSITION

There are various theories as to what exactly happens at the moment of death. Dr Elizabeth Kubler-Ross (*On Death and Dying*, 1969) talks of death being simply the shedding of the physical body, like a butterfly shedding its cocoon, followed by a transition to a higher state of consciousness where we continue to perceive, understand and grow. Bruce Goldberg (*Peaceful Transition*, Llewellyn, 1997) refers to death as our best friend, helping us to become aware of other worlds to which we're usually denied access on the physical plane. *The Tibetan Book of the Dead*, written centuries ago, describes the process of dying according to Tibetan Buddhist philosophy and gives instructions on how to proceed. *The Tibetan Book of Living and Dying* (Sogyal Rinpoche, Harper, 1992) gives a long discourse on the moments before, during and after the departure of the soul. There are also interesting accounts from healers, mediums, psychics and mystics who have either witnessed death or gleaned information through working with their clients; accounts obtained during past-life regression add to our knowledge, as you will see later from Eddie's story.

According to some philosophies, the soul leaves through the crown chakra at the top of the head, while some claim to have witnessed it leaving via the solar plexus or heart chakra. Others simply see a template of the body rise up from the physical body and either hover for a moment or simply make a fluid sliding exit and ascend out of sight. In the case of traumatic death the soul appears to leave in a similarly simple fashion.

Dr Ian Stevenson has offered a theory that there is an invisible electromagnetic field, which he has called the psychophore, which moves from one lifetime to the next carrying memory which is imprinted on the new foetus. The physical memories may appear as birthmarks and the emotional and behavioural ones as personal attributes.

Although the soul is returning home, as we shall discuss in the next chapter, there may be some confusion, exhaustion, sorrow or even anger at leaving. However, there's always a loving and accepting guide to offer to help deal with this, and as we return to that place that my mother referred to as the land of smiles, where there's only light and love, there's always a joyous welcome, reunion and celebration by those who have gone before us. Angels are present at the moment of transition and of course the souls of those who have preceded us and who have not yet reincarnated. We shall discuss the events immediately following the departure of the soul in the next chapter.

LIVING THROUGH THE MOMENT OF DEATH

Tibetan philosophy talks in terms of Bardos, which are phases of total life. They include the moments before birth, birth itself, the mundane phase, the moments before death, the moments after death, the soul life, then the moments before birth. The moment of death is not mentioned at all. This is significant and is due to the fact that there is no change except that the soul moves out of the physical and then continues on its journey as before. Living through the moment consciously is something to strive for, since in the very moment of death there can be a rush of consciousness that moves us towards enlightenment, perhaps to the point where we shall no longer have to incarnate. The meditations at the end of this chapter are intended to prepare us for a conscious transition – the first so that we can prepare ourselves, and the second for us to read to others (with their permission), or we may ask that those who care for us read it to us at the moment of our transition. At the end of the next chapter is another meditation to be read in the moments after transition.

Now let's have a look at several modes of taking our leave.

PEACEFUL TRANSITION

The vast majority of deaths are peaceful, even if they have been preceded by long degenerative illnesses or pain. Often family members are amazed that despite struggles in the previous weeks, months or even years, the final slipping away is so easy and the body left behind has an air of peace. A common comment is that it looks as though the person was merely asleep, all pain and discomfort gone. Such was the case with Jack, about whom you'll read later (see page 191).

SUDDEN DEATH

Sudden death, though chosen for the soul's ultimate growth, can nevertheless be a shock, sometimes leaving the soul trapped in the moment of death and unable to move on. Often the soul is not ready to leave immediately and may wander around the site of the death for some time (see Chapter 6). As we've seen, there is also the possibility of soul intrusion after sudden or traumatic death.

SUICIDE

There are various situations in which the yearning for death outweighs the desire to remain alive. Where hope evaporates and leaves behind only despair, people may decide that there is no other way forward but to take their own lives. Those who are very depressed need careful supervision, though sometimes it is as they start to get better that they have both the opportunity and the motivation to suicide and the energy to execute their plan. Terminal illness, especially if accompanied by pain, may well precipitate a decision to opt out early. Where there is severe physical illness or incapacity that leads people to need a lot of care, they may want to free others from the burden of having them around, although of course their suicide rarely achieves this, since those left behind inherit a legacy of guilt and pain. Often, however, where there has been great love, there can also be some relief that the loved one is no longer suffering.

Sometimes the motives are quite different and it's here that the soul may have some difficulty after the transition. Where anger, resentment, the desire for revenge or to teach others a lesson are the motivating factors of suicide, or where there is emotional distress and a spontaneous act of self-harm (parasuicide) that goes wrong and results in death (in some ways this is accidental death), the soul is released suddenly in pain and confusion, sadness and regret. Except in the case of terminal illness or incapacity, the soul may be unable to move on. We can help by surrounding the soul in light, instructing it to go to the light and praying for it. Soul rescue (see later) and healing as soon as possible after the transition is essential. We'll discuss this again in Chapter 6.

Suicide is particularly painful for those who are left since there is often a sense of guilt that we weren't there to prevent it, that the person died alone and that we survived and they did not. There is often also justified anger at such an aggressive act and frustration at never being able truly to voice this. Of course, those whose soul has chosen this route will kill themselves no matter what we do to try to prevent it.

TRAUMATIC OR VIOLENT DEATH

Sometimes problems in this lifetime give clues about previous lives and in particular the mode of death. Have a look at Eddie's story.

Eddie was a recovering drug addict who'd had a painful and abusive childhood; the third of four children, he had been a typical 'scapegoat child', always in some kind of trouble such as truanting from school, fighting and petty theft. He drifted from misusing solvents at twelve through marijuana in his teens to using amphetamines and cocaine. His drug-taking career had spanned fourteen years. At the age of thirty he'd been 'clean' for four years but remained unhappy and unable to enjoy life, finding relationships difficult. He said that transactions with authority figures were a nightmare despite the fact that he'd tried to deal with the problem with meditation, visualisation and affirmation. Though he'd done psychotherapy and healed a lot of the trauma he'd received at the hands of his father, he was agreeable to extending the search for the cause of his difficulties in past-life work. Our aim was to try to gain a better understanding of Eddie's relationship with his father and his ambivalent, often aggressive relationships with other men.

Within a few minutes of the start of the session Eddie found himself in America at the time of the Civil War. He reported having a large flesh wound in his right upper arm and feeling very tired, though he knew he was basically a very fit and healthy young man with a well-muscled torso — very different to his tall lanky frame of today. He had been running with his compatriots and had lost a lot of blood. He could feel himself becoming weaker and dizzy, and knew he would not be able to keep up with his friends for much longer. Without saying anything to them, he just allowed himself to slip back and reported that no one seemed to notice he was no longer with the group. He felt some relief at no longer having to keep up and conform and found himself slipping to his knees in the dry brown grass with a sense of calm and peace. He said he felt 'floaty' and comfortable; his arm was no longer painful and he dropped the gun he'd been carrying in his left hand. Suddenly his peace was interrupted by a group of rebel soldiers who appeared apparently from nowhere and now saw him kneeling vulnerable in the grass.

In my room his breathing changed and his voice became louder and more anxious as he went on to describe the scene where he was kicked and beaten, spat on and jeered. Finally someone was pointing a gun at him. He recognized this man as his father in this lifetime and tears started to run down his cheeks. Suddenly he relaxed again and his voice became softer as he began to give a more disjointed commentary. He was now rising out of his body, floating above it. He was being encouraged to leave but he was finding this difficult as with some fascination he watched his body and the men who had killed it. He was traumatized, shocked and ambivalent, finding it hard to leave. He reported wandering back to the previous battlefield and in a detached way looking at the bodies of his friends as they lay there. He found other souls wandering too, almost as though they were all trying to understand what had happened, perhaps not realizing that they were dead.

Over the next session we dealt with the emotional and physical aspects of that life and the traumatic death and in particular his feelings about his father. We noted too that the physical wounds, beating, etc. were imprinted on his etheric energy body and the humiliation on his emotional body. Both of these had some carry-over into this lifetime.

This regression demonstrates the hallmarks of a past-life traumatic death – ambivalence about leaving the site and wandering, then the carry-over to another lifetime where we reincarnate with someone from that previous life with whom there is still business to sort out.

Many such souls still wander at the sites of old battles. Healing at the time of a traumatic death is essential to help the soul move on, and we'll be talking more about this in the next chapter.

There are three other modes of making the transition that I feel I must mention here – euthanasia, assisted suicide and legalized killing in the form of the death penalty.

EUTHANASIA AND ASSISTED SUICIDE

Euthanasia is the act of inducing a quiet and easy death. In some places in the world this has become legal. The first legalized act of permitted, indirect and involuntary euthanasia in USA was performed at the request of Karen Quinlan. Assisted suicide means that a doctor writes a prescription for life-ending medication and the person takes the drug himself. For some there's enormous relief in knowing that this choice is available even though they may never use it. Both euthanasia and assisted suicide raise ethical questions that have been hotly debated for many years. Not only do most of us feel natural revulsion at the thought of killing another human being, but there is also the debate about Divine order. We could perhaps accept that whenever death occurs and by whatever means, whether life has been artificially lengthened or shortened, it is in Divine order and occurs at exactly the right time and is perfect for the soul's needs. And we could also say that the final decision is that of the soul, and the issue involves a simultaneous learning and teaching both for it and the soul of the person who is instrumental in either prolonging or shortening life. Once again we're faced here with the inner conflict between ethics and the desire to help prevent suffering in the case of severe intractable physical, emotional or spiritual pain, and where the person desires death. As a doctor, more than once I've been begged to help a patient die. One could say that wherever we withdraw treatment and mark 'TLC' (tender loving care, suggesting no further active treatment) on the notes, we are in a way assisting the patient's exit by doing nothing to prevent it. But does that inactivity in itself become a positive act of will? And who should decide – relatives, friends, medical attendants? And on what grounds – being old, sick or unwanted? Does abortion also come into this category? My feeling is that at the end of the earth life, just as at the beginning, the soul is in charge and the rest of us merely play a part.

LEGALIZED KILLING – THE DEATH PENALTY

When I first decided to move to Texas, one of the things that I thought about for a long time was the fact that Texas still has the death penalty. I had long discussions with people I trust about whether I could integrate into my being living in a place where legalized killing is a part of life. Finally I came to the conclusion that being here and spreading as much light and love as I could might in some small way help others to think more deeply about the issue and also help tip the balance in favour of peace and reconciliation rather than retaliation and revenge. Some time later, I read the following: 'When there is proper respect for the ultimate power and that understanding is attained and activated by enough people, the entire paradigm of humanity will be lifted above the belief of energy as a force. In the face of enough love, force loses its power to dominate consciousness. From that point forward, consciousness will awaken at quantum speed. It will be so powerful as to bring answers by the second' (Glenda Green, *Love without End*, Heartwings Publishing, 1999). Bearing in mind that it's not for us to judge, nor to forcibly end the life of another, and that should we do so we become murderers too, perhaps in time we shall be able to desist from legalized killing. Having worked with many people who have committed murder, raped and done other awful things, while having the utmost compassion for the victims and their families, I've always been able to see how and why the event occurred and still unconditionally love the perpetrator while despising their behaviour. My personal belief is that whatever the crime, we do not have the right forcibly to end the life of another, and that if we do so, we carry the imprint of that action on our soul just as surely as does the person we've killed. However, while we still carry within us remnants of that need for retaliation and revenge, it will continue. Each of us can hasten that awakening of consciousness by moving towards living in unconditional love, by understanding the positive intention in all acts and by dealing with our own aggressive impulses. This is something with which we may continue to struggle on a daily basis, as people come into our lives to challenge us to look at things from the perspective of unconditional love. I've often been asked how I would feel if there was an act of violence against one of my children or grandchildren. Could I still remain loving and not retaliate? I hope never to be tested in that way, for though I would answer now that I would still come from a place of unconditional love, only in that moment would I find out whether this were so. I do hope that I would never request the death of someone else. Nothing, including the death of the person culpable, could ever provide recompense for my loss.

THE DEATH OF LOVED ONES

In losing someone we love through death, although of course we grieve for our loss, ideally we can love the person enough to let them go in peace. Our ability to do that, however, depends not only on our love for them, but also on our inner strength, our sense of independence and of course, our own attitude to death. If you're stuck in your grief and unable to let go, please don't feel guilty. Talking it over with someone who can lovingly support you while you come to terms with this major life event will help.

One of the most beautiful clinical moments I recall was sitting with Jack, a man who was preparing to make his transition and who had been very worried about how his wife would be after he left. He himself was ready. The pain of his illness had wearied him and he had sorted out his life, dealt with his business and was calm and simply waiting for what he instinctively knew was going to be something wonderful. Still, his concern for his wife occasionally overwhelmed him and saddened him more than the prospect of actually dying. We had talked of this many times. He knew how deeply his wife Alice loved him, and that their forty-seven years together had left her more dependent on him than was wise. One of nature's gentlemen, Jack was now trying in his last weeks to find something to give this woman who had been his life and whom he loved so dearly; something that would somehow bridge the gap and soothe her. On this particular day he was calmer and pulled out from his locker a piece of paper bearing his beautiful fluid script.

'I've found this,' he said. 'I don't know who wrote it, but I want you to give it to Alice afterwards.' On the paper he had written:

If I should die and leave you here awhile,
Be not like others, sore undone, who keep
Long vigils by the silent dust, and weep.
For my sake, turn again to life and smile,
Nerving thy heart and thy trembling hand to do
Something to comfort other hearts than thine;
Complete these dear unfinished tasks of mine,
And I, perchance, may therein comfort you.

(*Turn Again to Life*, by Mary Lee Hall)

Within three weeks he had peacefully made his transition and I found myself sitting with his widow who, still held in his love, was stronger than Jack had imagined she would be. While she admitted that she would be lost without him, she was glad that he was at peace and no longer suffering. I gave her the verse and watched as she read and reread it, her tears flowing more freely for a while, but then being replaced by a beautiful smile.

'That's *so* Jack,' she said.

Although her grieving over the next few months did of course reflect her deep sense of loss, Alice went on to comfort other hearts, and I was struck by this continued loving between her and her Jack. Her love was sufficient to allow him to go and be where he now needed to be. Whereas some still hold strongly to the one who has passed, confusing the soul with their grief and distress that prevent it from continuing its journey in peace, Alice was able to understand that her connection with Jack would never be broken, that his essence had not died, and she integrated the loss of his human form into her life and carried on.

Euripides asked, 'Who knows that death is not life and life is not death?' In fact all is life, there is no death; both this earthly life and the life thereafter (what we may call the interlife or the interim phase), are real. From the material world where we learn and play, we return to where we truly belong and become once again free in that wonderful state that has been called heaven. However, it's up to us to create heaven here as well, and of course it's that for which most of us strive. Although many religions have taught for centuries that if we don't behave well and love God we shall go to hell, this is a fear-based mechanism of control. Many who appear not to behave well are in fact sacrificing themselves to raise the consciousness of the world. However, that is not to say that there is not a time of reckoning after transition – and we shall be looking at that in the next chapter.

✪ AFFIRMATION

I live lovingly and consciously for all my life, here and through the point of my transition and my continuing growth towards enlightenment.

✪ MEDITATIONS ON DYING

There follow two meditations, one for anyone to use as a preparation for a conscious transition and the other for relatives or friends to read to their loved ones at the time of transition. At the end of the next chapter there is a meditation that is to be read, preferably aloud, after the moment of transition. For the first I would suggest that you do it in your safe place, though if you are confined to bed, that's fine. Anywhere will do. It would be good to have a flower and a candle and crystal with you and perhaps someone you love to do the meditation with you. As always, take as long as you wish, with the phone off the hook. At the end of the meditation have a drink of water and take some time before you resume the normal activities of the day. Record whatever you wish in your journal.

⚙ MEDITATION ON MAKING A CONSCIOUS TRANSITION

Take a deep breath and then breathe all the way out, allowing your body to relax, let your shoulders fall and the earth take your weight and let anything negative flow out through the soles of your feet and your root chakra. Relax.

Take another deep breath and imagine white light coming in through the top of your head, shining down through every cell and every atom of every cell, cleansing, healing and balancing every part of you.

Now allow yourself to open to the wonder of leaving this earthly life to return home from whence you came, home to the freedom and joy of the soul planes, to meeting with loved ones you have not seen for a long time. Allow yourself a feeling of joy at this prospect and at consciously living through the moment of your transition from this plane to the next. Know that all the love you have created will live on in every being and place that you have loved. Your time here has been essential to every soul you ever met, and now your work is almost complete. Now it is almost time for you to rest. Know that at last you will be free, free of a physical body, free from pain and discomfort, free from fear, free to have absolute peace. Breathe into every cell of your being as you align with the forces of the universe and prepare for the wonderful journey you will undertake. Let go of any concerns now; let go of any worries and fears. Know that everything will be taken care of, those you love, those you care for, your home and your affairs will all be fine, just let go now and be in the moment. You are at the centre of this magnificent happening, you are the traveller on this journey, and you are at the point of power, moving into a new and exciting phase of your life. Let go now, let go and relax. Know that when you leave your physical body behind you will become pure consciousness, shining light, free in a way you have not been free for so long. Completely unfettered and unconfined. Simply imagine yourself now completely free. Free, floating, ready to enter the light, ready to meet with beings of light that are waiting for you.

Know that you are to be in absolute peace . . . no need for control . . . no need for fear . . . simply consciousness . . . Just allow yourself to feel that sense of weightlessness and freedom and know that when the time comes for your transition you will be ready and content to leave.

Visualize all those from whom you wish to take your leave. If there are any feelings of emotional discomfort, allow yourself the opportunity to look at these. Are there issues you need to address? Forgiveness to dispense? Things you need to say? Someone you need to reassure of your love? You can do this on a soul level — from your soul to that of the other person, or you can note to do this later. Just send a wave of gratitude that this wafted up from your subconscious, and with a single breath let it go. Relax.

Once again be aware of the peace, of knowing that you will be exactly where you are meant to be. Your transition will take but a moment and the pure essence of you will be released in the presence of dear ones who will guide and protect you. Know that your transition will be safe and that you will survive. Open to receive any wisdom that you need at this time. Breathe.

Stay as long as you wish, then start to prepare to feel your physical presence once more. For the moment you need to remain within the confines of your human body. So take a deep breath now and allow every cell of your body to be energized by it, feel the oxygen flowing to every part of you. Send gratitude to the highest source. Take another deep breath and again let every cell and every atom of every cell be revitalized. Make sure that you are well grounded. Start to feel your fingers and your toes . . . come back to a place of awareness behind your closed eyes and, taking your time, very gently open them. Stretch a little, have a drink of water, then record whatever you wish in your journal.

✪ MEDITATION AT THE TIME OF THE TRANSITION

This meditation is to be read aloud to the person who is at the end of their earthly life and in the process of transition. Read slowly, pausing between sentences. Simply intuit and repeat any sentence you wish. Remember yourself here too. Breathe, be as comfortable as you can and take your time. You are doing exactly what you're meant to be doing right now. All is well. Now . . .

Breathe and hold on to my voice, gently, gently feel my voice and feel that I am holding you through this moment, holding and supporting you whilst still letting you go to that wonderful home to which I am not yet coming. Hold my voice. You can still hear me and feel my love with you. You are departing now on that journey to pure consciousness, you are becoming pure consciousness. As your soul leaves your body just allow yourself to rise and float free and without fear or pain, free now, free again in the pure essence of who you are. Just allow yourself to be free and let go of your attachment to the Earth, without concern for those here on Earth . . . let go. You are free and perfectly safe, you are in the company of angels, let your loving guides take you now, in perfect peace and harmony with the universe just allow yourself to leave, leaving now through the top of your head, letting go, just allow yourself to rise up and be greeted by those who have gathered to collect you. You can still hear me and my love is still with you. Letting go now, letting go, you are safe and protected. My love goes with you. My love goes with you . . . You can look back at your body now but it is no longer of consequence to you . . . you are free in your light body . . . you are still alive . . . you are immortal . . . you have not died . . . You are your soul . . . listen now and let your guides take you . . . let go of everything that remains here and enjoy your journey now . . . Let guides and angels take you . . . Move towards the light . . . leave the earth plane behind you . . . feel the love . . . feel the peace . . . feel the

joy with which you are welcomed ... know that you are free ...
You are going home ... let the earth plane go ... Let me go ...
move towards the light ... go with my love ... enter into the
light and become at one with it ... let me go now ... I let you
go with love ...

*If you've read this meditation to someone who has now made their
transition while you helped them, take some time now for yourself
to allow your own needs to be met in terms of your own grief and
sense of loss. You are still here in the human realm and grief is
natural to us. Even though we may understand the process of transition very well, we still have our own wounds to tend, as the bonds
between us and the one who is going home are broken. Know that
they are safe and alive and that all is well. Give thanks for the privilege of having been with them and feel their gratitude to you for
having been strong enough to perform this sacred rite with them.*

✵ PRAYER

*I know that at some time I shall make the transition back to the
soul plane. Let me fulfil my karmic obligations and come to the
moment of transition in peace. I ask that I may have the presence
to live consciously through my transition and embrace my immortality with joy.*

> *How could the soul not take flight*
> *When from the glorious presence*
> *A soft call flows, sweet as honey,*
> *Comes right up to her, and whispers,*
> *'Rise up now, come away.'*

Rumi

❂

Part II

Life on the
Soul Planes

6 ENTERING THE COSMIC PHASE

I silently laugh at my own cenotaph,
And out of the caverns of rain,
Like a child from the womb, like a ghost from the tomb,
I arise and unbuild it again.

Percy Bysshe Shelley, 1792–1822

In Part I I dealt with the earthly life up to and through the moment of transition, and our immortal soul is now freed from the physical body in order for us to return home, the earth journey completed for this time. Now in Part II we move to the cosmic phase, also known as the interim phase or the interlife, on the soul planes. However, in each chapter of Part II, in order that we can, as always, see the practical value of the study, I shall view our experience of the wonders of the interlife from the human viewpoint too. It's been said that we shall never really know about what happens after 'death' until we finally make the transition ourselves. However, though it's true that we know less about the interlife than any other part of the journey, nevertheless there's information from a variety of sources – anecdotal, channelled wisdom, from those who can astrally travel (see later), from Instrumental Transcommunication, which I mentioned as evidence for survival of the soul in Chapter 1, and from past-life work where people actually have memories about this period – to allow us to piece together a fairly good picture. But, as always, we don't know what we don't know and I've no doubt that we are in for a wonderful surprise when we finally pass over. There's still plenty of room for research, and no doubt in the future there will be greater exploration of this vast, largely unmapped area of universal truth, more of which becomes clear as people become more willing to work on their inner lives and look to past-life memories as a rich resource. The more information we glean, the more able we shall be to understand the journey of our soul in its entirety, helping us make informed decisions about how we wish to live while here on earth. But more than that, recognizing those around us as great souls, no matter what their role in this lifetime, prompts us to be more loving and forgiving, and less judgmental, while learning to appreciate the positive intention in all things enables us to live in harmony and peace. The resultant increase in global awareness and consciousness is a transformative process already begun but now gathering speed and increasing exponentially. Although in our individual lives and in the collective human experience we shall continue to be challenged, this peaceful revolution will carry us forward along our path to enlightenment.

In this chapter I shall look at our arrival in the interlife, picking up our story immediately after the transition. We shall also look at the soul planes, how the mode of our death may affect our readiness and ability to ascend through the planes, and why some souls remain earthbound. As always, the chapter will conclude with an affirmation, meditation and prayer. In the next chapter we shall discuss the work of the soul during the interlife and then look at various soul connections* in Chapter 8 before we make preparation for a return journey to the earth plane in Chapter 9.

COMING HOME

For however long we remain at home in the interlife, most of us will once again find the peace, abundant love, joy and beauty which we left for a while as we voluntarily laboured in the material world. Here are our loved ones from whom we may have expected to be separated forever by the veil of their transition, along with our guides, teachers and those with whom we may have had serious conflict, but who we can now see were simply part of our mutual growth. Unless we've reached enlightenment and therefore have no need to return to human life (though some souls still make the choice to do so), when we have rested, we shall now continue our learning before making another foray into the school of human life.

Sadly, there's often considerable fear about what happens in this post-transition period. Children are still fed noxious myths about hell, while some religions believe that we're sent to purgatory when we leave our physical body. Stories of ghosts and ghouls abound, and the fear is perpetuated in horror movies, though happily fairly recently there has been some attempt by the film industry to balance the scales with some beautiful portrayals of the interlife. Although there may be some truth in these myths about what happens after we make our transition, let's examine what we know and set it all in perspective.

First, let's look at what and where 'home' is, how we arrive there and what happens when we do.

HOME – THE ASTRAL WORLD

The Greek gods were said to live in Astron, a place of the stars, and it is from this word that we have derived the term astral world – referring to that 'place' which is beyond the material world that many perceive as our only reality. The astral world is the true home of the soul, though it is not a geographical location, but simply a different state of being – an ever-present, non-physical reality of a differing vibration, existing here alongside us. From time to time, we choose to step into the denser reality of the material world, usually via birth (though there have been cases of materialization which we shall discuss on page 263) in order to experience more, and expand our growth.

The astral world consists of seven soul planes, which have been referred to as the heavens. Each soul plane differs in its vibrational frequency, though all coexist in harmony without interference from each other, much as radio waves, light waves and X-rays do. Our souls change in their quality and purity as we ascend through the frequencies, becoming only pure light. We still know very little about the very high planes, except that they are of an extremely high vibrational frequency and are generally inaccessible to the lower realms, but we do have a considerable amount of information about the lower planes.

THE SOUL PLANES

We live our earthly life on the material plane which has a low-vibrational frequency and is more dense than the soul planes. Here we, like many other life forms, manifest physically, while even the lowest of the soul planes is of a vibrational frequency which does not allow physical manifestation. Each of the soul planes has seven levels and each of those is divided into seven sublevels. They are then further divided into seven layers and so on for seven times, thus affording many different tiers so that each soul can go to the one appropriate to its development. From the lower to the higher, each ascending soul plane is occupied by beings more enlightened than those on the lower planes, and we may remain for long periods at any level (though of course time does not exist as we know it), ascending through as we progress spiritually. Depending upon our development so far, we may pass through the lower levels without pause, entering at that level most appropriate. Let's look more closely at each of the seven major planes.

The Lower Astral Plane

This is the plane closest to the material in vibrational frequency and the plane to which those souls that have not progressed beyond materialism, greed, selfishness and individual consciousness are assigned. The souls of those who have committed evil crimes, who are sadistic, cruel and self-obsessed, may remain here until they are able to acknowledge and repent their misdeeds and move on. The souls here may be troubled and may interfere with souls embodied on the material plane. Poltergeists (noisy ghosts) and demons are said to reside here as well as those who have not dealt yet with their karma and are wandering still, often shocked by their death and as yet unable to take responsibility for their earth choices. The souls of those who have committed suicide may well be here too (see the Cosmic Laws, page 313). These lower regions where souls may feel frightened and lost are what have been termed purgatory and hell.

The Intermediate Astral Plane

This is the plane upon which most of us find ourselves immediately after transition and where our soul, as our astral body (an exact copy of our physical body, connected to it by a silver thread that can stretch over long distances but which breaks on death), may stay briefly or for a considerable period. This is also the place to which we go in our astral body in our dreams, and during our earthly life we can reach this plane by telepathy, psychokinesis and clair-voyance (see Spiritual Gifts, page 96). Those who are able to astral travel during their human lifetime – that is, leave their body at will to have an out-of-body experience (I can't yet but I'm learning!) – describe the astral plane as a world similar in some ways to our own. After our transition our astral bodies seem much as our physical bodies did before. They appear to wear clothes and live in buildings of our mind's creation. Although colours are more vivid, and the whole seems to be formed and changed at will, nevertheless there are cities and landscapes just like our own. However, every soul appears to create its own particular world instan-taneously and can reshape it simply by willing it to be so. Many entities are found in the intermediate astral plane. There are others who are astral-travelling in their astral bodies, those who are recently 'dead' (see Eddie's story in Chapter 5) and other entities which have never incarnated in human form. We will be talking later about the phenom-enon of bringing new entities into existence through our thoughts. It is here that we shall find many of these. At this level our souls still feel emotion and have a fairly intact personality although they draw their energy from the cosmos rather than from any physical source. Animals are here also in their etheric form. Here we review our lives while we continue to learn and develop so that we can ascend further. Most of the communication received by mediums from the fairly recently departed originates here.

The Higher Astral Plane

This is the plane that has been called the summerland and is what we may think of as paradise. Inspired pure souls who have lived a good life on earth ascend very rapidly to this level and may appear to enter here, while others may ascend to it over time via the lower and intermediate astral planes. The astral body is now starting to disintegrate and emotions and individuality also begin to disappear. Nevertheless, many souls here still make an effort to communicate via mediums and, for the benefit of their loved ones, to present at least some features of their human personality in order to give proof of survival. However, the personality may start to appear blunted and less recognizable to family and friends now that the transition from personality to powerful soul is taking place. Even if the soul does manifest as the personality, the messages begin to be of a different quality as the soul introduces itself in its true power, wisdom and glory to those who want to have contact. One soul with whom I truly love to have contact is that of a young man who made his transition in 2000. Now on the higher astral plane, he does still manifest sometimes as his personality – bright, funny, mischievous and almost flirtatious – then occasionally as a more mature man as he would have been had he not made his transition. Gradually, however, he is introducing his true ancient powerful soul to those he loves, and the content of his communication as well as the 'language' in which I receive it has taken on an eloquence which marks his rapid development on the soul plane.

The Mental Plane

The mental plane leads us into the higher regions, which for centuries have been referred to as heaven. Here, though, there is still some structure, less solid than that of the astral plane, and while each soul continues to create its own reality, everything is composed of shimmering light, its form often defined only in outline. Here we exist only as pure intelligence, having left behind all other vestiges of our human life. Spiritual leaders, great teachers and guides are at this level though they may from time to time reincarnate to help humanity. Those who were good and just leaders on the earth plane continue to inspire and guide from here, as we shall see in the next chapter.

The Celestial Plane

We know little of the very high planes, but on the celestial plane there is no physicality, simply unity consciousness and the purest of love. The ascended masters, Christ, Buddha and Mohammed and others, are on this level as well as angelic beings. Highly evolved souls may remain on this plane for hundreds of years before reincarnating and indeed may choose never to reincarnate again, instead aiding the universe by making available the highest teaching, wisdom and healing to be channelled for the good of humanity.

The Causal Plane

This is the place of cosmic consciousness and the plane on which the legendary Akashic Records, sometimes referred to as the Book of Life, are stored and where the Halls of Learning are found. (Akasha is a Sanskrit word meaning the primordial substance from which everything was made.) Recording Angels in the Halls of Learning maintain an Akashic Record for every soul, documenting every thought, word, intention, experience and deed in its many lifetimes thus far. In deep meditation during our human life, we can ask to be shown our Akashic Record, and though the information released to us may appear strange or fragmented, it is always accompanied by a sense of revelation and insight that prompts us to trust it.

The Seventh Soul Plane

This is the so-called seventh heaven, the highest of the soul planes, about which we know little.

OUR JOURNEY TO THE ASTRAL PLANE – WHAT DO WE KNOW?

The events occurring after death are not quite the mystery they used to be. Descriptions which come from near-death experiences (NDEs), past-life regression, mediumship and channelling concur almost entirely with ancient writings. *The Egyptian Book of the Dead* (1300 BC), a guidebook for the interlife, the original title of which was *Going Forth into Light, The Tibetan Book of the Dead*, eventually written down in about 800 BC after centuries of oral tradition, and the *Katha Upanishad* from India, written in about 600 BC, are remarkably similar in their descriptions, despite coming from different cultures in various parts of the world. Dr Raymond Moody Jr, in his groundbreaking book *Life after Life* (Bantam, 1975), first reported the stories of many people who had been pronounced clinically dead but survived. Dr Michael Newton's, *Journey of Souls* (Llewellyn, 1995), gives a great deal of very detailed information about the interlife gleaned from his clients in regression therapy. Many books have been written about the phenomenon of the NDE by attendants to the dying, researchers and also by the survivors themselves. Reports from those who have had out-of-body experiences have also contributed to our knowledge. There is some fascinating technological data too, to which I shall refer, and of course there is my own experience with clients and my own channelling.

As far as the physical body is concerned, the brain continues to work for a few minutes after the heart and lungs have stopped. In the case of NDE, consciousness leaves the body and often brings back an account of a reality that most of us are not privileged to perceive, showing us that the soul can operate independently of the physical resources of the body. The information from whatever source is so similar that we can only conclude that it is real. Most NDEs are positive and life changing, but even those that are not, prove that there is a life beyond the physical realm – that the life of the soul continues free of a physical existence. NDEs have been dismissed by sceptics on the grounds that they are hallucinations, or due to the failure of neurotransmitters, or are caused by medication or anaesthetics, or even that they result from memories of being forced down the birth canal. However, many people now agree that these experiences do in fact show us the events that occur shortly after death.

So let's piece together what happens. It may help for us first of all to have a summary of the core experience as we know it from NDE reports.

THE NEAR-DEATH EXPERIENCE

Usually some or all of the following components are present, though not necessarily in this order. We shall briefly discuss each of these elements, adding what we know from sources other than the NDE.

- Leaving the body and hearing the pronunciation of death
- Hearing a loud sound
- Floating and observing the body and the scene
- Being supported by guides and loved ones
- Becoming aware that we still have a body, but that it is different
- Moving towards a tunnel and a bright light
- Emerging from the tunnel and meeting a being of light
- The life review
- The return
- The aftermath

Some of these events may overlap, occur in a different order or appear absent. Let's have a look at each of them in more detail.

Leaving the Body and Hearing
the Pronunciation of Death

In some circumstances, for example if there's considerable pain or shock, the soul may leave the body before it dies. Depending upon where the death takes place and whether there are any attendants, the person may hear themselves pronounced dead either immediately before leaving their body or shortly afterwards. The soul leaves by slipping out of the body through the heart chakra, solar plexus or crown, and for a while floats above it. Betty Eadie in *Embraced by the Light* talks of being drawn out through her chest as though by a magnet, and others have likened leaving the body to the reverse of the birth process. Those having out-of-body experiences claim a strange sensation, then a strong tugging before finding themselves outside their body though remaining attached by the silver thread which we mentioned page 205 (note that this remains intact during NDEs, but breaks irrevocably at death). Any pain or discomfort of the dying body is left behind, but the soul is conscious and there-fore can feel emotionally, has thoughts and a heightened sensitivity and intensity, often with some sense of confusion. Most of all, however, there appears to be a feeling of expansiveness, freedom and peace. If we remember the sense of loss of freedom and restriction of the soul on birth, we have here the reverse of that. Suddenly we're released into that free state from which we came, though it may take a while to adjust, especially if we haven't been prepared for the moment of transition.

Hearing a Sound

Often a loud noise, the last human sound, accompanies or momentarily precedes the soul's lifting out of the body. People who are adept at leaving their body voluntarily in OBE (out-of-body experience) also comment upon this sound. It has been described as buzzing, ringing, roaring, rushing and numerous other adjectives, and most seem to imply that it isn't a particularly pleasant noise. It may be that since the last of our senses to disappear when we die is that of hearing, this is the final withdrawal from our sensory perceptions as a human being.

Floating and Observation of the Body and the Scene

Most survivors then report floating and hovering above the body before a pulling sensation urges them to rise higher away from where the body remains. There appears to be relaxation and curiosity rather than fear, as the body and what is happening to it and around it – for example, the medical team doing the resuscitation or people arriving at the scene of an accident – is observed with fascination and compassion. On their return many near-death survivors have been able to describe the scene exactly, for example reporting in detail the conversation that took place between medical staff. Often the reports include details about things the person could not possibly have seen or heard from an oper-ating table or hospital bed, such as descriptions of events taking place in adjacent rooms.

Being Supported by Loved Ones and Guides

Angels, guides and the souls of relatives and friends may have gathered during the hours or days leading up to the transition, and as the soul leaves the body they are waiting to welcome it lovingly, to encourage it to leave the body and, giving comfort and assistance, to accompany it on the next stage of its journey. Some souls may be relieved and anxious to leave, whilst others are reluctant or confused. Some may remain on the earth plane for years and become earthbound souls (see later), but once encouraged to begin the process, most do so without fear. The often palpable sense of emptiness that pervades the room after someone dies is due in part to the departure of their soul, but also of all the other souls who now leave with the soul they came to collect. Rarely does a soul make the transition without the help and support of a guide, whether this be a loved one who is on the soul plane or a highly developed spiritual teacher. Highly mature souls may not have a guide but ascend through the whole process very quickly.

Becoming Aware of a Different Body

The soul then becomes aware that although it is released from its physical body, it does still have a form, albeit now glowing with light energy radiating from it. A sense of euphoria develops as the soul becomes aware that it is free, suspended in air, weightless and able to drift gently, with neither limits nor obstacles. Sometimes, however, there is a sense of frustration with the lack of response from grieving relatives as the soul, unaware of its invisibility, tries to communicate that it has not died.

Moving Towards the Tunnel and a Bright Light

There are references to the tunnel to which NDE survivors refer in ancient writings and it is also beautifully depicted in *Visions of the Hereafter*, four paintings by the fifteenth-century Dutch painter Hieronymous Bosch which can be viewed in the Palazzo Ducale in Venice. This tunnel is the portal to the astral plane. The position of the tunnel has been described variously as close to the physical body and high above the earth. In the work that I've done with lost souls (see later), I've witnessed a vortex of energy which opens sometimes only perhaps 20 feet above the earth, with constantly swirling energy, dark only in contrast to the amazing brightness of the light above it. The energy of the vortex spirals upwards, drawing everything gently into its centre, and souls have simply ascended into the light or 'walked' into it. On the morning of 11 September 2001 while in London, several hours before the attacks on the World Trade Center and the Pentagon, I had visions of a gathering mass of thousands of angels above a swirling vortex over a city I couldn't recognize. This vortex equates to the tunnel. It would appear that both the previously described sound and the tunnel are congruous with the shift in electromagnetic frequency necessary for souls to ascend to the astral world. There are also reports that within the tunnel there may be other souls, some of them moving quickly and others seeming to linger. The maturity of the soul seems to dictate how quickly it traverses the tunnel and ascends into the light. This is the only time when the soul is alone, having been lovingly encouraged before entering the tunnel and then met as it emerges into the light.

Emerging from the Tunnel and Meeting with a Being of Light

Once out of the tunnel there appear to be layers of energy of varying brightness. Some report utter silence while others speak of gentle sound vibrations, buzzing or music, all of which appear to help create an atmosphere of tranquillity, love, peace and total acceptance and, for most, euphoria at returning home. There is now infinite space, though some describe cities with buildings, which may of course be the imagination creating images to ease the transition. Loved ones await us with tenderness and affection, and are recognizable even though they may appear only as masses of energy. The meeting with a being of light is usually the event which is remembered best, and which is also reported to be of most comfort and having the most life-changing effect upon those who survive near-death experiences. Our religious or spiritual beliefs may well come into play here, though many with no such previously held values talk of this being as Jesus, one of the saints or an archangel. Others simply talk of a glowing being of light from which pure, unconditional love emanated. Some can hardly articulate the wonder of this experience, yet remember forever with humility the radiance and the feeling of being held compassionately in absolute love beyond anything of which they could normally conceive. For most, it appears that this being or a beloved guide is present for the next event, which is the life review.

The Life Review

Scriptures have talked of the Day of Judgment, and perhaps this review of our whole life is just that. Instantaneously we're able to see every event of our life and relive not only our feelings but also those of everyone who was involved with us. As we are faced with how we have lived our life we may be filled with guilt and shame, despite the fact that we are held in love and compassion, never blame, condemnation or punishment. We are lovingly supported by a guide as we try honestly to appraise and make sense of it all, and are encouraged to integrate what we perceive, the emphasis as always on learning, growth and healing. In fact, should we be too self-critical, we're helped to reassess the situation in the light of the good we've done. There is judgment by no other being but ourselves.

The Return

In the case of an NDE, we're then told that this is not our

time to leave the physical world and are encouraged to go back. Many have reported a reluctance to do so, having felt the peace, love and joy of the soul plane and knowing now that that is our true home. However, having once made the decision to return, instantaneously, with a thud and some discomfort, we're reunited with our body, often shocked by the sense of restriction and by the return to the physical pain we had left behind. Though time does not exist on the soul plane (nor here for that matter!) most people report having felt that they were out of their bodies for a very long time during which they were shown amazing wonders and appeared to travel so far that they could hardly believe that they may only have been 'dead' for minutes.

The Aftermath

Although obviously people do talk about their experience, many are reluctant to do so, finding it too difficult and too personal to describe. The experience has almost always been a positive one, but very occasionally beings are encountered whose energy feels negative. Even then, however, the NDE is a life-changing event. In almost all cases of NDE, those who return undergo a shift in personality, being kinder, calmer and more grateful, understanding and loving than they were before and they may wish to become involved in some kind of service. It could be that where there has been a negative experience, it can act as a catalyst for positive change – a timely warning perhaps to start to live a more positive and useful life.

Although the language is different, the information gleaned from NDEs is almost identical to that given in *The Tibetan Book of the Dead* which was intended to be read to the dying to help them on their way and also to inform those grieving about what is to happen to their loved one so that they can let go and allow the process to proceed. It is of course possible that people reporting their NDE experiences did so after reading such a book, but this is very unlikely and could not account for the near-death experiences of children.

CHILDREN'S NEAR-DEATH EXPERIENCES

In 1983 Dr Melvin Morse published in the *American Journal of Diseases of Children* an account of the near-death experience of a little girl. He eventually followed this up with his book *Closer to the Light*, in which he reviews several such cases. The descriptions, whilst childlike in their honesty and simplicity, are in many ways similar to those reported by adults, leaving us in no doubt that children do have near-death experiences. A study, known as the Seattle study, showed that the majority of critically ill children have NDEs and they are not caused by drugs but are part of the natural process of dying.

THE EFFECT OF THE MODE OF TRANSITION

As we saw in the last chapter, the mode of transition is significant with regard to what happens immediately afterwards. In peaceful death the soul leaves easily, and after a brief while moves on. Even then, however, especially in the elderly, there may be some slight confusion.

Shortly after my father died I distinctly felt him sit on the bed beside me and simultaneously felt my heart open and start to beat fast. That very first time was different in that he seemed desperate to reach me, worried that I might not feel him there. We sat together on my bed and I was able to cry softly and have him know that I was aware he was with me and that though I was happy that he was free, I missed him. And it was OK. Comforting for both of us.

There are many anecdotes that would lead us to think that even in sudden death, the soul knows that the transition is near. Poignant stories about people making declarations of love, making unusual phone calls, contacting people from whom they have been estranged or tidying up their affairs very shortly before accidental death appear to confirm this.

My friend Jennifer was grieving for the death of her husband, and as we talked only hours after he'd been found dead, she recalled incidents that had occurred over the previous few days and in particular during the last hours. Almost a week earlier he had told her that in case anything ever happened to him, he wanted to remind her about where all his important papers including his will were kept and they had laughed together as to what had prompted him to do that since he was not the most organized of people. Generally he was not given to being particularly tidy, and she ruffled his hair and teased him about what had got into him when a few days later she found him tidying his desk, sorting out old paperwork that he no longer needed and seemingly spring-cleaning his office. The day before he was killed he called his mother and uncharacteristically told her at the end of the conversation that he loved her. An hour or so before his death in a hit-and-run accident, he had left the meeting he was attending and rang Jennifer at home saying that he was running late but telling her never to forget how much he loved her. She had laughed and said she knew, but then joked that she was getting a little concerned with all this attention and asked if he had done something he needed to tell her about. They closed the conversation, their last, with declarations of love. Jennifer said that it was almost as if he knew.

Of course on one level he did.

As we shall see in later chapters, the past-life death is of utmost importance to the next life, as any thoughts, feelings or behaviour at the end of the life – that is, at the moment of transition – that have not been resolved will leave a karmic imprint and be carried over to the next life, and may manifest as some relationship difficulty or perhaps as a fear or phobia. This makes it crucial in doing past-life work to heal the past-life death so that we can deal with any imprints that have moved into the next life.

MOVING ON

Sometimes the soul feels some resistance, wanting to comfort the loved ones left behind, trying to talk to them and tell them that they are still alive even though their body has died. Many remain earthbound until after the funeral, whilst others are quite eager to leave and go home to the peace of the soul world. The soul may be very sensitive and exhausted during the weeks after its transition, almost as though it has returned from a combat zone, and may enter into a deep sleep which allows it to heal and regenerate. During this time it is prepared for the higher realms. The less highly evolved the soul, the more rest and recuperation it needs, whereas mature souls, who have made this journey many times before, move quickly through the various stages. Some don't know that their body has died and become stuck, as we shall see later. The more we know in life of what happens after death, the more quickly we appear to move on, but unfinished business or unresolved addictions, lack of belief in something beyond ourselves or the fact that we shall come again, appear to make it harder to leave.

Detaching from our personality (which was merely useful in helping us play our part to maximize the benefit from the earth life) as the astral body disintegrates, the mental energy of the soul carries on, immortal, and we begin to remember who we really are. The soul may have yet another regenerative 'sleep' before it ascends to the mental plane where it spends a variable time being prepared for rebirth. We shall look at this again in Chapter 9.

NOT ENTERING INTO THE LIGHT: EARTHBOUND SOULS

For several days the soul may remain in close proximity to where the body died and during that time may attempt to contact relatives, talking to them, trying to touch them and sometimes feeling confused that no one responds. Because of this, should you feel the presence of someone who has passed on, it would be kind to embrace it, talk to it, but then encourage it to go to the light. Eventually, after a period of time, the souls of our loved ones can return and be around you at will, as we shall see later.

Although we would like to think that all souls ascend into the light, as we saw in Chapter 4, this is not always the case. Sometimes the soul may be confused and lost, concerned for those it's leaving behind, perhaps guilty and ashamed about some life event, desperately wanting to contact someone, to protect loved ones or to complete some business before moving on. These are termed earthbound or lost souls. Where a soul is still disturbed by some unresolved issue, it may remain for many years living among us, meaning to cause no harm but wanting to draw attention to its plight. Occasionally, inadvertently or by design, they do cause us problems, as we shall see. Whether they cause us difficulties or not, they *are* lost and need to be gently persuaded to move on.

Let us look at some of the reasons for souls becoming earthbound.

Traumatic or Violent Death

Fairly recently I was asked to clear the energy in a large office block in London. The secretaries there were having constant headaches, no one felt very happy and product- ivity was lower than it might have been. Although the people in the upper part of the building complained less, in the communal secretarial office, in the basement, the atmos- phere was certainly uneasy. I decided to begin there and asked to have access also to every office, cupboard and store- room. First of all I found a smallish hole in the wall of the office opening above the desk of one of the secretaries. The energy coming through the wall there was unsettling and I felt a flurry of activity in my chest as I approached it. The hole led into a storeroom with no natural light. Leading from the storeroom was the boiler room. As soon as we entered, the energy was cold and heavy and the woman who had accompanied me this far beat a hasty retreat. There in this cold, dark place I found the earthbound soul of a young woman who had been accidentally killed by her lover in the early 1940s. She was pregnant and she and her married lover had been quarrelling. She wanted him to leave his wife as he had promised and be with her. The fight became heated and physical, she was pushed and, stum- bling against the wall, struck her head. Her lover, shocked and afraid, left her body there briefly before taking it that night to a building which had been bombed. Everyone assumed she had been killed during an air raid. Though the soul had been encouraged to leave by those who had come to guide her, she had refused, wanting someone to know the truth of what had happened to her and her baby. We summoned some of her ancestors to help and she was finally quite happy to leave.

This is not an uncommon situation where there has been violent death. Murder especially leaves behind it a heavy, dull atmosphere, which affects those who are living or working in the area, whether or not any lost souls remain there. Some years ago I went to view a house which was for sale at an extremely good price. Right on a river and very attractive, it had stood empty for the last several months, and the previous two families had lived there for very short periods before moving out. Immediately I stepped inside I was aware that the temperature changed and there was palpable anguish. The estate agent was obviously some-what uncomfortable, and when I looked questioningly at her she told me that she must divulge the information that a young man had killed both his parents there and then committed suicide. It was very easy to get permission from her to go to the house later and do some clearing of the energy. The souls of all three were there, stunned, shocked and still unable to release their grief and anguish and find their way to the light. There was no sense of anger or revenge. The boy had been mentally ill and had killed his parents in an act of compassion since he thought that something dreadful was to befall them all. There was simply a sense of deep love between them all and gratitude towards me as they were finally released.

In another incident in a private hospital in the south-east of England, the owners had done a wonderful job of reno-vating a very old building and making a paradise for people recovering from serious illness. However, there was one room that was almost just as it had been when they bought the building. It was clean but undecorated and they said that every time they almost got round to decorating it so that it could be properly used, something would happen. The deco-rator's ladder had broken; the paint had not arrived; the door got jammed; someone slipped on the shiny floor and the project was delayed while they dealt with her injuries. I just happened to be viewing the facility with a view to referring patients there. In the corner of the unoccupied room there was the soul of a young woman. She had been there for many years, just where she had died a traumatic death at the hands of her father. She had never caused anyone any problems but somehow she protected the room until someone could come and hear her story and help her to move on.

Of course, where there has been violent death there may sometimes be a desire to exact revenge, and these earthbound souls tend to cause disturbance and noisy hauntings. They may interfere physically, psychologically and spiritually with those living in the location (who are not necessarily those who were involved in their death), causing annoyance, leaving people feeling drained of energy, ill or below par, often experiencing bad luck and difficulties arising in relationships. Usually such souls are found either where they died or where they were buried.

In cases of an intensely traumatic death, for example during torture, ritual killing, dismemberment or during an explosion, where there is severe destruction of the physical body, there may also be fragmentation of the soul which prevents it from leaving the earth plane. In this case fragments of the soul may then find another host to whom to attach. Usually some of the soul will reincarnate very quickly with little rest or recuperation, little preparation or guidance and without having moved into the light, setting up difficulties for the new incarnation.

Sudden Death

It is not only violent death that keeps the soul earthbound. There are earthbound souls everywhere. There are many reports of souls wandering in hospitals. Apparently an American talk show host claimed that for nine days, while his body lay attached to life-support machinery after a massive brainstem stroke, he wandered around the hospital talking to people who had died and who were still trapped on the earth plane. He claimed that they appeared to be unaware of any higher consciousness and were lost and afraid to go on. When he awoke (recovery from such a serious cerebral incident is rare) he reported an incredible experience where he had helped many souls move on. He described glowing energetic beings that could shape-shift. A young man who passed on fairly recently told me that during surgery a few months before he died he left his body and saw many souls wandering in the operating theatre and in the corridors and that for a while this made him frightened of dying.

The Grief of Relatives and Friends

Sometimes the grief of those left behind, or indeed the grief of the one who has died, keeps the soul here trying to comfort or be comforted. The sensitivity of the newly released soul can be disturbed by loud emotional displays and this may prevent it from doing what it needs to do and enter the light. However, in many societies it is considered only proper to externalize grief in a very flamboyant manner. In some African societies, for instance, the whole tribe will take the opportunity of a death to express both their current grief and all the emotional pain which may have accumulated since the last funeral. With loud wailing and show of emotion, days are spent having a communal catharsis, after which there is a huge feast and celebration to honour the soul and send it on its way to the light.

Confusion or Reluctance to Let Go of Human Identity

Following accidental death, the soul may feel disoriented and unwilling to move from where it is, despite the welcoming souls who are present to encourage it to leave. Also, if the ego remains attached to the current life and there is unwillingness to let go, or if the soul doesn't know that its body has died, it may continue for a long time living the life it always knew, carrying on with what was its usual daily routine sometimes for years. In a house that I cleared in Sussex where the family complained that, if she were allowed to, their dog would stand for hours looking into the corner of the sitting room, sometimes barking and sometimes wagging her tail, the soul of an old lady was sitting as she always had in life, even though she had died many years ago. She had made her transition in hospital but had made her way home and had been here ever since, not knowing that there was any other place she should go. She was so delighted when her husband, who had passed several years before she died, was summoned to take her home. The dog never barked at the corner again.

Addictions and Suicide

Where a person has been addicted to drugs there is often soul damage with loss of fragments and attachment of foreign fragments or even whole entities. This may prevent them from leaving (see Soul Loss and Soul Attachment, pages 146 and 155). The results of suicide are variable and the reason for the suicide seems relevant, some souls moving on quite naturally whereas others appear to remain stuck. Where there has been severe illness such as cancer, great pain – either physical or emotional – or terminal illness, the soul is usually at peace and moves on with comparative ease. Where there was great anguish before the suicide, the guilt and despair the soul feels may hold it earthbound. However, Peter and Elizabeth Fenwick in their book *The Truth in the Light* (Headline, 1996) reviewed three NDEs of people who had attempted suicide and survived. Two of these survivors commented that the depression vanished after leaving the body and that there was an awareness of peace and of something beautiful happening. The third appears to have reported the kind of experience that one might think would lead to obstruction to the soul's onward journey.

Widespread Loss of Life

In areas where there have been multiple deaths over a comparatively short period of time, for example during war, the holocaust, natural disaster or terrorist attack, many souls may still be wandering. One of the greatest privileges of my life has been to do work with lost souls in Berlin. I love Berlin and work there a good deal, although as with many cities I visit, I see much less of the area than people imagine, since my itinerary is usually quite tight. However, on perhaps my fifth visit I was urged by my inner guidance to ask to have my translator and dear friend, Gaby, take me down along the site of the demolished Berlin Wall and through what used to be East Berlin. At one point I suddenly became almost incapacitated with emotion. My heart chakra was so painful that I was forced to sit crouched in the car with my knees up and my hands over my chest while my breathing became laboured, and I was obliged to ask Gaby to take me back to my hotel. I had an important meeting over dinner that night, and she came back to collect me a couple of hours later when I had composed myself somewhat. However, over dinner I could hardly speak and was certainly not my usual self. My eyes kept filling with tears and I was unable to concentrate on what was going on. That night I was very restless, with pain in my chest and a deep emotional longing that wasn't mine but nevertheless felt so strong that it was as though it could break my heart. The next day was the last of the four-day work-shop when I usually leave time for special topics – things that people want to ask, or things they would like me to deal with. However, in my meditation that morning my guidance was that I must take the time to do some healing of the lost souls who had gathered here. Some of them had been here for a very long time; some of them were from the Second World War; some of them had died trying to cross from east to west, and some were from very long ago. I followed the instruction I had been given, which was to ask permission of the group to use this time for a project of my own and to have them simply spend the time, eyes closed, in quiet meditation supporting that. One of the men in the group, a healer himself, was to sit directly opposite me in the circle to hold the energy and Gaby, as always, would be beside me, partly to translate, but also because of her beautiful energy.

I spent only a moment giving silent gratitude about having the privilege to do this work before requesting that we open up a vortex of light above us. I then silently asked that any souls that wanted to use this place of peace to come to, and finally enter the light, were welcome to do so. They would be held in love and supported and their loved ones would gather to greet them. What happened next was so moving that it is difficult to put into words. Initially one by one, and then in an increasing wave, souls came, and with feelings of love, joy and great gratitude as they passed by, they entered into the light. The process went on and on, and as it did, I sat with tears streaming silently down my face. Eventually I was guided to ask that the vortex rise even higher, which it did, and that the process could continue while the group was now involved in some way. I broke the silence by suggesting that we give thanks, then make sure that we were grounded and come back in full awareness to the room. I was not prepared for what I saw when I opened my eyes. Almost everyone in the room was crying and most people were very eager to report what had happened. Almost invariably, with their eyes closed, they had seen what I saw. Though their accounts varied very slightly – some had felt warm touches of gratitude, others had felt presences gently brush past them, some had felt or seen children, others had felt exquisite pain in their heart chakra, some felt love they couldn't describe – no one was left untouched by the wonderful experience we had all shared.

I am by no means the only person who has done such work in Berlin and other places where tragedy has prevented many souls from returning to the light. And there remains much work to do throughout the world. Sadly, while writing this, the dreadful events of 11 September 2001 during which there was great destruction and loss of life in America, in both New York and Washington, occurred. Although many people began working immediately to help the souls reach the light, I have no doubt that there may need to be further work in New York for some time to come. Wherever there have been battlefields, souls continue to wander, though some will also have made their way home. We can do much to heal the planet by lovingly helping to release these souls, though we also need to be skilled and willing to accept guidance about whether it is actually our work or whether we are being guided by an inflated ego.

KNOWING WHEN TO DO NOTHING . . .

Some years ago I spent some time in Egypt where the work was wonderful and the experiences could fill another book, and may well do so! In the Cairo museum I was initially drawn to the mummy room, but when I was almost at the door, there was suddenly a very strong field of energy pushing against me and preventing me from entering. The message was that it would not be good for me to go there and that it was neither my job nor the right time. In 2000, quite by accident (except there is no such thing!), an Australian friend put me in touch with a lady in America who had recently returned from a trip of Egypt where she and a friend had been guided to go and do some work helping the souls of the mummies to depart to the light. Their work was at exactly the right time and they were the ones to do the work that I had wanted to do some years before. Had I gone ahead and attempted to do it then, it would have been an act of my ego rather than my soul and, I have no doubt, would have led me into difficulties.

In all these cases, a gentle, compassionate, empathic but sometimes firm stance is called for, with the willingness to discuss and answer questions the soul may have, but nevertheless to encourage them to go home.

So now we know what happens as we re-enter our true home, the soul plane. However, though we can now rest and recuperate for a while, for most of us there is still work to be done. In the next chapter we shall look at soul work for our own benefit and also in the service of others.

✿ AFFIRMATION

I live every moment of my life here and on the soul planes with integrity and unconditional love.

✿ MEDITATION

This meditation is different to the others since it is intended to be read out loud immediately after the physical death of the body. If someone you know is almost ready to make their transition, then you could check out with them whether you should have this meditation read for them. If the person dying is someone to whom you are very close and you feel that in the moments immediately after death you would be unable to trust your voice to read, then why not ask someone close and similarly spiritually minded to read it while you simply bear witness? You can also use this should you find yourself for instance at the scene of an accident where someone has been killed. If you yourself are nearing your transition, why not nominate someone to read it for you when the time comes? In the box at the end of the meditation there is a separate ending for you if you are grieving for the person for whom you've been doing the meditation. Take care of yourself!

Having a candle, flowers and some incense would be nice. Sometimes of course this is not possible, for example in hospital rooms where there's oxygen, so please check first. If it isn't possible, or if you're somewhere where you can't read this, simply ask for guidance for yourself and allow yourself to say what you know to be right. It will be fine. Protect yourself and the whole area with white light, ask for angels to be present, then gently, softly and slowly, remembering that the soul is very sensitive at this time begin to read or say . . .

May you be in peace at this moment and always as you now prepare to leave this place. Arise now and leave your body, blessed vehicle of your human life, and be free once more. Free of the material world and free to return home. Look down at your body and know that you have shed it and you still live. Look at it with compassion and gratitude for all that it has done for you. Feel your freedom, feel the peace. Allow your-self clarity. You are going home. Have no fear or concern for us. Our lives have been enriched by your courage to be here with us on the earth plane. Now is your time to be free and we shall meet you in the future on a higher plane. Leave behind any pain. Do not hesitate. It is time for you to go. Let go of your earthly life, and move into the peace and the light. Allow your guides to take you gently, as we in turn take our leave of you with love in our hearts. Move towards the light now. The white light will gently draw you as you ascend into the tunnel, which is the portal of the soul planes. Allow yourself to return home to the love and compassion of those who wait for you. Feel the love that embraces you. See the light and know that you will be held in the utmost love. Allow yourself to feel the peace and enjoy. You are travelling upwards in the light and love. Allow yourself to move towards the light. Go to the light now. Ascending, ascending. We wish you well on your journey. You are greatly beloved. Go well. Goodbye, beloved one.

Now take a moment for yourself and give gratitude for the priv-ilege of being with someone at their transition. If this person was close to you, it's now time for you to feel your feelings whatever they may be. No matter how enlightened we are, we are human beings and if you need to cry, that's fine. If you need to be quiet, that's fine too. Allow yourself just to be. When you feel up to it you may wish to have a ritual and celebration of the life of the person and the love, friendship or whatever you shared. Whatever you do now, it's time to take care of you. Your loved one is in safe hands. Give yourself some time, and then you might like to do the following brief meditation. Where I have left spaces, you might like to use the person's name and, as always, adapt the words to make them your own.

Wherever you are — in your safe place, in a hospital room or wherever — make yourself as comfortable as you can. If it's possible, it would be healing to have your candle, flowers and perhaps a beautiful crystal and some memento. Take a few deep breaths and close your eyes and relax. Just take another deep breath and this time allow your out-breath to take with it anything you don't need. With another breath, ground yourself and feel the earth lovingly supporting you. You are here in the material world where you need to be right now. Take another deep breath and this time surround yourself by white light. Relax. Let your shoulders fall. Let your chair or the floor take your weight and let anything you don't need simply discharge into the earth. Relax.

Now allow yourself to feel whatever feelings are uppermost. Simply allow them to surface in any way that is safe and comfortable for you. When the crescendo of emotion is over, ground yourself again. Now allow yourself to bring to mind the person who has made their transition. Bring to mind any memories you wish to savour and spend as long as you like with this. Then . . .

I give thanks for the presence of this person in my life. For all that we have shared, taught and learned, given and received, I give thanks. For the honour of being chosen to be present at the time of transition, I give thanks. I give thanks that my life was enriched by (the name of the deceased person) being in it. I ask that I may be blessed at this time and that my wounds may soon heal. I wish freedom for my loved one and also for myself, and ask that light may heal my heart and cleanse the bonds that have been ruptured by (the name of the deceased person's) departure. I welcome the highest possible healing masters to heal me now.

IF YOU ARE GRIEVING NOW . . .

Allow yourself to feel the peace and, with a sense of awe and humility, know that angels are in attendance. Breathe gently, knowing that with every breath you bring yourself closer to wholeness. Know that you have rendered a great and loving service to the one who has made their transition and know that there is gratitude to you. Take as long as you wish and allow yourself to feel whatever you need to feel. Allow yourself to be the centre of attention now as you ask for love and comfort for your wounds in letting go of someone for whom you care. Give yourself whatever you need in this moment and allow yourself some pride in having helped your loved one to make a good transition. Breathe. Observe your own energy and in particular your heart chakra and ask for light to heal where bonds have been broken. Ask for a flood of light now to enter in through the top of your head and fill every cell and every atom of every cell, then breathe it into the space around you, filling your auric bodies with light. Visualize the light healing you and bringing all your chakras into harmony and balance. Feel yourself coming into alignment and regaining your strength and a sense of calm. Know that you may need to repeat this again and that this is quite normal as waves of grief may wash over you. Allow yourself whatever time you need . . .

Then when you are ready, give gratitude and start to return to this moment. Make sure you are present and well grounded. Check your chakras once more, then be fully aware of your physical presence, and when you feel fully alert, gently open your eyes. Have a stretch and a drink of water, then record whatever you wish in your journal.

When someone we love makes their transition, often our heart chakra and the bonds between us are broken. Homeopathic arnica is good for the shock and to help reduce any trauma to your heart chakra. Since the heart chakra is responsible for immune function, taking some immune system support would be good. If your grief remains unresolved, some homeopathic ignatia would be useful.

✪ PRAYER

When the time is right and we have completed all that we came here to do, let us joyfully and peacefully make our transition to the soul realms from which we came and to which we shall return, knowing that we are blessed and cherished at every moment and that we are assured of a loving welcome home.

7 SOUL WORK IN ANOTHER DIMENSION

Lo there do I see my father
Lo there do I see my mother, and my sisters and my brothers
Lo do I see the line of my people back to the beginning
Lo they do call to me
Bidding me take my place among them
In the halls of Valhalla where the great may live forever.

Ancient Viking Prayer

The famous teacher and clairvoyant Rudolph Steiner talked of the plane of consciousness between death and rebirth as being merely a continuation of life, and saw time spent on the soul plane as one of rejuvenation and restoration, rather like sleep in the earthly life. Other models imply that there is an afterlife – a place to which we go after death or, rather, after life, and where we await the Day of Judgment. Well, let us look at the possibilities and ask ourselves whether we believe that our souls will simply sleep and restore and forgo any further growth, or indeed whether we will be held in some terminal awaiting the end of the world. Or is it more likely that though we may begin our life hereafter with rest and recuperation, there is work to be done on the soul plane before we are ready to return to human life again? I believe the latter. As in the human life, some of our work needs to be self-focused and for our own personal development, balanced by service to others.

The measure of our greatness is how we cope with life's challenges and integrate them into our being. It was Tennessee Williams who said that high station in life is earned by the gallantry with which appalling experiences are survived with grace. If we are unable to integrate the learning from our challenges or survive our experiences with grace during the earthly life, here on the soul plane we have another chance to expand our perspective. Letting go of our personality and human identity, which has been rather like a cloak obscuring our wonder and magnificence, we are once more revealed in our true essence.

According to the 'afterlife' model, our destination after our transition depends upon our behaviour during our earthly lifetime, the choices being heaven, purgatory or hell. The term interlife (though the most commonly used), is misleading, implying that the real life is the earthly one and the other merely time between, whereas nothing could be further from the truth; as we discussed in the previous chapter, the soul plane is our real home from which we venture now and then.

In fact, though what happens in the interlife is not easy either to document or authenticate, there is considerable evidence of continued dynamic growth with continuing education and also the opportunity for service. Unravelling what happens to each of us on the soul plane is a bit like spiritual psychotherapy, and understanding can lead us to make better-informed choices here on earth, which can lead to healing of all aspects of current human life. That, as always, is my hope and aim here. To bring all this together, then, I will be using the same tools as before – reference to ancient and modern writings, case studies and my own channelling and experience. Although we shall look at the experience from the point of the soul, it's essential that we also relate this to our life here so that we can incorporate our knowledge into our current life.

WHAT DO WE DO IN THE INTERLIFE?

After reviewing and processing all that has happened in our most recent earth life, then putting that into the context of the whole journey of our soul thus far, we continue our growth and learning. Many souls continue to have a powerful interaction with life on earth as they serve others still in human form, while others have the opportunity for service within the soul planes. Much of this depends upon the development of the soul and its natural aptitudes – much as we find here on earth. Eventually, with the help of guides, and always of our own free will, we make decisions about what we still need to experience and make plans regarding our next life. Much of this appears to happen simultaneously, but let's sort it out into some sequence even though it may not happen exactly in this way.

Setting the Scene

First let us set the scene. Those who are able to regress to memories of the time between earthly lives often describe the interlife in physical terms. Just as we create our reality here on the physical plane, so, it seems, we do in the interlife also. Thus we perceive that we still have a body, albeit not a physical one, and live in cities with buildings, or in natural landscapes or gardens, according to our choice. There are healing places and temples and of course other souls; colours are perceived as brighter and more vibrant, while structures are less solid and permanent than on the physical plane. Everything appears to have its own life energy and even musical expression, while the reality, perfect for our needs, is described as constantly changing, being remodelled and moulded by our thoughts, according to our individual needs and perceptions. Thus the surroundings may not necessarily be perceived as similar even by souls in close proximity to each other. We are able to do things with ease and to communicate telepathically, having wonderful and intense encounters with souls we have always known and loved. Everything is experienced in an atmosphere of love, peace and compassion. Although each soul has the opportunity to have exactly what it needs for its development and the completion of its work in the interlife, not all souls necessarily perform all the tasks we shall discuss. The most enlightened may appear to have little of the former and progress more quickly to the point of service. Some souls may spend many, many years without the desire or need to reincarnate, instead dedicating themselves to the service of others both in the interim phase and also on the earth plane.

But first there is a time of rest and recuperation – which may be termed cosmic sleep – and then we are ready for further growth.

Soul Work for Our Own Development

We begin our work on the astral plane, where in many ways life appears to be similar to that on earth. We are surrounded by spiritually evolved beings whose only wish is to help and guide us and to be available to us as we progress. Before our last excursion to earth we had already learned a great deal, but many of those skills needed to be 'forgotten' so that we had maximum benefit from the challenges we set for ourselves. Now we also recap on all we have learned in all our lifetimes thus far. In the process of our development our light is purified and changes from white light progressing through yellow and eventually to blue and finally violet.

Let's break down some of the tasks so we can understand them better.

Reviewing Our Last Life

We have dealt to some extent with some aspects of the past-life review in the previous chapter. I will only reiterate that the accent is on growth and learning and not on judgment or punishment. We are here to be objective about our life experiences, to learn from them and integrate them, enabling us to further our development and help us to make decisions about future lives. The process is witnessed and guided by souls who love and cherish us and may then be able to help us with later decisions. We are at last able to put into context and fully understand various interactions on the earth plane – to recognize the souls who came into our lives, and how all of us behaved as we did for our mutual learning and growth. At last there is understanding and the recognition that not only is there nothing to forgive, but souls may have made sacrifices on the earth plane for our higher good by doing what we experienced as painful or abusive, and so gratitude is more appropriate. Often those who behaved in ways we did not like, who pushed our limits, prompted us to make changes, to move, to grow were those who loved us most and sacrificed their own potential joy in the relationship for us. The value of each and every soul who transacted with us becomes clear, as well as our own essential role in the lives of others. With compassion for ourselves we can release ourselves from the bondage of guilt and shame, being free now to rest and enjoy a time of renewal, healing and restoration as we reacquaint ourselves with our true home and our loved ones.

Lesley's story demonstrates the value of the life review, but also shows how understanding the concept in this current life can help us make changes now.

When Lesley came to see me she was a smart, sharp, no-nonsense fifty-five-year-old who had neither married nor had children, having struggled all her life with her identity and with her sexuality which had never been allowed to blossom. She was angry. In fact she had been angry for much of her life. Her mother had lived alone since her father died nineteen years ago, and during that time Lesley had made regular dutiful visits despite the fact that she felt no love for her mother and was actually repulsed by the thought of touching her. Recently her mother had become forgetful and had had a series of falls and now Lesley found herself having to make decisions about long-term care. In doing so she had found herself even more angry than usual, sometimes erupting into fearful fury, trapped by feelings she didn't understand. Ideally she would just have liked to put her mother into a home and be finished with what had been a lifetime of rejection and disappointment with regard to their relationship. An only child, she had neither sibling nor family support and was even more angry at having to consult someone like me.

We looked at her fury, which Lesley traced to her mother's apparent coolness and lifelong rejection. She said that her parents had been very much in love and were so wrapped up in each other that they should never have had a child – or they should have had more than one so that each would have company. Besotted with each other, her parents had paid her little attention, any possibility of affection from her father being blocked by her mother who was jealous and constantly craved his attention. After her father's death her mother had withdrawn even further – a grieving widow, she had made it abundantly clear that even Lesley's father's memory was more important than she was.

I asked Lesley to look at what she had gained from choosing this woman as her mother. Initially this concept, alien to her, simply fed her fury, though eventually she was able to see that many of the skills and qualities that made her so strong, cool and efficient in her business came from the independence she had learned in childhood. Though with reluctance she acknowledged this, it did nothing to quell her feelings of rage towards her mother.

One day she came to her session saying that she had read an interesting, though in her mind preposterous, article about past-life therapy and asked my views on it. She appeared to find it an interesting intellectual exercise and, though she was sceptical, agreed to try it. Under regression she recalled a past life where she had had a turbulent relationship with her mother. In London in the 1800s she was the only boy with five younger sisters, all living in squalor with their depressed and suicidal mother and drunken father who was regularly violent to all of them. She found herself often taking care of all the other children and her mother, tending wounds inflicted by her father. She squirmed in her chair as she recounted how furious she was with her mother for not protecting them. Tears of angry frustration streamed down her face; the first time in any session she had allowed herself to cry. She saw herself eventually killing her father and suffering the death penalty for her crime. Throughout, she blamed her mother for her actions and for the punishment she received.

Passing through her death experience, we paused at her life review. Her expression softened as she reported becoming aware of her mother's sacrifices during that lifetime. Her mother, a soul-mate with whom she had spent many a lifetime, had forfeited the love, respect and affection between mother and daughter so that her son might fulfil his role in this family karmic agreement of violence.

After the healing Lesley gently returned to her normal state of consciousness and began to talk about her current life. Her mother was not the same mother as in the life she had just visited, and in some ways she found little connection between the two lives. But what was striking for her was that, because of the life review, for the first time she could see what it must have cost her mother to play her part. She saw that they had both lost a great deal in this relationship, but that she, Lesley, had indeed gained also. Her compassion for her mother was evident. Although their relationship has still not been easy, there have been shifts and Lesley is certainly happier than she has ever been. What's more, having resolved some issues with her past life and her current mother she is able, for the first time, to review her life afresh, allowing herself to look at the fact that whereas heterosexual relationships have never worked for her, a lesbian relationship might.

Putting It All in Context

Now that we have finally understood the roles that we have played in the lives of others and how others have taught us too, now that we are aware of how intricately our experience is entwined and how those who may have hurt us were in fact helping us, it's time for us to review our whole progress. Surrounded by the joy and admiration of those who have not only witnessed our growth but been an integral part of it, our task now is to review all of our lives hitherto. This allows us to integrate our latest learning into the context of the journey of our soul thus far. All of our experience, from our soul's conception through all those lifetimes even before we were human and all our lifetimes since, has been essential to our evolution. Though we may yet have many lifetimes to come, we have progressed a long way on our voluntary quest to experience all there is. Now is the time for further development, and we will be assigned to the level most appropriate for us. The speed with which we move on depends upon our level of enlightenment. Many highly evolved souls will have little to gain from further learning and instead will move directly to their work of service. The souls of children also usually move on quickly.

Continuing Our Growth and Learning – Ascension to Higher Planes

Our review complete, we may remain for a considerable period on the astral planes. Only if we are unable and unwilling to process and acknowledge our immediate past life, to forgive and find compassion for those for whom we may have felt anger and hatred, do we tarry a while in the lower astral plane, where we have the opportunity to experience more until we are ready to ascend. Through our willingness to acknowledge our behaviour and come to an understanding and acceptance of positive intention and love, we eventually move up through the astral planes and thereafter ascend to the mental plane. We now shed our astral body and shimmer as pure light energy with little solid form. The mental plane, you may remember, is a higher dimension of pure intelligence, where knowledge is expanded and where the masters and angels who are to continue to work with us welcome us in an atmosphere of pure, unconditional love. Here are the halls of learning, with the sense of a celestial school where, without effort, we simply absorb knowledge and understanding. With calm, peace, tranquillity and love pervading everything, the whole of our journey is clarified as we receive insight after insight, telepathically communicating with the great masters and wise beings. In this place of pure thought, where there is no time, we shall spend much of our interlife, continuing with our own personal work, helping others also, and meanwhile having the opportunity to learn from interaction with the earth plane.

THE HONOUR OF SERVICE: OUR CONTINUING SOUL WORK

As on earth, an essential part of our continuing spiritual growth is to be of service, and we now have the opportunity to continue our work in a variety of ways. We may choose to work with those who are on the soul plane by taking up our place as witnesses, counsellors and guides, as many have already lovingly done for us, or to target our work on those who remain in physical bodies, or to work more globally with the evolution of humanity and the planet earth.

SERVICE ON THE SOUL PLANE

Helping to Guide Those Who Have Recently Made Their Transition

As we saw in the previous chapter, the soul leaving its physical vehicle and making its transition to the soul plane is accompanied from before the moment of 'death' until it enters the spiritual world. We may now be one of the souls already on the soul plane who gather around the body of the person they know and love as they approach the moment of transition, to lovingly support and guide, to encourage the soul to leave the body and move on towards the tunnel. Or we may be present to greet the soul as it emerges from the tunnel, though usually a single being of light will be present at this time. Nevertheless, as one of those well known and beloved by the newly departed soul, we may be present to help orientate and welcome. In the case of massive and sudden exit of souls from the earth plane, such as in war zones and where there are natural tragedies, there is often an amassing of welcoming angels and souls, as I described on page 214 regarding the events of 11 September. The events of that day have been extremely well documented, and I mention it here only to highlight the work of these angelic beings and great souls who gathered to welcome the thousands of souls who agreed to leave the material plane simultaneously that day, once again to highlight lessons to the world and raise consciousness.

Helping Those Undertaking Life Reviews

As we have seen in Chapter 6, loving souls are always present at life reviews to support us and prevent us from being too harsh with ourselves. They often then continue to counsel and guide. The following case history demonstrates this and several other aspects of the interlife. In her current life, Renee is a natural healing channel who is now in training. Her past-life regression includes a description of part of the interlife as she experiences it, and her work as a member of the panel of a past-life review.

Renee had done much work on herself and her relationships and was now training as a healer. She wanted to do some past-life work and I took her to a time in the interlife so that she could view her experience there. I then asked her to pick up on the life she had just left and the one she was about to begin.

She found herself in the warm, loving, expanded consciousness of the interlife and said that she was surrounded by other glowing beings who were part of the group assisting with a life review. Their job was to be witnesses and to encourage the soul to be less harsh and self-critical. Renee said that they did this not with words but by simply radiating soothing love – the messages were simply automatically absorbed. The soul was one she knew well and loved dearly. They had incarnated together within a group on many occasions; most recently he had been a pupil, and now she was honoured to be of assistance in this way. She described the scene in various qualities and hues of light, with a structure that she found difficult to describe except in terms of colour and a sense of density. The soul which had arrived was glowing with yellowish-white light, whereas she herself was tinged with blue. Other beings had different hues, one of them, exceedingly wise and loving, glowing in purple light.

The atmosphere was one of unconditional love, difficult for Renee to describe. As she struggled to depict the scene, things seemed to change. The surroundings, she said, appeared solid but changed shape instantly from time to time, and without apparent movement everything became different. The only constants were the feelings of love and security. She felt that she had been in the interlife for a very long time, even though time didn't really exist. She knew that she was to incarnate again but that plans had not yet been made. Her role for the present was that of guide and counsellor.

We shall pick up on Renee's story again in Chapter 8 since it also demonstrates beautifully the weaving of relationships through several lives.

Guides and Counsellors

Throughout the whole of our time on the soul planes, guides and counsellors are available to us to help us in any way. We may find that these are souls we knew on the earth plane – those who incarnated perhaps as grandparents, parents or friends – or perhaps members of our soul group (see page 272) with whom we have incarnated at other times. All of us therefore have the opportunity to be of service to each other on the soul plane. There are also those guides who specifically help with next-life planning and we shall discuss this in Chapter 9.

SERVICE TO THOSE ON THE MATERIAL PLANE

Here on earth, we are constantly being guided. Becoming aware of this can change our lives dramatically and bring us great joy. Although we are now looking at this process from the point of view of the soul plane, you should try to keep in mind also your earthly self and how this knowledge can affect you now. We shall come back to this later.

Offering Comfort and Evidence of Survival

It is important to us to know that after 'death' there is survival, and as we discussed in the previous Chapter, many souls on the soul plane are involved in giving us whatever proof they can as a message of hope for the future as well as comfort to those who are grieving. Obviously communication from the soul plane cannot be exactly as we perceive it on earth. However, every attempt is made to bring us information as succinctly and accurately as possible. Souls will gather round whatever channel they find available to them in an attempt to communicate. Sometimes this may be a medium or channel who literally acts as a connection between the two worlds. Many people use this form of communication as a common part of their lives and consult mediums regularly to open the possibility of this communication with their loved ones who they know will be trying to contact them. (Queen Victoria is reported to have used this method of receiving messages of comfort from Prince Albert after he died, whilst Abraham Lincoln also used a medium to seek the counsel of souls who had passed on.) Often, however, communication is direct as souls in the interlife hover around us giving us signs in various ways that confirm their presence and survival. How those on earth perceive these messages varies according to their sensitivity and openness. Communication may be perceived either as words, sometimes spoken, sometimes written, or as visions, a scent or more subtly as simply a feeling, a sensation or a sudden rush of emotion.

Carletta B'Hahn writes beautifully in *Benjaya's Gifts* of the communication with her son Benjaya who, after his transition, would give her messages through automatic writing. Benjaya actually talks of his need to move into his great soul self (much like the young man I mentioned in Chapter 6), telling his mother that though he is a 'whole wiser self', he comes to her as his boyself since that is what she draws from him 'like a magnet attracts certain metals'. He describes how, whenever his mother thinks of him, he knows about it and often comes instantly to be with her. 'I can come to you instantly without disturbing anything I'm doing at the time. I can just carry on doing that thing as well.' He talks of having to free himself from his boyself and his human thoughts to grow in the new world. In common with the souls of many who make the transition as children, he also reports having felt more trapped in his physical body during his short earthly life than most children do, having been a free spirit enthusiastically seeking expression in a restricting world. 'I came to express myself as spirit as fully and wholly as possible and it was my job to do that within the rest of life's restrictions.' He asks that his mother should not now 'box (him) into boy-consciousness'.

Communication from departed souls may come in a very different form as they search for ways to give us proof that they are still alive. The following examples show how souls on the soul planes are trying to contact us to give us proof of survival, but we who are still here need to do our part and expand our willingness to receive. Sometimes those of us who have worked in the field of the paranormal for many years still fail to recognize such communication for what it is. Read on!

About three months after my father died, one Friday afternoon I suddenly became obsessed with the idea of building a cupboard. I had the whole plan in my mind and it seemed quite urgent to do it now. I still had some clients to see, but nevertheless felt that I had to get away as soon as possible and buy the materials, which I did – wood, screws, glue, handles for doors and drawers, glass for shelves and even shelf paper. I was asked if I would like delivery, but said that I wanted to take it all with me even though I couldn't close the boot of the car. I drove home in a state of excitement and somehow managed to get all the wood out and into my kitchen though I was now finding it heavier than I had done before.

Suddenly, with a bit of a thud, I was grounded and looked at all the materials I had bought and wondered what on earth I had been thinking of. I had never done woodwork before and had no real idea of how to proceed. I felt rather stupid and eventually went off to bed feeling a bit low. The next morning I got up and there on the kitchen floor was the pile of wood and all the bags of screws and hardware. I made my way to the kettle and made a cup of tea while wondering whether the store would take some of this back since I had no idea what to do with it. I must have been crazy the day before! Then as I sat in the middle of the mess I heard my dad's voice.

'Go and get my tools,' he said.

In my garden shed I had a box of his tools, some of which had belonged to my grandfather and all lovingly cared for over the years. I went and lugged out the box, hardly able to shift it. I opened it up and found myself choosing at random various tools and I carried them back down to the house. Over the next few hours, guided by my father, I built a beautiful cupboard. When it got too heavy to lift I simply asked him to help and he did. By the end of the day it was complete and I sat there with yet another cup of tea admiring what we had done.

Now, this may not seem to be the most inspiring of guidance, not like channelling or speaking in tongues, but it was warm and loving and practical and gave me the utmost joy in having another unexpected day with my dad. For him, I later perceived a whole new sense of peace. He had managed to reach me and knew that I had understood. Not only that, but he had established with me a form of practical communication which we now use regularly. If ever I am in difficulty, for instance trying to lift something very heavy on the ranch, I call to him and know that he will hear and help me. I have no doubt that he is communicating in other ways with my sister and our children.

There are many similar stories of fairly newly deceased relatives coming to help their loved ones, often in times of stress and need rather than, as my father did, just to lovingly share time and comfort.

Sometimes the communication only makes sense to the person receiving it and might appear fanciful to others. However, for the person who has asked for some sign of survival, the answer may be unmistakable as the person requesting proof has in so doing opened a channel through which the communication can be given.

A delightful patient of mine was overwhelmed by the death of her father and we talked about survival, though she didn't really believe in such a thing. Her mother had died some years earlier and she said that she would be so comforted if at least she knew her parents had found each other and were together. We talked of how, if she asked, they might give her a sign that this was so, though if she was expecting words of comfort she might be disappointed. She tearfully said that she would be open to any sign they could possibly give her. That same night, unable to sleep, she was standing in the dark, crying, looking out of her upstairs bedroom window and watching snow gently falling. At 2 a.m. a car drove very slowly up the quiet private road and stopped right in front of her house, paused for a moment and then made a three-point turn. As it drove away she was stunned to see its tracks making two perfect hearts in the newly fallen snow. From that moment her grief began to ease and she emerged with a new and strong spiritual conviction.

Offering Protective Guidance

Spiritual guides stay with every one of us both from before incarnation and throughout our lives, and though they never interfere with our free will, they constantly guide and protect us, never abandoning us despite the fact that we

may override their guidance, ignore them or be totally unaware of their positive effect in our lives. The same highly
evolved beings often guide us from our very first incarnation as a young and innocent soul, remaining with us also
on the soul plane, helping us to review the life we have just
left, guiding us as we choose a new one, and then following
us again, our welfare being their purpose. They communicate with us in various ways, but being open and ready to
receive their communication is up to us. Sometimes I observe
such clear guidance being put in the way of people I know
although they haven't detected it for themselves. Sometimes
what we may perceive as a sudden idea or intuition is in
fact guidance. Suddenly finding ourselves on a road we
didn't intend to be on is often due to our guides' protection helping us to avoid a problem on the route we had
planned. Making a sudden decision, for instance, to travel
on a different day or do something that delays us so that
we miss an aircraft that later crashes are not mere coinci-
dences, but are due to guidance that we perceive on a subconscious level. Asking for the help of your guides, even if
you don't believe in them, can sometimes be astounding in
that it opens a way for us to become aware of their ever-
present help, although of course the sceptic will always be
able to rationalize the events that follow. That's fine! They
don't ask for our gratitude!

Some souls are assigned as guardian angels to particular
souls and will remain with them through lifetime after lifetime and also during the interlife too. They may also incarnate with us at times and share at least part of an earthly
life with us. For example, a beloved grandparent or great-
grandparent may have been a guardian angel for eons and
on this occasion come to help prepare our way in the early
part of our life, leaving when we're well established. Many
of my patients have told me stories about being visited in

dreams by a grandmother who had died when they were young, of being guided in some way by her and of her being uppermost in their minds at times of crisis. A dear friend when having a difficult time said that she would have visions of her grandmother brushing her hair and soothing her and that she then felt able to sleep and manage another day without resorting to the self-harm that was uppermost in her mind. I have no doubt that the soul of her grandmother is her guardian angel.

Some years ago I was returning late at night from a teaching engagement in Yorkshire. I was travelling over the moors at almost midnight, going back to my home in Sedgefield. I knew that I was low on petrol but thought that I would make it, and in any case there were no garages open for miles so I had little choice. Suddenly the car spluttered to a halt at a point where the road was going uphill, miles away from anywhere, with no road lighting. I steered it off the road and almost into the heather. If any traffic had come along it would have been quite dangerous. I sat for a moment wondering what I was going to do. It looked as though I would be stranded there for the night. I had no idea where the next petrol station might be and setting off to walk in the dark across the moors was not a particularly good idea. There might be another car at some time that would give me a lift, but some would consider even that risky. This was in the days before mobile phones, so it appeared that I needed simply to sit in the car and hope for some help to arrive and that my husband wouldn't be too worried about me.

I then decided to call for help and simply asked that if there was any way I could get out of this, now would be a good time to have some guidance as to what I should do. I suddenly knew that I had to take my shoes off and get out of the car – this in November at midnight on the Yorkshire moors! I did as I was guided and left my high heels in the car as I followed instructions. I was told to turn the steering wheel and walk beside the car – not really push it, just walk with it – which I did. With no resistance whatsoever, the car moved out of the heather and on to the road and, in my stockinged feet, I simply walked it uphill with one hand on the steering wheel and the other on the door. Though I probably walked for about three miles, it took me very little time and absolutely no effort whatsoever, and what's more, my feet were not cold, nor did I make holes in my stockings! Suddenly at the brow of another hill I saw a petrol station in the distance. I was then told to get into the car and simply free-wheel down to it, which I did. I was home at about 2 a.m., to find my poor husband wondering what had happened to me as I arrived absolutely elated and with a very strange story to share.

Giving Help When Needed

I have many similar stories of having received exactly what I needed exactly when I needed it and asked for it from those working with me on the soul plane. There may well be instances that you have experienced yourself that you simply have not interpreted as coming from a similar source. However, such help and guidance are never far from us, and even when we have not thought to ask, we're constantly gently nudged in the right direction, although of course we have free will and may refuse the offer of help. In many cases we may wonder why something, someone, God, did not appear to help us when we needed help. But our guides will not interfere if we are learning from what appears to be a bad situation unless we ask them to. Sometimes, however, we have been guided to avert disaster and what happens to us may be far less serious than it otherwise would have been.

When I was working as a doctor in Zambia in the mid-1970s, troubles were building up both in Zimbabwe (then Southern Rhodesia) to the south and in South Africa. Angola, to the west, was in the midst of armed conflict, and the Caprivi Strip, the narrow piece of land to the south-west forming a border with Botswana and administered by South-West Africa, was a prime target for freedom fighters who laid mines and generally caused havoc to raise awareness of the plight of the African people. It was not unusual therefore for men to be flown into the hospital from the border, often with horrendous injuries. On one such night, a helicopter brought in several men. There were few of us on duty and all of us were needed to help get these men in as quickly as possible. I paused for only a second to ask for help, and suddenly was aware that I had developed enormous strength way beyond my normal capability. I found myself bodily lifting men much bigger than myself on to trolleys and running with them up to the emergency room. There was neither stress nor strain and afterwards when I felt myself return to normal, I was neither stiff nor sore. I simply gave thanks and got on with the job in hand, being once more myself.

Healing

Healing energy is constantly available, being lovingly and willingly channelled to us. All we need do is open to that possibility and great souls are ready to help. Thus those of us who are called healers do not actually do the healing ourselves but simply make available a pathway or channel for this energy to flow from healing souls, masters and angels who themselves are conduits for the divine energy that has the power to heal. That energy then passes through the 'healer' and helps stimulate the innate capacity of the other to heal himself. Sometimes, however, while channelling healing energy we can simultaneously perceive beings of light around the patient and ourselves as they work alongside us, dissipating any negative energy as it is released, flowing in healing light, guiding our hands and hearts to where the work needs to be focused and giving us insight about what the person we have the privilege to be working with needs. Sometimes while doing psychic surgery, for instance, we may appear inactive while great things are none the less happening on an energetic level as great master healers do the work. When teaching healing I suggest that healers in training just allow their hands to move without thought or effort since they will, if they have enough humility, be guided to the right place to do the right thing. During a healing session, whether the person is with me or absent, I receive a constant stream of help in the form of mental pictures of what has happened in the person's life, what they suffered in past lives and how this is relevant to their current problem. All of this is the guidance and healing of the masters who work with me. The mark of the great healer is to acknowledge that in fact we had nothing to do with the healing except by being a willing and open instrument. Discarnate beings are drawn to us as we invite their help to protect the whole healing area and cleanse everything with light. All we need to do is to get ourselves and our egos out of the way and to detach from the outcome, and the most wonderful guidance will pour down through us. Sometimes souls choose a particular healer with whom to work and the healer perceives a constant, unchanging guide. Sometimes, as in my case, we are not aware of any particular named presence, but only that the energy comes from an ever-present, very powerful source. Sometimes the particular guides of the patient are working as part of the healing team, protecting so that I can get on with what I have to do. Often, I'm afraid, I am impolite and fail to ask for help, but thankfully it's always generously available. I always try to remember to give thanks afterwards, though on a busy day sadly I may forget that also. It is in the nature of the remarkable, palpable, unconditional love of the great discarnate master healers who help us that they continue to offer what we need despite our occasional lack of good manners!

From the soul planes other masters are continually flooding the earth and the hearts of men and women with healing energy and light to help us evolve as a race and assist with global healing. The great changes in our acceptance and understanding of spiritual matters through what has been called the New Age movement are the results of the healing and intervention of beings of love and light who are working with us and through us from the higher soul planes. They help open masses of hearts and minds to meditation and healing and the acceptance of concepts that those in the East have acknowledged for centuries. They are constantly encouraging us to make their work our own by accepting our calling to be in active partnership with them for the advancement of the world, spreading the philosophy of love and light as we in turn transmit to those around us directly by teaching, writing, workshops, etc., or by example and modelling unconditional love, the messages which these powerful masters on the soul planes constantly broadcast to us. What is so wonderful is that this wisdom from the masters is now available to us all. We have moved somewhat from the times when all gurus meditated and dispensed their wisdom and healing from caves and mountain tops. Now very ordinary men and women living ordinary lives, dealing simultaneously with relationships and heartache, working to make ends meet and bringing up children, are doing very extraordinary things, and, in partnership with souls working on higher planes, are acting as messengers for their fellow humans.

There is nothing to stop each of us being more open to receiving the messages and passing on the flow of unconditional love and healing that the world so badly needs. Those of us who have had a loved one depart can validate their lives and experience by doing just that. Here we can continue the work that they begin on a higher plane. In the mental plane they are passing on messages of love, whether or not you feel able to pick up their broadcast. Take the courage and opportunity to pass that on with a smile and a kind word, with a move towards integrity, with a loving hand or gesture, with a cessation of anger and anguish, with forgiveness while still here on earth.

DOING YOUR SOUL WORK NOW . . .

We shall all reach the mental plane at some time, and we shall eventually be in the position of doing our own global healing. This knowledge can prompt us to make a choice to begin now. In this very moment, by the power of your own will and by the power of God that resides within you, you can change the world. Someone once said that vast social change occurs in the heart and mind of one man at a time. Are you ready to make that shift to produce vast social change? Could you from this moment listen anew to the loving messages that are everywhere? Could you shift your attitude even a little and come from a place of optimism and joy that will comfort and change the lives of those with whom you come into contact? Could you smile at the next person you meet and with a light and joyful voice bring pleasure to their day so that they might pass that on? Could you open your heart with love in this moment and send healing and peace to those around you? Could you let off the hook those you have been torturing with criticism or passive aggression, sarcasm or complaint? (Although you still have a right to say you no longer want them in your life). Could you start to see everyone around you as equals, no matter what their colour or creed, no matter what you perceive them to have done? Can you let go of judgment and see that they are on their own path and simply trying to survive just like you? You do not have to wait till you reach the soul plane to do this soul work. There is opportunity in every second of every day to make a difference. And maybe the place to start is in forgiving yourself for the past. In acknowledging that, as in the life review that you shall no doubt attend at some time, there can be compassion, lack of judgment and only learning. You do not have to wait. You could do your own life review right now and make the rest of your life different.

Education

Many entities, some of which have been embodied and have been on the soul planes for centuries, and others who have never opted for an earthly life, are working to give us information previously not available to us on the earth plane about the nature of the universe, our soul's journey and the workings of God. The Bible and other sacred works offer us ample evidence of such communication with the people through prophets and saints in more ancient times. Over the last forty or fifty years there has been a marked shift, and these souls are working with many more of us here on earth to bring about a rapid increase in our knowledge. We mentioned some of these in Chapter 1 when discussing the survival of the soul. Much of the material freely given to us is very beautiful, sometimes perceived in rather unusual language. In fact many of those chosen by those on the soul plane to channel such information are astounded by what they hear coming out of their mouths and are stunned when reading or listening to what has been recorded since what they have talked of is far more than they as ordinary human beings actually know. Though many are sceptical that we can be given information in this way, perhaps the most persuasive evidence that it is so is that if these channels were able to produce such material themselves, why would they not claim it as their own? Souls are eager to communicate with us and offer the service of expanding our knowledge. No doubt the criticism that is often levelled by the sceptics, that some of those 'channelling' are charlatans, may have some validity. However, you have only to read some of the work and perceive its effect upon you, the sense of rightness in the words and the contrast between the channelled information and the usual speech or writing of the channel to know that there is something of great value here. Beware of the pretentious speech, the flowery, the judgmental, the commanding and demanding. In my experience true channelled wisdom bears none of these human traits.

Offering the World New Experience and Ideas

Great souls on the mental plane who had particular skills during their earthly life often continue their work and communicate it to those who are still on the earth plane. Here they generate concepts which will manifest on earth in the minds of men and women who are still within their humanity and the material world. Many of our greatest ideas are in fact generated in this way as the souls of the departed continue to work with us as guides and teachers, ever extending their brilliance as a gift to the world, handing it down to us so that we may manifest it for the good of the whole human race. They come to us with such creativity in meditation or even in sleep from which we then wake (or are awoken) with a fully formed idea or solution. In much simpler ways, we may search for an idea or a concept, then ask for help, and are rewarded with a veritable flood of consciousness which feels wonderful but which we sense instinctively is not our own. As always, the more we are open to receive and gently ask (not demand or beg) to be a channel for creative wisdom and are willing to use it well, the more likely we are to be chosen as a recipient. In practical terms, for example, I'm sometimes asked to give workshops or speak at conferences and have no idea what I'm going to offer as a topic. I then sit for a few minutes and literally ask for help about what I should talk about and I'm given a title almost immediately, often with nothing else attached. Sometimes I look at it and wonder how on earth I can produce several days of work around a title which may at first appear foreign to me. However, I have only to ask again, and as long as I can get myself out of the way, I can receive a ready-made synopsis and later the details of the workshop, all of which have been generated on the soul plane. It's then just up to me to express it as best I can and give it openness, enthusiasm and unconditional love, and we have a winner! For years I was unaware of this and found myself still working hard at producing something even while on a train or a plane on the way to the venue. My beloved assistant and friend, Scott, would often be sitting anxiously beside me on our way to Turkey or Spain, while I commented that I still had no idea what I was going to be teaching. Bless him, he would be so lovingly supportive while trying to hide his concern, when suddenly the whole thing would just come flooding through and there we were. My daughter is the best medicine in such cases. I sometimes comment that I still haven't prepared and she simply and wisely tells me that both she and I know that it will be fine. Nowadays I don't worry about it. I ask for help, take it whenever it's offered (though sometimes I have to say my guides leave it quite late to help me!) and just know all will be well.

Global Evolution

Collective minds of great discarnate beings are constantly flooding the planet with light, though unfortunately many of us are completely unaware of their contribution to our well-being, choosing instead to focus on the negatives. However, more highly spiritually aware people are becoming more conscious of this and are inspired to use their heart chakras to spread unconditional love so that the ripple may become a wave and the wave a tidal wave of healing that will eventually encompass the planet and all that resides here. You can join in with that at any time you wish, whether you can personally feel the guidance or not. I assure you that if you start to behave as though you do, you soon will! Blessings pour upon us when we dedicate ourselves to be part of the movement of peace and love that is spreading through the planet. As we make our presence felt, great souls begin to gather around us to inspire and guide us and support our work. Sometimes we can feel or see it – rays of light scintillating down from the heavens and surrounding us as we flood with joy and can hardly breathe – hardly *need* to breathe – as we behold the majesty of it. Sometimes we may be stopped in our tracks for a moment as a flood of delight fills our hearts, and sometimes we may feel nothing, but at these times – perhaps more than at any other – we need to trust that great souls are doing their soul work and are around us, charmed by our childlike desire to do good and lovingly touched by the fact that we continue even if we cannot yet perceive them. Sometimes when I have been in that inner place where I am working hard but seem to be unable for a moment to feel their loving support, they offer me a gift – a feather suddenly drifts down and lands unex-pectedly at my feet; a leaf blows from a tree and lands right in my hand; the light changes in the room; I suddenly recall part of a lyric and start to hum it; someone calls me and gives me a loving message; a child looks at me and smiles and I see something ancient in the depths of its eyes; I hear my mother's voice or my eye alights on one of her musical boxes and I'm directed to wind it up and play it; a book falls off the shelf; the wind suddenly gusts against my window; the flame of my candle suddenly wavers; I smell the tobacco in my father's pipe; I feel warmth spread across my back; a bird hovers very near to me; one of the humming birds at the feeder on my porch comes to hover in my crown chakra; I look up and see an angel in the pattern of the clouds. Once you're open to receive the signs, they are many. They become almost an extra language that we can use every day, finding more and more joy in the apparently little things that speak to us constantly whether or not we are listening, and that can lift us out of the mundane. Suddenly we are living fully in our humanity but with an eye and an ear open to the soul planes and to the wonder of those who have gone before us and are no longer fettered by a dense body, but are lovingly and attentively part of our lives and our learning, warmed by our effort, delighted by our success, soothing our pain but giving us ample room for free will.

Loving Concern for Us

Those in the spirit world are always watching over us and are to some extent affected by our actions. Although emotion does not exist as we know it, nevertheless there can be sadness to see us having a difficult time and a desire to help us. At the same time they will never interfere with our right and need to learn from the experiences we have set for ourselves, lest, being thus rescued, we shall need to complete the learning at yet another time.

SEEING SOULS

Very occasionally we are blessed by being able actually to see a soul that may materialize before us in a kind of bodily shape, or perhaps just as light or almost like vapour. If you are so blessed, there is no need for fear. Many would give their right arm to have what you have! If you can, it would be best to embrace the situation, see what you are to learn from it and then allow the soul to leave. If you are frightened, however, you only have to ask firmly that the soul leave you. Most such apparitions are on peaceful, loving missions bringing you evidence of survival, messages from loved ones. It is not wise to ask them to stay. Lighting a candle will often help them draw energy from that instead of us and allow them to leave.

There is an old saying that we should always be willing to entertain strangers for in doing so we may be entertaining angels. Those doing their heavenly soul work are constantly guiding us and sometimes they manifest briefly here with us. There are well-documented instances of some of the great Indian gurus who are working on the soul plane also appearing here in the flesh. There are others whom we would never recognize, but rest assured that unawares we have transactions almost daily.

AFFIRMATION

I open to receive the great guidance that is available to me. I take responsibility to share it with the world unobtrusively and with humility.

✪ MEDITATION

This meditation will help you to be open to receive guidance from those working on our behalf on the soul plane and also to commit to doing your own soul work. The power of the meditation and your ability to receive will improve with repeated use. Don't expect too much the first time. It might be an idea to set yourself a time limit at first (start with no more than five minutes) but be willing to extend this if you find you receive a flow of information or creative ideas. As you become more comfortable with the concept, by all means extend the time you're happy to give to the collection of information. Eventually it will flow quite fast, almost immediately you settle down and ask. Have your notebook or some recording device ready as you may want to record what happens. You may find that you feel urged to write or speak and that afterwards you're surprised at what you have said or written. You may also find you have little recollection of what happened, hence recording is essential. Try to record without thinking about what is happening, otherwise you may begin to add your own interpretation and lose the true wisdom of what you are being given. If you find that suddenly you appear to have lost a sense of connection, don't worry. You will learn to get it back quite easily. Try to have a feeling of gratitude to those on the soul plane who are gathering to work with you at all times. If you are hoping for communication with a loved one, it would be useful to have a memento with you and to be as calm as possible.

Prepare for your meditation as you now know well how to do. Then . . .

Take a deep breath and breathe all the way out and as you do so let your body relax. Let your shoulders fall, your chair take your weight and anything negative flow out through the soles of your feet and your root chakra. Take another deep breath and this time allow white light to pour in through the top of your head, shining down now through every cell and every atom of every cell, cleansing, healing and balancing as anything you no longer need simply discharges into the earth from the soles of your feet and your root chakra. Relax. Now take another deep breath and this time let it flow through your physical body and out into your aura. Feel the peace as you allow the healing energy to flow through you and around you. Know that in this moment you are protected and blessed. Feel the angels gather around you to support you and allow a wave of gratitude to envelop you. Breathe it out as far as you can to touch everything. Know that there is no space between you and the whole universe. Know that you are one with all the wonder and beauty of all time and all space. Take another deep breath and, as you breathe out, relax even further.

Send a wave of love out beyond you into the soul plane. Just imagine a place of beauty and joy inhabited by loving beings who have only your growth and well-being in mind, longing only for the manifestation of peace, love, harmony and beauty in the universe. If you feel ready, but only if you do, perhaps you could begin to affirm . . .

I am open to receive the loving guidance from the soul plane and to start from this moment to do my soul work here. I am able to begin to change the world, one heart and mind at a time. I begin right here and make changes within me. I acknowledge the love of all my ancestral line, the passion and joy and love and toil that has preceded my life here. I validate all that has gone before and now take up my soul work in honour of my ancestors. I acknowledge my human self in all its integral parts — my personal self, my intimate self, my child self, my adult self, my social self. I acknowledge the wondrous spiritual being that I am. I acknowledge my soul. I open now to receive the loving guidance that I know is here for me, surrounding me, supporting me. Even if I do not perceive that today in any concrete form, I know that it is there for me, healing me, helping me grow to be the best that I can become. I acknowledge that flood of love and give gratitude for it today, passing it on with graciousness to those I meet, those I know and those I shall never know, so that I play my part in the healing of the world and the advancement of the human race. I take the responsibility for my soul work and for increasing the peace in the world. I take every opportunity to spread love and peace so that bit by bit it may fill the hearts and minds of all men and women. I rededicate my life to this purpose – to my spiritual growth and the spiritual growth of all, to teaching, to learning, to healing, to peace at the farthest ends of the earth and in every human soul. I give thanks for all that I have been given and for the new understanding that opens my eyes to the powerful difference I can make in the world starting with just one smile, one kind word, one pause before I would usually judge or criticize. I dedicate my life to this change and thank all those who are constantly working for me on the soul plane.

Add anything you wish to. You may want to name souls you have loved and who have departed but who are working constantly with you, and thank them for their love. Even those with whom you may have had difficulty on the earth plane are loving you. Think back to the work on forgiveness – all was in Divine order – you were simultaneously teaching and learning – let there be forgiveness now, release yourself, release them, let it go. Bring home that part of your soul that has been stuck in lack of forgiveness. Feel yourself become more whole as you do so.

Allow yourself to be open to the glow of the love that is around you now. With your inner vision let yourself see whatever you are ready for. Allow yourself to perceive the joy and the warmth that pervade your space. Feel the peace. Be aware that you are hardly breathing!

See your energetic body with all your chakras spinning in beautiful colour. Scan them now in your mind's eye, pausing at each to wonder at its beauty and the gifts it brings. See your root chakra deep ruby-red ensuring you security and stability; your sacral chakra bright translucent orange ensuring flexibility and flow in every aspect of your being and your life; your solar plexus spins with bright yellow light — feel its power and know that it enhances your will, your motivation and your intellectual self; see your heart chakra emerald-green but filled with the pink light of love and compassion; see your throat chakra filled with blue or turquoise light ensuring good communication, truth, integrity and purpose; see your brow, deep indigo-blue and know that it will provide you with wisdom and understanding as well as accurate vision; and finally see your crown chakra purple or white extending way above your head, sparkling and scintillating ready to open your connection with the soul planes and the Divine. Note that running between them all is a central channel, connecting them and allowing energy to flow freely from the earth via your root chakra to the heavens via your crown. And with a single gentle breath watch that energy flow as all your chakras expand slightly and your crown opens. Feel the energizing, loving, cool and gentle energy that now fills you. Let it nurture all of you.

Enjoy . . .

Allow yourself to be willing to join with the stream of higher energy and ask that whatever happens now is for your higher good and the higher good of all. Accept that in this moment you are aligning with the Higher Will and that it will assist you now to receive whatever is good for you to receive. Ask now that what you receive will be from the highest possible teachers, the highest possible guides and masters, from those who are working in love and peace and whose intention is for the higher good. Send them gratitude for being willing to work with you and a loving welcome. Now, commit to being open to receive and simply be still and allow anything positive simply to float in through your open channel and know that you will receive it. Note any sensations in your body, shifts in emotion or changes in atmosphere in the room. Give yourself whatever time you allocated for this part of the meditation.

Whatever has happened, give thanks. (Failure to receive anything does not mean that communication with you was not being attempted. Perhaps as yet you were not quite ready. Don't give up!)

Take a deep breath and imagine a beautiful flower at each of your chakras and allow them one by one to close their petals. Feel yourself contained, whole and secure. With your eyes still closed, affirm that you are ready to be involved in soul work for the higher good of all and that you will be open to interpret the signs and synchronicities as they appear in your life.

Once more, send gratitude to the Divine and all the souls and beings working for us and with us on the soul plane. Feel the warmth and love with which they respond. Stay as long as you wish. Enjoy! Send a stream of gratitude as high as you can, thanking all the angels, souls and discarnate beings for their continual help and love.

Then very gently give thanks and take a deep breath, filling all your cells with oxygen, enlivening them and making yourself aware of your physical presence. Feel your fingers, feel your toes. Take another deep breath and allow a wave of strong energy to keep you well grounded in your physical presence on the material plane for this is where you belong right now. When you feel fully grounded, come back to a place of awareness behind your closed eyes and when you are ready, gently open them.

Have a stretch and then a drink of water. Take just a little exercise – walk around your room or stretch a little – gently! – then record whatever you wish in your notebook. Be aware of your grounding all day, drink plenty of water and herb tea, and if necessary do some grounding exercise, move to music or go for a walk. Be open to the signs – there will undoubtedly be some!

✦ PRAYER

I give thanks to the realms of souls who daily love, guide and protect me. May the Great Spirit and my guardian angels be with me throughout my earthly journey. Let all those who come to travel with me be held and embraced by love. Let our relationships be blessed with love.

8   SOUL CONNECTIONS

*Life creates a place for you infinitely again and again according to
your love and in relation to your loved ones.*

Love without End, Glenda Green, Heartwing Publishing, 1999

It has been said that we have lived and loved so many times
that we've had relationships with just about everyone we
meet! When we return to the soul plane, we have equally
loving relationships with everyone. However, as we have
seen, those with whom we have most recently incarnated
(parents, grandparents, great-grandparents) and those with
whom we had partner relationships (husbands, wives, lovers)
and have gone before us are usually waiting for us at the
moment of transition. Some may act as guides, others as
teachers or they may simply be there to give us loving support
and help in the interlife.

In our current life, there are many souls with whom we
have ancient connections, having incarnated with them many
times in a variety of roles, and our reaction to them when
we meet them can often give us some clue about our previous,
or most recent, relationships with them – how we have
supported and shared with each other, taught and learned
from each other, loved and hated. Learning about them and
coming to recognize the parts we have played can resolve
conflicts and hurt in this lifetime, help us to understand our

reactions and move us from places where we feel stuck and lost.

So . . . in this chapter, first of all I want to take a brief journey back in time, and then present you with some friends of mine and their stories to illustrate some of the complexities of our relationships.

BEFORE WE WERE HUMAN

In searching deeper and deeper, back and back down the line of our soul, we begin to feel a yearning, almost like homesickness, that somehow we can hardly grasp but which is profound and full of longing. When I go back like that in meditation, I come to a point where I am no longer human, way back before Atlantean times, way before coming to this planet, way before I had any physical matter at all . . .

Long, long before there was anything concrete, just gases and perhaps water, as we've seen, we existed – the essence of us – combined in that great essence, the force that we may call the Divine, God. Then we split off, myriads of God particles, dispersed into the universe, drifting sometimes without seeming purpose but already wisps of consciousness, souls, pure energy without the need for a body, exploring the space and experiencing. These souls were androgynous, complete – carrying all the characteristics of the divine masculine and the divine feminine. However, before becoming human our soul split into two – twin souls, one bearing the divine masculine and one the divine feminine. These two halves then incarnated, sometimes at the same time, but more often separately. For centuries, while developing and evolving, they yearned to be once again reunited with their other half – masculine and feminine, the negative and the positive, the yin and the yang – in harmonious, dynamic balance. This yearning for completion is the basis of human love. The feminine aspect may from time to time be incarnated into a masculine body and vice versa, allowing each the opportunity to experience and understand the other. While on incarnation we forget who we are, the soul never does, and it continues its search, being attracted to those who somehow remind it of its other half. Only when we have achieved completion within ourselves are we ready for reunion with our soul twin, the balance of masculine and feminine being perfect as we reunite for eternity. We shall talk of this again later.

SOUL GROUPS

As we began to incarnate, so eventually we came with groups of souls to inhabit the planet. We were initially five groups making five different races – the red, the black, the yellow, the brown and finally, in the Caucasus Mountains, the white. Edgar Cayce, that wonderful healer and prophet of the nineteenth century, said that he found at least two distinct soul groups – one which had incarnated in early Atlantis, then in early ancient Egypt, in Persia and Palestine, then at the time of the crusades and in colonial America. The second specific group he found were incarnated in late Atlantean times, late ancient Egypt, early Greece, Rome during the time of Jesus, France during the time of Kings Louis XIV, XV and XVI and again in the American Civil War. These very large groups, he felt, incarnated as whole generations. However, we could choose to leave our generation group from time to time and come with a different group, or decide to remain in the interlife. Within the large, generational groups are smaller soul groups who incarnate perhaps as a race, a nation, community or culture, the majority of whom share at least some common philosophy or idea. However, as we shall see, we often incarnate across those groupings

– experiencing what it is like to be part of a different race or culture. It has been said that the quickest way to incarnate into another racial group is to have hateful, judgmental feelings about it! (See Sarah's story later.) Smaller groups then come together perhaps as families, friends or colleagues, who may incarnate together most of the time, but occasionally miss a generation and belong briefly to another group.

The same souls have been incarnating together within those smaller family groups almost since that time, changing here and there but otherwise choosing again and again to be with those souls they now know so well – learning alongside each other, teaching each other and loving each other enough to play a host of roles to help each other experience whatever their soul needs. Although there are those towards whom we may feel great animosity, anger and rage, it's likely that these are the souls who have loved us enough to fulfil the roles which stretch and challenge us, making us grow in ways we would otherwise avoid. As I said in *Affairs of the Heart*, one of the tasks I set for myself in this lifetime was to learn about betrayal, but I could never have done it if there had been no soul willing to betray me and put up with my pain, anger and resentment when they finally did for me what I needed.

Let's pick up on Renee from Chapter 7, then look at another modern-day example of how a group of souls are wonderfully and magically interwined through human lifetimes and the interlife as they come together again and again to learn with and from each other.

In her past life therapy, Renee and I moved to her last past life and she found herself in a large, imposing building, possibly a castle, built of grey stone. She was working in the stables, her job being to prepare the horses and present them when the lord and lady of the castle wanted to ride. It was a pleasant task. She loved the horses. She knew that although she was a poor and uneducated man, she was wise and respected. Her employers were kind and cared well for her and their numerous other employees. She then moved to being an older man. She was still working with the horses but younger men were doing much of the work. She smiled as she recognized the soul in the life review as a young stable boy of whom she was particularly fond and who she felt would eventually take over her work here. As the man she was then, Renee now wore a smart uniform and was at the front of the house as the door opened and his beloved mistress, now an elderly woman, appeared. He let down the steps of the carriage and she touched his hand lightly as he was privileged to help her to her seat. She smiled at him and he knew that there was deep respect and a kind of friendship between them that would never be expressed in words. He ensured that the lap blanket was inside the carriage before closing the door and once more met her eyes with his own as he saluted and the carriage drove off.

We moved to the past-life death as in his small room he lay with no one in attendance, his solitary state reflecting his solitary life. He had pneumonia but was fairly comfortable, the souls of his grandparents and his mother now appearing. He allowed himself simply to slide gently from his body, hover for a moment and then leave quickly. The movement through the tunnel was fast and he found himself within an instant home with souls he had always known. He recognized the lord and lady of the castle as a brother and sister of another time, and the warmth of their greeting confirmed the mutual love and admiration he had always felt. He knew that they had lived many lifetimes together and that the mistress had been also his daughter and his mother as they had learned many things together. He saw that in this immediate past life his role was to care for her from a distance and be an important part of her life, even though in all the years of service hardly a full sentence had been spoken between them.

We then moved on to Renee's next life where she found herself ready to be born in a small village in India. Her mother, a very young woman of perhaps fourteen, was unprepared for her labour. Her father was a much older man. He felt that there was respect between them but not love. Renee had chosen to be a boy and the body was prepared. She had been fleetingly inside the body of the foetus and knew that the body had defects which were an important part of the next life. She carried the solitude of her last life with her and would utilize it in this lifetime too. She would become a beggar and would learn much about compassion and suffering. Her mother – the lady of the castle – would die in child-birth and the child would carry the guilt and shame of having lived at the expense of his mother's life. He would be shunned by his family, partly because of his deformity and partly because of his sin of having killed his mother as he was born.

Renee learned much from this past-life sequence and was able to see how she had integrated all of this into her current life. As a healer she had brought to her work wisdom and patience along with humility, compassion and empathy for the suffering. She also accepted that her work might set her apart and she had learned to live in comparative solitude to prepare for this. Her ability to recognize the simultaneous vulnerability and majesty of the human soul was to make her a great and compassionate healer who would positively influence many lives, while she herself might feel unful-filled as a woman in her personal life. Happily the latter predic-tion proved to be only part of the lesson as in her own later life she was once again reunited with the soulmate – the mother of her Indian life and the lady of the castle who was now herself a compassionate and powerful healer.

The following account is from a series of sessions with my patient Sarah and demonstrates also the shift from one polarity to another to experience what we deride most.

Sarah was in difficulties. She had to agree with her husband that she was so obsessed with the safety of Tim, their youngest child, that she was inclined to neglect their three older children, the eldest of whom, Jay, was now a surly teenager, acting out his jealousy of the attention lavished on Tim. Sarah was also creating a problem for Tim since she refused to allow him the normal rough-and-tumble of a small boy's life. She found herself, almost against her will, peering into the school playground to see if he was all right, complaining to other mothers about their children, telephoning when he was playing at some other child's home and talking about him incessantly in conversation. Otherwise she was a healthy, attractive, forty-four-year-old Jewish woman, happily married to Jonathan and deeply involved with her community. She had had a good education and had gone off to spend a year on a kibbutz before university. She and Jonathan had met there on the kibbutz, although their families had known each other for years and were very supportive of the couple and their children. There were no financial worries and they had a good social life. Although she had given up her career as a barrister in order to have the children, she was happy to have done so and felt that she would eventually return to work when Tim was older. She was in good physical health and the only blot on the landscape was that she was seeing a psychiatrist – me – something that no one else in the family had ever done.

After a few sessions exploring and being open to anything that might help, Sarah agreed to embark on some past-life work. Very quickly we were in a life in biblical times and Sarah found herself carrying a dying child. She was begging for someone to help, but people were backing away from her rather than helping. She noticed that she was limping and also then that one of her thumbs was missing. Aghast, she looked at her feet to find that one foot had no toes. She was a leper. She was begging for help for her child from healthy people who were terrified of her. She looked at the child and saw it was Tim and watched as he died. Her grief was tremendous and though we paused to allow her to feel, we then moved on to the death of that lifetime. She was lying on dusty ground but with something soft under her head. There were people around her, their faces grotesque because of their disease, but they surrounded her with love and she was at peace.

Then she reported floating, hovering above her body, and a sense of relief, amazing peace, wholeness, love and comfort. Some being was there to guide her, and she felt held in a wonderful love. She recognized the guide as Jonathan and smiled.

In the interlife she reported being with Jonathan from time to time, communicating with him, mainly telepathically, and constantly feeling held in love and peace. At her life review he was there, and as she planned her next life he helped guide her thoughts and shape her plan.

The next life she moved to was in Dover. She and her husband and children were swimming in the sea. It was a lovely, joyful day and she felt very happy. She watched the children playing and felt very blessed. Her husband was swimming far out. He was fairly close to some rocks. Then she couldn't see him and felt a sudden wave of panic and a sense of doom. She wanted to get to him, but was concerned about the safety of the children. She called to them to get out of the sea but they appeared not to hear her. She felt her panic rising further and knew that something awful had happened. Torn between her loyalty to the children and to her husband, she was paralysed. Finally, the children safely back on the beach, she struck out towards the rocks – too late. In my consulting room she began to cry softly. 'It was Tim. He was my husband. He drowned.'

The following week we resumed our past-life search, though already Sarah was beginning to understand her fierce protection of Tim. The life we visited that day held the most painful but important revelation for her. She found herself as a Nazi officer in a concentration camp. Here in this lifetime she was Jewish, her grandparents having narrowly escaped the holocaust while many members of her extended family had perished. I asked her to breathe into the pain and see why she had chosen to visit this life. There was a young Jewish woman, Salomea, her hair short, almost shaven. She was the officer's personal servant, dealing with all his daily needs. He found her attractive while nevertheless finding her Jewishness repulsive. They were in bed. He was trying to suppress his feelings. He was falling in love with her, a very dangerous situation. He had simultaneously to protect her but appear cruel to her. The conflict was tearing him apart. Sarah recognized the young woman as Tim.

We moved on to her death in that lifetime. There was shooting. Her male self of that time was running. He felt searing hot pain in his back and fell to his knees. There was blood staining his jacket and making a pool on the ground. He was lifting out of his body and felt strangely detached, watching other uniformed men falling. They too seemed to rise out of their bodies. He felt himself wandering, looking with detached interest at what was happening. A gentle presence was beside him, soft and loving, gently encouraging him to come away. He felt suspended – peaceful, but unable to move. He looked again at his own body, then became even more aware of the loving presence beside him. He recognized the loving, glowing warmth of Jay and finally allowed himself to be guided to the light.

She knew she needed to reincarnate quickly and that she would choose to be Jewish and that her beautiful guide would be her first son, and Salomea her last.

In the next few weeks Sarah made peace with her past lives and also with her need to protect Tim. She began to release the control and allow him to have the freedom of any ten-year-old child. Her relationship with Jay took on a whole new depth and she started to find in him the wisdom she had loved so well in the interlife. Though she has not yet shared her experiences with the children, she has told Jonathan, and their love for each other, always deep and supportive, has become even more so. She has

not shared her Nazi past with her parents – there is no need –
but she has started to talk more in terms of reconciliation and
peace.

Sarah showed a similar inner conflict in at least two of
the lives she found here, and the deep emotional turmoil
that she had carried with her was again causing havoc in
her life and that of Tim. Jonathan, however, at least in the
lives we uncovered, remained a guide and teacher in both
the human life and the interlife, though it is uncommon for
us to partner in this way in the mundane phase with one
of our guides – they are usually in our extended family. Jay,
loving guide over centuries, is here once again to prompt
Sarah's growth. No doubt if we were able to explore
Jonathan's past lives, and those of the children, we would
widen the net even further and find Sarah in various roles
in their other lives, as they have lived and loved and taught
each other over centuries. Other members of Sarah's current
family would also be present in her past lives, and, time
permitting, we could go on searching and uncovering the
magical pattern that holds them all together.

SOULMATES

Those like Sarah, Jonathan, Tim and Jay who have been
together in many lifetimes and in many guises – as lovers,
parents, siblings, friends, colleagues, enemies – are soulmates. When we meet soulmates, we feel an instant sense
of knowing them, or of reacting in a way that seems exaggerated or inappropriate. We discussed this in Chapter 3.
Often we search throughout our earthly life to find a soulmate – one with whom we can have a loving partnership.
However, we frequently miss those who are in our lives in
other roles – soulmates who are simply not to be our loving

partners this time but who nevertheless know us so well. Recognizing them can deepen relationships with those around us and add richness to our lives as we simply move from day to day, preparing ourselves for that union which will bring us to the sense of completion we all, on some level, yearn for – reunion with our one twin soul.

Our past-life memories can help us rediscover who we are and who those now in our lives are too. Where we have either feelings of attraction or revulsion, unexplained feelings of desire or fury, there is often past-life memory that remains unresolved. Have a look at the case histories that follow.

Angela was suffering in a same-sex relationship in which, despite her obvious intelligence and training, she had allowed herself to be emotionally and sometimes physically abused. After each episode she determined to leave the relationship, but within a few weeks she had settled down again, feeling enormous love and compassion for Freda and wanting the relationship to work. Freda's drinking and aggressive behaviour were damaging to both herself and Angela, and much of Angela's anger was directed towards herself for allowing the situation to continue. She had read all the books on codependence and knew what she should do, but somehow she was convinced that there was something deeper that kept them entrapped.

We decided on some past-life work to see if we could find why Angela was willing to allow herself to be harmed, but also to see if there were, as she suspected, any past-life connections with Freda. I gave her instructions to pick up from any past life anything that would be helpful.

No sooner had we completed the induction than Angela began to cry. She was in a wood where it was cool and the sunlight was just reaching through here and there. The ground was soft with centuries of fallen leaves and she looked down at her male sandalled feet. Around her were several men, some dressed like her in coarse woollen shirts and trousers, while others wore rough leather trousers and boots and cloaks over cotton shirts. In her hand she held a long stick while some of the other men had similar sticks and some of them swords. Lying on the ground in front of her lay a young man in finer clothing, his cream-coloured knee-length stockings and green trousers soiled with earth and his white cotton shirt and cloak blood-stained. His blond hair hung over his face and blood was trickling from his nose and mouth. In the consulting room Angela continued to weep as she described how she lifted her stick and with the others continued to beat the young man until finally he was still. In a soft and shocked voice she whispered, 'It was Freda.'

After a slight pause she moved into another lifetime where she found herself standing on a pebble beach in Scotland. She was chilly. It was the early morning and she wrapped a coarse woollen blanket over her cotton nightdress. She turned to go into the small croft where two children were asleep in a wooden bed and another bed lay empty. A fire was beginning to crackle in the grate. She began to dress, then lifted down an earthenware jar of oatmeal. The door behind her opened and she turned to return the loving smile of a huge man who had just returned from hunting. In the consulting room she smiled softly. 'There's such love between us. He's Freda,' she said.

We tapped into two other lifetimes in that single session. In one they were brothers between whom there was considerable sibling rivalry and competition as they vied for the attention of their father, the owner of a small textile business in Lancashire. Angela was the elder son who had not been particularly involved in the business but nevertheless was the heir, while Freda, as the younger son, had worked hard. When their father died, despite the business title, Thompson and Sons, the whole business was left to the elder son. Years of animosity, bitterness and resentment ensued, with the younger son cursing his brother who refused to share the inheritance.

In the final lifetime we visited, Angela found herself in France, a young military officer at the time of the Revolution. He was standing by the guillotine when his heart opened with love and recognition as a young woman with her hands tied and stripped of her finery, but very obviously of high birth, was dragged forward. This was Freda. Tears streamed down Angela's face.

'How could I?' she murmured.

Over the next two sessions we did considerable healing of her past lives and deaths and also of the soulmate connection with Freda. Though initially Freda was unwilling to be involved in this 'crazy stuff', eventually she agreed to come along at least to discuss some of what Angela had discovered, and together they started to make more sense of their relationship and Freda's fury which came out mainly when she had been drinking. She was able to forgive Angela and free herself of the subconscious fear that Angela might kill her as she had done at least twice before. Angela was able to take care of her own guilt and shame and heal her wounds and become more self-assertive in the relationship, while Freda began her own journey of self-discovery. Finally they were both able to enjoy the love which, as soulmates, had spanned centuries as they had lived out several polarities together.

Angela shows two lifetimes linked by the victim – persecutor polarity where she has the chance to learn the feelings and lessons from each side of the coin in order to integrate the whole into her soul's growth. Although Angela tuned in to these particular lives to help resolve her relationship with Freda, we could have explored many other lives and found them in other roles, along with members of their current families and social groups.

Now have a look at June and Max's connection as it plays out in this single lifetime. Though we did not do any past-life work, I have no doubt that had we done so, we would have found June and Max together in many guises over many lifetimes. Their desire to be together, yet do other work with other people first, is fairly common with soul-mates and twin souls. Note how the universe brings them together, then allows them to part and yet somehow holds them in parallel patterns, making it easy for them to find each other again. Though Max has seemed somewhat oblivious of the situation over many years, June always has a strange sense that something keeps bringing them together.

June was a delightful fifty-eight-year-old who had met and fallen in love with Max while they were both at university in London almost forty years ago. Though it had seemed for a while that they would marry, each had been pulled in different directions geographically and within a year of graduating they had both drifted into other relationships. June married Jim and was quite happy. They had two children and after a career in hospital administration she finally found herself exploring her spiritual life and moving into complementary medicine, uncovering her natural healing talents. About fifteen years ago she was invited to a wedding in Manchester and was delighted to meet Max again. He was looking well and prosperous and they happily introduced their partners and the four of them shared news of their families, all parting at the end of the day with a hug. June later reported however that she was aware that something of the old flame was rekindled in that brief time together. On her return home she thought little more about the meeting, but five years later while visiting a friend in a hospice she was surprised to meet Max in the car park. Looking pale and drawn, he told her that his wife was dying of breast cancer. Three years later, she found herself lovingly attending her dying husband as he gently and peacefully slipped out of his body. Now she was completing her grieving, while also trying to sort out her emotions. Six months ago, only a year after her husband's death, she had seen Max in the Tate Gallery in London and had been shocked by the sudden flow of joy and girlish embarrassment she had felt, accompanied by a deep sense of knowing that their time had come to be together. She reported feeling shy and strange and was not surprised when some weeks later she received a call from him.

She said, with no hint of disloyalty to her late husband, that what she felt for Max was entirely different to anything she had known with Jim, whom she had nevertheless loved dearly. She reported a feeling of having come home and of knowing that it was with Max that she would now be for the rest of their lives. She knew that it would not necessarily be plain sailing, but that it would be as she felt it always had been, that they simply belonged together.

It may be that June and Max are in fact soul twins. (See Tony's story later which demonstrates a twin-soul reunion.) Old connections are not necessarily with someone with whom we have a family or partnership role, and they are not always pleasant! Remember that where we react strongly and often irrationally or with an exaggerated response, we may have some old business that is begging for completion. Also, as you'll see in Pauline's story, we don't have to have the recognition of the other person to do the work and make considerable changes. Remember that in any closed system such as a relationship of whatever kind, if something changes, everything changes. So if you find yourself in a similar situation, you can do the work yourself and change your behaviour and almost miraculously there is a shift. It may be of course that the shift is a geographical as well as emotional one! Sometimes doing the work allows us to understand so that we can part.

Pauline was a counsellor in a small hospital where all the staff worked together as a team – in some ways like a family. However, just as in a family, there were sometimes frictions which could usually be dealt with very successfully within the staff support group. However, over a period of about eight or nine months, ever since she joined the hospital, Pauline had been aware of animosity between herself and the medical director, Dr Paul Leonard. She reported that this had been obvious to her from the day she began work there and now their relationship had become so difficult that it was a burden not only for the rest of the staff, but for the patients too who could not but be aware of the strained atmosphere and sometimes scarcely veiled fury with which the medical director referred to Pauline. Attempts to confront the situation in the staff group were unsuccessful, Dr Leonard pulling rank and then for several consecutive meetings being unavailable to attend due to pressure of work. Pauline was becoming more and more undermined by the situation, feeling constantly criticized and put down and unable to use her usually excellent skills to deal with the situation self-assertively. She remarked that she had got to the point of looking behind her sometimes and lowering her voice when talking to other members of staff, almost as though she was being spied on and about to be stabbed in the back, as she put it. When she finally came to me for help, she was at the point of resigning, though she said that she had talked to her husband about the whole situation and he felt she would have a case for constructive dismissal. We started to look at what happened to her when she tried to confront this situation as she would any other, and at the second session I asked her if she had ever thought of there possibly being a past-life connection. She immediately looked relieved and said that she had had a recurrent dream in which this man was interrogating her and that the dream always stopped at the same point, where she felt sure that she would not live for much longer. On the days after the dream she usually felt quite bruised, since it was so real that she was sure it was not an ordinary dream.

Within minutes we were into a past life where she was being interrogated during the time of the witch hunts. I asked her to rise above the pain so that she would not remember or feel any physical sensations but to allow herself to recognize anyone who was in her current life. Although there were several men involved in what was in fact torture, with some horror she recognized the chief inquisitor as Dr Leonard. We dealt with the past-life death and released the karmic memory trapped, and I asked her to move to any other life which would be relevant to the current issue.

The next life Pauline visited took us to South Carolina where she described a beautiful wooden house built on high stilts, extending down towards the beach. The view was magnificent she said, the sea was amazingly beautiful. The weather was hot and steamy and she saw herself in an attractive dress with a tight waist and flouncy skirt. She wore a bonnet and held a parosol. She was obviously amused at the scene because it seemed that she had strayed into *Gone with the Wind*! She estimated that she was in her teens and from a very rich family. She did not belong in this house but was visiting, her home being a large plantation house at the other side of the Ashley River. There were slaves serving drinks and she and her friends were rudely ridiculing them. She then found herself in Charleston at the slave market. She commented on the heat and the flies and the dreadful scene as men and women in shackles were inspected and sold. She commented that her father had bought her a child slave for her very own. His name was Jacob. The scene then shifted once more and she was at home in the large and beautiful plantation house and Jacob was now about sixteen. Her father was very angry and was shouting. Pauline dissolved into tears as she tried to describe the abuse of the slaves at her father's hands but also her shame at her own attitude which was one of apparent unconcern. Rising above the pain so that she could simply learn whatever she needed to, we then did healing of the past life and she asked to be brought back out of the session. She recognized the child Jacob as Paul Leonard.

After a pause I regressed her again and this time we went from that lifetime to her past-life death and into the interlife. Now an old woman and quite peaceful, she reported floating out of her body but was surprised, at the moment of her death, to find that the guide who lovingly came to accompany her was Jacob, who had passed in his thirties after a lifetime of harsh cruelty. She then recounted how she knew him as a beloved soul with whom she had had many lives. He accompanied her at her life review and suggested that she be less harsh on herself in judging her part in his demise.

I asked her to move to her next lifetime and here we found her in Wales in the 1920s. She was a man in his forties called David. He was returning home from work in the mine and was black with coal dust. He was both unhappy and angry, with a sense of fore-boding. He had a hammer in his hand as he approached the miner's cottage. He was walking with determination . . . Pauline then moved quickly to find herself in the cottage and gave a commentary on the scene as David went quietly up the stairs and, with apparently no emotion, murdered his wife with the hammer. She then winced in the consulting-room chair. Watching the bleeding face and head of the wife David had just killed, she whispered, 'Oh God. It's Paul Leonard.'

Over the course of these lifetimes, these two souls had con-tracted to be together and to learn with each other various aspects of being human. Again and again they had played out the faces of love and betrayal, hatred and desire, each time during the inter-life recognizing each other with love, compassion and gratitude for the willingness to sacrifice soul peace to teach each other. Again and again they had returned to the interlife traumatized and exhausted and had acted as loving guides for each other. And now here they were again and it was important to find the message in the present lifetime so that the karmic chain could hopefully come to an end.

Though usually I ask that both parties be present at such healing sessions, Pauline felt that her career was already threatened enough by what had happened thus far and we decided instead to do the work on a soul level, having first asked permission to do so. Over the next month or so, things gradually began to improve. Someone was admitted under Dr Leonard's care who had previously been Pauline's client and they found themselves in the position of having to discuss the patient's needs. At the end of the session Pauline was unexpectedly complimented on the depth of her insight and was asked if she would like to continue with the work while the patient remained in the hospital. Over the following six months their relationship steadily improved as Pauline herself began to let go of her judgment of this man whom she had found so difficult that she had at one time felt hatred towards him. The last I heard of her, the team was once again working as a functional family, with Pauline as a respected equal within it.

TWIN SOULS

Twin-soul relationships are what we're all striving for, though relationships with soulmates are rich and rewarding and enhance our lives. The souls that were divided all that time ago may find each other here, but may spend lifetimes searching. Often I have refused to teach about these relationships, since I see people rejecting good, strong, loving and potentially wonderful partners in favour of the half-remembered dream of the twin soul. As we said earlier, the split was so that we could perfect our inner balance and finally bring wholeness to the reunion. Our work over many lifetimes is helping us to develop that sense of inner masculine/feminine balance. It is not something we can rush or avoid. There are no short cuts. As women we must also develop our masculine characteristics and get them in balance to support our feminine ones, and as men we learn to honour our inner feminine and allow it to soften our masculine characteristics. Until there is absolute balance and wholeness within ourselves, we are not ready for the reunion with our twin soul. Thus doing our soul work, respecting our need for spiritual growth, cleansing, healing and balancing our energy system, exploring our past-life connections and becoming aware to the level of unity consciousness are essential precursors to that final meeting with our twin soul. Sometimes people come to me with the express purpose of finding their twin soul but are unwilling to do the work necessary to become whole and happy within this life. The wholeness we need to be ready for our twin soul renders us content. Usually we will have had other relationships, often with soulmates, that have helped us learn and grow and develop our soul. Usually we will have learned at some time to be happy living in chosen solitude as we spend time with the Divine, loving and enjoying our soul experience, being happy and content with who we are. However, even then, we are aware of what has been called divine discontent – our soul's yearning to continue to grow and to reunite with the Divine.

Then when we may least expect it, the twin soul arrives . . .

Twin souls always have parts which reflect each other completely – similar interests, yearnings, passions, and desires. Their lives may show parallels as they have moved through this lifetime, sometimes passing each other on the way, but not recognizing each other until the time is right and they have both done the work they need to do to render them ready. When finally they meet and recognize each other, often in their mid years, they both know that they will never be parted again, even though geographically they may not be together from time to time. Although, as in all relationships, there may be some conflict, this is always of a minor nature, and the thought of separation never occurs to them. They are now united forever. It may be that Max and June are twin souls – time will tell – but Tony and Libby most definitely are.

Tony, now seventy-eight and coming happily to the end of his life, tells his story of the amazing love that he and Libby found together, albeit in their later years.

They first met in the 1930s. Libby was a nurse at a sanatorium where Tony was a patient, having contracted tuberculosis. She was engaged to be married, and he thought at that time that he would not survive his illness. However, he recognized some ancient and wonderful spark in Libby though he never spoke of it at that time. While he remained there, Libby married her childhood sweetheart, Grant, and moved away from the area. From time to time he heard snippets about her and her life, the fact that she had three children and was happy. Recovering, he also married and was happy with his wife, Margaret, with whom he had two fine sons and a daughter.

After the war, his life had changed considerably. He had witnessed things in a prisoner-of-war camp that had changed him irrevocably, and while he saw some of his colleagues who survived becoming bitter and angry, he found himself turning more to the religion he had left behind as a boy. Then he had felt restricted by the dogma of religion and had started to read more and more about Eastern spiritual philosophy, learning to meditate and finding at last his personal connection with God. Sadly, Margaret suffered a fatal heart attack in her early post-menopausal years, and Tony had learned to live alone with the loving support of his family around him. He had never wanted to remarry, since his love remained with Margaret, and in any case he was content as he continued to explore his spirituality, teaching also his grandchildren and anyone who was interested the amazing truths he was learning.

Libby, meanwhile, had brought up her children and had eventually returned to nursing. She had for some while belonged to the Spiritualist Church and found herself more and more drawn to using healing touch with the people with whom she worked. She found in particular that she felt truly fulfilled working with the dying and was quick to respond to the call for nurses to join the newly formed hospice movement. Just when their lives seemed to be set for a pleasant cruise into their twilight years, Grant was diagnosed with colon cancer and deteriorated rapidly and died. Libby's joy was to be with him, doing healing with him as he made his transition. Though filled with grief, she continued to work, and found herself healing and coming to a sense of peace within herself. She had had a good loving marriage with ups and downs, but generally with a great deal of love.

At fifty-nine and sixty-three respectively, Tony and Libby found themselves enrolling for a series of evenings studying the teachings of Parahansa Yogananda, the great Indian yogi, and at the first break stood next to each other as they drank their tea. Tony remembered the feeling that engulfed him at that time. Rather like a mild electric current, Libby's presence made itself known to him. This woman who stood beside him, whom he thought he had never met, was affecting him both physically and emotionally in a very disconcerting way. It took another two evening sessions before he finally spoke to her directly about what happened to him when they were at close quarters. Only then, as they finally spent some time looking directly at each other and acknowledging that there was an undeniable connection between them, did Libby recognize that, although they both were beginning to realize a past-life connection, they had also met in this life, albeit some forty years earlier.

From that moment the two of them were inseparable, devouring every possibility to be together, to share old experiences and new understandings, eager to find out all about this lifetime while knowing on a deep level all that was essential. They were thrilled to discover that they both loved gardening – Libby had won prizes for her roses – and travelling – they had both cruised the Nile only weeks apart, and had a passion for Africa. Both had plans for a trip to the sacred sites of India. Both had a commitment to a life of service and had lived in contented solitude exploring their spirituality and their spiritual gifts. Where there were differences between them, they found these enriching too. Libby hated to plan but was full of spontaneous and joyful ideas. Tony was meticulous in his attention to detail and found much of the joy of his travelling in the planning of the trip. She, childlike in her enthusiasm, would infect him with the joy of movement and dance, while he introduced her to the classics which she had previously shunned. Finding each other was the icing on an already very rich cake!

Their relationship had blossomed into a spiritual partnership that had continued joyously and peacefully until Libby's death almost a year ago. Tony was content in the knowledge that they would never be parted again even by death.

Twin souls may not reincarnate together. Indeed, they may be so spiritually enlightened that they chose not to reincarnate again. They may have found each other in a previous lifetime and come again to teach others, forfeiting their closeness, being with other soulmates while never harming their union and being content that they are one. One may incarnate alone, being guided and inspired by the other who remains on the soul plane. They are often advanced souls expressing themselves and their love in some earthly form, manifesting on earth the deep and abiding soul love that flows between them. In such cases there is no yearning, but instead a conscious contentedness as they flow endless love into humanitarian pursuits. Where the yearning continues, the reunion is yet to occur, obstructed still by their need to resolve karmic and personality issues. Sometimes the path to find each other may be painful and difficult as they search constantly, experiencing disappointment in the relationships which could offer them love and comfort and an opportunity to find the balance within their chosen identity which they need.

In the interlife, all is clear. No doubt the souls of Tony

and Libby came together there many times on the way to their final reunion, while knowing that the time was not quite right and that each had more development to do before being ready to crown their spiritual and human union. It is unlikely that they will reincarnate again.

So liberation from the earthly life into the interlife brings us face to face with a multitude of souls who have known us during different incarnations. We are then called to give equal love to all, much as we are learning to do in our development of universal consciousness on earth. Each of us is an individual and unique expression of divine love, each of us is a part of the body of God to which we shall finally return after we have completed our work both on earth and on the soul planes. And each of us shall be known to the other by the uniqueness of our love. Once again we shall unite in the one Spirit. However, before then, there may be another incarnation for which to prepare. This we shall deal with in our final chapter.

☼ AFFIRMATION

I open my eyes to view all those around me with compassion, seeing that we are all entwined, each supporting the other in our mutual growth. I offer my love and understanding to each of them today and the hope that our paths may become clear.

☼ MEDITATION

This meditation is intended to help you open to the wonder of the vast network of souls who have connections with you both in this current lifetime and others. Try to keep a sense of grounding and openness with the accent of love and forgiveness.

Take up your place as usual in your sacred space, and then . . .

Take a deep breath and breathe all the way out and as you do so let your body relax. Let your shoulders fall, your chair or the floor take your weight and anything negative flow out through the soles of your feet and your root chakra. Take another deep breath and this time allow white light to pour in through the top of your head, shining down now through every cell and every atom of every cell, cleansing, healing and balancing as anything you no longer need simply discharges into the earth from the soles of your feet and your root chakra. Relax. Now take another deep breath and this time let the light flow through your physical body and out into your aura. Feel the peace as you allow the healing energy to flow through you and around you. See yourself as a shining being filled with light, surrounded by light. Know that in this moment you are protected and blessed. Feel the angels gather around you to support you, and allow a wave of gratitude to envelop you. Breathe it out as far as you can to touch everything. Know that there is no space between you and the whole universe. Know that you are one with all the wonder and beauty of all time and all space. Take another deep breath and as you breathe out, relax even further. Allow yourself to be suspended in this wondrous peace.

Now . . .

Be aware of your heart chakra and with a single breath, allow it to open, like a huge rose. First of all let the green sepals unfurl, then within pink petals, opening and opening to become a full-blown rose. Feel the warmth of it. Feel the radiance as its loving energy now pours out to fill your whole being. Feel yourself fill with compassion and note any physical sensations and emotions – there may be simultaneous feelings of excitement and peace and a tingling in the middle of your chest or the centre of your back. Breathe gently, allowing the love to reach every cell and also fill your whole aura. Send out rays of love now to those people currently sharing your life for whom you feel love and visualize those rays touching and entering their hearts. Send them a message of gratitude for being in your life and for being willing to share learning and growth with you. Pause and enjoy the sense of connection. Now send out rays of love to all those who are in your life but are perhaps a little more distant – friends, colleagues or neighbours. Note that they are all in your life for a reason, whether or not you have discovered what that is. No one is in your life by chance. Again pause and note any sensations you may have, any changes in the atmosphere in the room. Now extend your rays of love even further, to those you may never have met, and note that they are here on earth at the same time as you by design – people in different countries and communities, politicians, entertainers, those who have committed crimes, those who are sick, those who are imprisoned, those who are alone, those who are dying, me – allow your web to widen as you see the intricate connections with every other human being. If you can, let rays of love from your heart reach them too. There may be those whom thus far you have felt unable to reach – those with whom you have disagreement, anger, hatred, lack of forgiveness. Take a gentle breath and if you can, but only if you can, send rays of light or love from your heart to theirs. This will not form a new connection where you have fought hard to separate, it will simply hold an opening for the meditation. Now raise your attention to the soul planes and to the souls there who have all had a part to play in the journey of your soul, send love to them also. Pause and visualize yourself at the centre of a vast network of connections. See that there is a never-ending pattern of each of us connected to each other with no space separating us, each of us important to the other, each of us teaching, learning, giving, receiving. If anywhere in that whole network you feel resistance or a block, pause and ask yourself why. What is it you cannot let go of? What is there that you still do not accept or understand? Where do you still need forgiveness? Breathe! Be gentle with yourself. You do not have to do everything today, just note where you feel stuck.

Know that you are protected, that your guardian angel and

other loving beings surround you and hold you in peace and love. Know that nothing can harm you. Pause and allow yourself to feel the wonder of being intimately connected with every other soul. Know that all of these souls have loved you in some way, that in universal consciousness we are all part of each other, that we have shared intimate connections since the beginning of time. Feel the might of such an amazing powerhouse of love and information. Be open to become aware of any connection in this lifetime or past lives that you need to know about now and can receive in safety and love. Know that everything that has ever happened has had the power of positive intention within it. There is no blame, no shame, no guilt. Breathe. Send love and gratitude where you can.

Stay as long as you wish. Wherever you can, send love, forgiveness, compassion and healing and note that all of these are yours in abundance. Feel yourself bathed in light, love and healing.

When you are ready, send gratitude to the Divine and to the whole universe, all of which has played a part in your spiritual growth and development. Feel yourself still held in love and know that those souls who work with you constantly will be taking care of you now and always. Start to withdraw the rays of light and love, knowing that you will remain connected as you always have. Allow your heart chakra to close gently, holding within it an abundance of love.

Take a deep breath and fill your whole being with life-giving energy and start to become aware again of your physical presence. With your eyes still closed, move your fingers and toes, give thanks for all that you are and all that you are becoming. Take a deep breath and fill all your cells with oxygen and come to a state of full alertness. Make sure that you're well grounded, and when you're ready, open your eyes, have a stretch and a drink of water and record whatever you wish in your journal.

✪ PRAYER

May we be open to understand rather than judge, to praise rather than criticize, to love rather than to hate. May we let go of resentment and anger. May we rise above the need for retaliation and revenge as we send gratitude even to those who teach us painful lessons. May we invite the wisdom and clarity of our souls to be ever present in our daily transactions, bringing us finally to reunion with the twin of our soul and with the Divine.

9   PLANNING THE RETURN
       JOURNEY

Not in entire forgetfulness
And not in utter nakedness
But trailing clouds of glory do we come
From God, who is our home:
Heaven lies about us in our infancy
Shades of the prison house begin to close
Upon the growing boy.

Wordsworth

Joel Whitton, a fellow psychiatrist, commented that although the interlife is our natural home in which there is an atmosphere of lightness and love, most of us still choose to be born and 'venture forth on arduous journeys of physical embodiment' on our endless search for enlightenment. So here we are, almost at the end of this turn in the ascending spiral of the journey of the soul, ready to look at planning and preparation for the adventure of another earth life, our immortal soul consciousness once again bringing forward its karmic memory – all that we have experienced in all lifetimes thus far – to imprint upon the foetus as it sets out on its new mission. Just as death was merely the transition from one dimension to another, leaving the physical body and liberating the soul, rebirth is the journey from the soul plane to the physical once more.

In this chapter we shall look at the theory of reincarnation, our choices in planning a new life, karma and the cosmic laws and our preparation as we approach the perinatal phase, that is, the time immediately surrounding birth back into the physical. This will include the construction of the auric bodies, conception, life in the womb and finally, birth and the immediate post-birth period.

So first of all, let's talk about the roots of the theory of reincarnation.

ANCIENT AND MODERN, EAST AND WEST – WHAT DO WE BELIEVE?

Since ancient times, cultures far and wide have believed that we live, 'die' and are reborn. The Egyptians wrote of reincarnation in the *Egyptian Book of the Dead* around 1300 BC and mummified their kings, building pyramids with stores of jewels and goods to ensure that the pharaohs would have the same body into which to be reborn, as well as riches. The Tibetans, in *The Tibetan Book of the Dead*, talk of having repeated lifetimes alternating with periods of 'cosmic sleep' as we evolve in order to improve ourselves. In Greek, Native American and African cultures there were similar beliefs although the traditions to provide for reincarnation vary. Then we have the ancient myth of the phoenix which lives for 600 years then builds its own funeral pyre, burns to ashes and dies only to rise again reborn and ever young. Looking further East, Hinduism, which is more a culture than a religion, believes in the presence of the soul or atman, which travels from body to body, from reincarnation to reincarnation, by a process known as transmigration, and is awarded a particular station in life (caste) according to its previous behaviour. In the sixth century BC, Buddhism arose from Hinduism with the belief (the Anatta doctrine) that consciousness and patterns of thought rather than a soul are transferred from one life to another. On reaching Nirvana – a state of bliss and nothingness – rebirth is unnecessary. In Buddhism rebirth is believed to occur immediately after death, as the consciousness moves directly into the body of a newborn child and continues.

Both Christianity and Judaism originally had reincarnation as part of their doctrine. The Kabbalah, which was part of Jewish law until the nineteenth century, represents the esoteric side of Judaism and refers to reincarnation as Gilgul – the revolution of souls – in which souls enter the physical world sporadically, expanding awareness through a series of incarnations, and ultimately return in a state of perfection to be reunited with God. The Gnostic gospels, discovered only in 1945 but written approximately 100 years after the birth of Christ, make reference to reincarnation, karma and ultimate salvation. Up to the third century AD there was a firm belief in reincarnation, and only in AD 529 did the Synod of Constantinople outlaw the doctrine, at which time most, but not all, references to it were removed from the Bible. (For example, in Matthew, Jesus identifies John the Baptist as Elijah reborn: Psalm 90, verse 3, 'Thou carriest them away as with a flood; they are asleep; in the morning they are like the grass which groweth up'; John 8:58, 'Jesus said unto them, Verily, verily, I say unto you, before Abraham was, I am'). Partly because of their continued belief in reincarnation, the Cathars became the target of the Church in the twelfth and thirteenth centuries. Now, with both the Catholic and Protestant Churches officially opposing such doctrine, Christianity is the only world religion that does not believe in reincarnation. However, in the moving *Love without End* (Glenda Green, Heartwings Publishing, 1999), which is purported to be channelled wisdom from Jesus, we have: 'You were created in perfection and perfect love and do continue to remanifest infinitely . . .' a refreshing update on the teachings of 2,000 years ago.

WHAT DOES REINCARNATION MEAN?

As we have seen, reincarnation appears to be interpreted differently by various cultures and religions. However, I believe John van Auken sums it up well in the first few lines of his book *Past Lives and Present Relationships* (Inner Vision, 1984) when he says, 'The idea that you and I have reincarnated is somewhat of a misconception. The "you" and "I" that we consider to be our normal, everyday selves have actually not reincarnated . . . However, there is an inner part of us that has been alive before. This part has incarnated in the Earth's dimension many times.'

Thus, I, as the personality Brenda, have not been here before. But my immortal essence – my soul – that is now clothed in Brenda's body, has. Over centuries it has created many different personalities, sometimes male and sometimes female, which have come into the world in order that my soul can experience all aspects of life. In fact it may choose to be reborn into several bodies simultaneously in order to gain maximum experience.

Having remained in the interlife in the astral world briefly or perhaps for hundreds of years, eventually, by our own free will, we make the valiant decision to reincarnate and to forgo the freedom and peace of the soul planes. The purpose of each new life as we have seen is to resolve karma, to develop our consciousness and allow our soul to evolve to the point where we are able finally to integrate with the energy of the Divine. We come to complete old business, and in order to accomplish this of course we need each other's help, and this to some extent governs some of our choices as we plan our return. When we finally balance our transgressions against others and against the laws of the cosmos (we shall talk of these later) with good works, grace and spiritual evolution, we shall reach a point where we no longer need to incarnate in human form, but remain in the astral world from which, as we saw in Chapter 7, we simply work for the good of all.

Many people think that they haven't ever lived before, but have you? Have a look at the following.

HAVE YOU BEEN HERE BEFORE?

Have you ever . . .

- been drawn to a particular place or a particular time in history, or to art, clothing or jewellery from a particular place?
- had a yearning, almost like homesickness, for that place?
- had a skill for which you had no training?
- found it almost second nature to speak another language?
- met someone and had an instant feeling of familiarity?
- met someone and felt love, hatred or fear at first sight?
- had dreams that are very real and of which you remember every detail, unlike those that you remember for a few minutes after you wake then lose?
- had some special gifts since very early in childhood?
- had recurrent dreams from which you awake just as you're about to die?

Any of the above may well be signs of some past-life memories that are just waiting for you to gently explore them. Some people are very aware of past-life connections, feeling a sense of recognition when they meet people or visit a 'new' place, whereas others are closed and cynical about the possibility of having lived before. For some, the thought of having to come and live another life is daunting, especially if this one has been difficult. However, the truth is that we have all been here before, though some not as often as others, and the vast majority of us will be coming again – probably many times. Certainly some of us have incarnated more than others, and are occasionally referred to as 'old souls'. Those who have little interest in spiritual matters are sometimes referred to as 'young souls', though this is a misnomer. It may well be, however, that they have chosen to remain on the soul planes rather than have many earthly incarnations.

PLANNING A NEW LIFE

Planning for a new life will usually begin on the mental plane. Imagine preparing for a great expedition. Rebirth planning is like this, and just as in human life, some will wish to prepare with meticulous detail, keen to achieve their goals, while others will tend to rush through with little planning at all. As we've seen, for various reasons, some incarnate again very quickly. For example, those suffering traumatic death may rush to get back to the material world, and those who die in childhood also. Many of those who died traumatically during the Second World War are already reincarnated, and most of the children in Dr Ian Stevenson's study discussed on page 24 reported a past life on average of only ten years earlier. Although the choice is entirely ours as to when and whether to reincarnate and what to learn while on the earth plane, we do have advisers, guides and teachers in the interlife (see Chapter 7) to help us make a good choice. After our embodiment, those same guides and masters will help us here, keeping us safe as we work through the life events we have chosen.

Our decisions about what we want to achieve will to a large extent govern other choices. Sometimes the life we choose can be very difficult as we opt for a great deal of growth in one lifetime. What personal characteristics and socio-economic status will help us most? Do we need a perfect physical body or would there be greater advantage for us in having some handicap? Are we coming mainly for our own growth or for the greater good of humanity and the planet? Are we bringing a particular gift to help humanity? How are we to manifest that gift? With whom do we need to incarnate to have the best possible chance of achieving all that we need to do? What are our karmic obligations? Where are our soulmates with whom we have unresolved karma to be reincarnated?

In deciding upon a new incarnation we are opting for new experience, new learning and new growth that will enable us to transform and rise above some of our passions and desires, evolve and fulfil our potential, coming ever closer to the possibility of reunion with our twin soul and also finally reunion with the Divine. In being reborn, each of our cells is to contain all the intelligence and consciousness of our whole new self – every experience, every memory will be there, including those passed down through generations of the lineage we now choose. However, we also come into a world with a collective inheritance and we must assume responsibility to take our part of the collective that needs to be processed. We shall discuss this later. Several factors (which I have referred to as the invariables) – our parents, place and time of birth, sex, race and any birth defects – need to be chosen now. It's essential that the soul chooses well so that it has the best possible launch into the new life to enable it to learn the lessons that it has set for this time. As we saw with Sarah (see page 276), in different lives we may choose a different religion, race, sex and economic status to give us maximum understanding and maximum perspective. We may also choose how long we are to stay – for instance, we may opt to stay for only a short period of time, our emphasis being on teaching rather than learning, or to live a very long earth life during which we have great opportunities both to teach and learn. We have the option to accept any special mission too. Though we shall have a detailed life plan, we also have free will to play the cards we have chosen however we wish, and of course we are not to live our life alone. We will be challenged by the choices and behaviour of those who incarnate with us. The way in which we deal with life's tests and challenges will dictate our karma for the following life.

So to recap, in reviewing what has been learned and what still needs growth and healing, and with the help of guides and teachers, we select a new life and the circumstances that will set us off in the right direction and launch us into life.

Let's look at the choices we need to make.

OUR PARENTS, SIBLINGS AND ANCESTRAL LINE

As we saw in Chapter 8, we reincarnate again and again with souls we know and with whom we have played many previous roles, and within our family there may be some old and some new connections to give us challenge, balance, love and support. The ancestral line we choose gives us characteristics, qualities and tradition, while ancestors often connect with the newborn as guardians who will watch over their growth and development throughout the earthly life. The meditation at the end of this chapter will help us to honour all those who went before us in our ancestral line and whose power and passion brought us into being. We chose our particular ancestral family in order to inherit their qualities and characteristics – perhaps courage, pride, forbearance or musical talent – as well as some of their weaknesses – perhaps difficulties with intimacy, addictions or metabolic defects – in the exact blend that we need to complete our mission.

Our parents are usually souls we have known for eons and with whom we have old unfinished business. We opt to be incarnated with them, though of course they come ahead of us. They will give us our genetic inheritance and also our temperament, both of which we need either to integrate or overcome in the process of our human life, and their own life script will determine how they will nurture us as parents. Our siblings complete the picture. As we saw in Chapter 4, all the members of our family may have opted for a single lesson such as violence, which each of us experiences from a different perspective – perpetrator, victim, witness, etc. As we grow together we impinge on each other's inner strengths and weaknesses, test each other and force each other to grow as we blend into a common existence, but always with unique perspectives and perceptions. Our choice of family will also govern the economic status into which we are to be born, though whether we choose to stay there is up to us.

Sometimes we may incarnate into a completely new family to heal them, bringing them new perspective and helping them break patterns that may have trapped the lineage for generations. Often, when we do this, we feel that we don't belong, that the family seems foreign to us, or that we were born in the wrong place. Of course we never were!

PLACE AND RACE

The environment we choose will give us our cultural inheritance, and whether we choose a culture that is at peace or at war, affluent or in poverty, it will give us the best possible chance of experiencing what we came to learn and either integrate or overcome. The place may also dictate to some extent our life's work and economic status – we choose to be born in a remote fishing village, for instance, usually to live a life associated with the sea – or to overcome that and move to something very different. As a child in the north-east of England during wartime, I chose a very different cultural inheritance than if, for example, I had been born in a fishing village on the shores of the Aegean Sea in peace-time. The place and country of our choosing will always be where our roots belong and to which, even subconsciously, we usually hold loyalty. However, part of our challenge is to ascend to the point where our loyalty is to the universe rather than to a small section of it. While loyalty is a fine quality, it can become misplaced and be the cause of sepa-ration and ultimately racism. In choosing a closely knit community, sometimes this is one of the lessons we have come to learn.

As we saw in Sarah's story on page 276, often a soul learns to grow, love and let go of judgment by becoming what, as a previous personality, it most despised.

TIME AND SEASON

Just as a good astrologer can draw a chart which shows us the planetary events that can shape our lives, so angels help us choose the exact time and place for our birth so that we have the ideal astrology to launch us and complete our mission. No matter whether we feel that doctors or midwives may have interfered with the time of our birth or that of our children, the soul dictates the time of birth and all is in divine order even if there has been induction or delay. For instance, though I laboured in County Durham during the birth of my son, in the last few hours events occurred that forced our transfer to a regional hospital in Yorkshire where he chose to be born. That delay and geographical move of even 30 miles changed his natal astrological chart. Note the difference in our personality make-up depending upon the season we chose. Even if you have little faith in astrology, just do a little scan of yourself and your friends. Do you see the Virgos as meticulous, dependable and loyal and the Scorpios as passionate and secretive and often stinging when threatened? Are the Arians around you butting their way through life and the Leos proudly lording it over others if they're not careful? We chose to be born as we are, but that doesn't mean we can't change. Balancing and overcoming those innate qualities might be exactly what we're supposed to be doing. The Scorpios can learn to trust more and sting less. The Leos can learn to have more humility and stop wanting to change everyone else's life. The Virgos can learn to relax a little and splurge into a bit of mess sometimes. What did you choose?

Our natal horoscope reveals our past and also our probable future, but, as always, we have free will and we can also override our karma by grace. We, and only we, are the architects, instigators and active participants in whatever has occurred and is currently happening in our lives, and are therefore fully responsible for what happens to us. Those around us are merely playing parts in our drama, as we simultaneously return the favour. The good news is that since we created everything by our own action, and since we possess amazing spiritual resources, we can, by our positive actions, triumph over any limitation we have created and overcome anything we have set in motion. This is part of the challenge of our lifetime.

GENETICS AND BIRTH DEFECTS

It has been said that all human ills have a spiritual basis, arising from some transgression of universal law. The roots can often be found in previous lifetimes, particularly in the experience of past-life death. If we need to experience some disability in order to learn something new, then at the moment of conception, when we lay down our etheric body (see later), we shall create a matrix for a new body which may dictate that it is not perfect. It will bear past-life memory and the plan for the physical being. Our genetic inheritance is part of the legacy of our ancestral line and greatly underlies our choice of family.

MY CHOICES

It might help to put this all together if I share my choices with you.

One of the things that I set myself to do in this lifetime was to overcome poverty and to do so with integrity and love. I therefore chose a poor background in a depressed area in wartime, but also chose parents who were good people, industrious, honest, conscientious and with integrity. I chose to be female and Caucasian and to have a healthy body though I carry a birthmark on my right leg which is probably a carry-over from my last life, though as yet I haven't discovered its meaning. The exact time when I was born in my mother's bed, in a tiny village not far from the sea, was also chosen carefully. I chose an ancestral line with the characteristics of courage, stamina and fortitude and also the north-eastern culture with people who have toiled long and hard for centuries overcoming adverse weather conditions in the winter and working in unpleasant environments such as mines. I also inherited the warmth and friendliness of my natal area along with, in my early life, the sense that we of the north were in some way inferior to the people of the south whose behaviour, dialect and manners were considered preferable. Some of this I was to integrate, and some of it I was to overcome. Thus the stage was set and I just had to walk out on to it and play my part, make good choices (though they haven't all appeared good!) and work hard. My natal horoscope – I'm a Leo – has borne out my development to this point and I know more or less what else I'm here to do.

I also set myself the task of learning to deal with betrayal without revenge – something I hadn't mastered in previous lives. And so when I was small, my mother – the perfect mother for me, chosen with great care – told me stories about the folly of revenge; I heard about it in Sunday school; I read about it in books. Then came the moment of betrayal – not once, but several times – and thus far I haven't exacted revenge. Hopefully I've proved that I know this and won't need to be betrayed again. My anger is something else I chose to deal with, since it has led me astray in other lifetimes. I chose a father and grandfather who had hot tempers, and I have the same predisposition. It seemed that I had overcome that, but recently it's been severely tested again by someone who is obviously a great teacher of mine. I guess I'll be back here again dealing with that one! Abuse? Yes, I chose to deal with that too, but I didn't have the courage to opt for the horrendous lessons that I see some of my beloved patients suffer.

On the whole I chose wonderful things and wonderful people and acknowledge and thank everyone who has shared my life in any way. You have all been my teachers.

ACCEPTING MORE THAN OUR FAIR SHARE OF TROUBLE . . .

Human pain and trouble belong to us all, but some of us, with great courage, accept more than what appears to be their fair share. Sometimes we may find ourselves beset by trials and painful events which seem to make little sense. We may try to rationalize them by seeing them as punishment or a way of redressing the balance. The latter may sometimes be true, but it may be that we have already taken much of the collective joy and are now called upon (or willingly opt for) more of the pain. Those who commit murders and other crimes may be acting out that part in all of us that is capable of such deeds so that some of us can be relieved of dealing with our own violence in this lifetime. None of us has a right to stand apart and judge those who have the courage to hold the pain on our behalf. As each of us, no matter what we have done, reaches the point of grace and acceptance of where we are and who we are, divine love can lift us out of the illusion of fear and pain and back to the inner reality of health and happiness where the river of abundance and love is constantly flowing and we are safe.

KARMA

As we said in Chapter 3, karma is a merciful, educational and evolutionary process that helps us carry forward to another time – in another life if necessary – that which we have not yet understood. There's also a sense of balance to it – every action has a reaction, whatever energies we put out into the world are reflected on us – and thus we determine our destiny by our own behaviour. The Bible sums it up: 'Whatsoever shall ye sow, so shall you reap.' In planning our next life we meet with one of the lords of karma who guides us as to how we can best make restitution. As always, we have free will. We can opt for whatever we wish to accomplish – perhaps to help humanity for instance, or to teach medical science by presenting an unusual illness, or to be a politician or statesman or even perhaps to commit some crime that helps highlight our need for penal reform.

In each life we have new lessons and new obligations too, thus we are constantly moving forward, but often picking up more baggage as we go. For instance, I may have learned to deal with betrayal without resorting to revenge and can let that go, but I haven't yet mastered anger and need to relearn that and also make restitution. Although most of the time I feel humility, sometimes my Leo pride gets in the way and I still have to sort that out. If I haven't managed to master those things (and that's not all!) by the end of this lifetime, then I shall have it on my agenda for the next. The plan is constantly to raise our vibration so that love, charity, kindness and compassion are the essence of who we are, what we do and what we share with the world. Everything we experience moves us forward inexorably towards the goal of enlightenment, though it may appear from time to time as though we take two steps forward and one step back. Every lifetime has at least some influence on those that follow it. This is especially true of our mode of death. Those with whom we have karmic obligations reincarnate with us and we find ourselves down the line interacting in a way that might not be comfortable, but is nevertheless beneficial to both parties in the long term. The story of Angela and Freda (page 280) demonstrated this. Ideally we get to a point where both of us can acknowledge the karmic agreements that are being played out between us – just as Angela and Freda did – so that we can pay off our undischarged debts, as it were, and have our good rewarded and our wrongs reversed according to the law of justice.

THE COSMIC LAWS

There are three main cosmic laws, which are encoded within every soul and by which we should aim to live. Even though we may be consciously unaware of them, on a deep level we all know these laws, which set out the basics of expected human behaviour, to be true, honourable and just rules by which to live. Unfortunately our weakness, desire for instant gratification, emotional or physical relief or revenge during our earthly life often leads us to forget them. Violations against these laws are recorded in what is known as the Trianic Record held in the Halls of Learning, and we are reminded of the need to make restitution for our transgressions as we plan our next life.

The laws state:

- that the soul should function as part of the one unified consciousness and for the benefit of all. (We talked about raising to unity consciousness in Chapter 1.)
- that we should embrace experience in order that we will have evolutionary advancement. (Wherever we avoid experience or the consequences of our behaviour, we break this law and set up new obligations for the next lifetime.)
- that we should never destroy the body. (Suicide and self-harm breach this law and set up karmic obligations.)

There are also three codicils:

- that self-sacrifice for the sake of another is a sign of approaching enlightenment since the soul recognizes that all others are a part of itself. (This is nothing to do with acting as a martyr in relationships! It does, however, call us to act with courage and bravery and to extend ourselves for the higher good of all.)

- that acceptance is the seed of humility, the most precious of all virtues, and leads to bliss. (Remember that acceptance is not synonymous with complacency, nor humility with humiliation or false modesty.)
- that it is love that leads us back to union with the Divine. (This offers us a choice at every moment, in every transaction, with every person. It also encourages us to look for the spark of the Divine in everyone and to love it.)

Being consciously aware of the cosmic laws can ease our lives enormously. All of us will transgress from time to time in moments of weakness, but remember that karma can be erased by grace and love. It's never too late to rectify or make restitution for our blunders. If we haven't done so by the end of one life, then we're encouraged to schedule opportunity into our next life plan.

APPROACHING THE PERINATAL PHASE

Though we looked at birth in Chapter 2, here we view it from a different angle, that of the incoming soul. The choice is already made to return, our invariables have also been chosen, and now, as the process unfolds, we descend through the soul levels from the most fine until at last we're ready once more for our entry into the material world.

Let's break up the return into several stages.

Life Preview

At this time we have a preview of the life to come, with our major tasks and opportunities set out before us, though once incarnated we will have free will to proceed as we wish and of course to react to those who are incarnated with us. We're reminded of any major humanitarian work we're to do and the advanced masters who will guide us give us blessings.

Although as we incarnate we forget this preview and may appear to be in uncharted waters, our soul knows its way partly because of the imprinting of the cosmic laws and partly because of this glimpse at its life map. It may be that *déjà vu* experiences are actually memories of our life preview. Sometimes we may become spontaneously aware of our life preview and just 'know' our way forward from that time. Often this may be quite daunting, depending upon what tasks we have set for ourselves. At the age of about twenty, during hypnosis, I found myself back at my life preview and became aware of what I was going to do in my life. I remember that initially I was simply in disbelief and then almost angry and a little overwhelmed on seeing the enormous responsibilities I was going to have, which, to my young self (that little girl from the north-east), seemed way beyond my capabilities. Of course I've grown into them, and my way of being has become a natural and easy part of me. However, I would never have got here without the love and support of all the wonderful friends, guides, mentors and helpers with whom I've been blessed along the way. What seemed like a very lonely and awesome pursuit when I first saw it has actually been a journey of unbelievable joy, wonder and passionate adventure for which I'm grateful every day.

Preparing on the Energetic Levels

The construction of our energetic body takes place in stages as we descend back through the soul planes towards our re-entry into the material plane to manifest once more in a human body. If we're to have a special mission, then advanced beings and masters will help prepare our soul by increasing the intensity of its light and encoding information about our work, since almost all of us will forget who we are when we arrive in the material world so that we can complete our early human tasks. Only when we have completed much of our human work will we start to remember who we really are and find our mission. (Many people come to see me when quite young and are anxious about finding their true purpose. Often, however, they are still at the point where their purpose is simply to learn to be a mature human being. Usually our spiritual mission is revealed later when we are more ready and able to begin to fulfil it. As I said earlier, knowing at a young age, as in my own case, can be a bit scary.)

The human energy field or aura, what I refer to as the energetic body, consists of seven layers – the auric bodies – each discrete and with a particular function, each associated with a major chakra. Every action of every life leaves a memory trace on an energetic level which we carry from one life to the next. A brief discussion of the auric bodies will help us understand their development better.

The Etheric Body This is the auric body closest to the physical body and associated with the root chakra which is the first of the major chakras to be activated or developed after birth (its maximum development being in the first few months and continuing until the age of about three to five years). The etheric body is pale bluish-grey in colour and extends to about 3 cm from the physical body. It follows exactly the contours of the physical body including the internal organs. It is laid down at conception, forming a matrix upon which the cells of the physical body will manifest. The etheric body is influenced not only by the karmic memory of the soul, but also by the soul's intention. If the soul has decided that, in order for it to accomplish those challenges that it has already chosen, the body will have some defects, these are laid down within the etheric body during this stage of development. Birthmarks, which are carry-overs from last-life trauma (particularly last-life death trauma), are also laid within the etheric body. At the level of the root chakra and etheric body we are at the point of individual consciousness. Karmic memory is also carried at this level. The energy of the etheric body is the most dense of all the auric layers, with the frequency becoming higher and the energy more fine with each successive level.

The Emotional Body This extends beyond the etheric to about 9 cm from the physical body and is associated with the sacral chakra, the second major chakra to be activated, usually between the ages of five and eight. It consists of masses of coloured light. This body deals with the emotional aspects of human life, as well as sexuality and inner masculine/feminine balance. The emotional body and the sacral chakra allow us to begin to move into group consciousness. All the chakras except the crown and root open on to this level, an important consideration for chakra healing and balancing. This body also carries karmic memory, particularly of an emotional nature. Since each successive body can negatively affect the one below it, should there be painful past-life memory carried within it, painful past-life emotional patterns that are ignored and not dealt with can manifest as physical illness.

The Mental Body Associated with the solar plexus chakra and extending to about 24 cm from the physical body, the mental body is yellow in colour and deals with the intellectual and mental aspects of life, along with power, will, motivation, ambition and drive and also the so-called negative emotions of bitterness and rage. The solar plexus chakra is the third to be activated (usually between the ages of eight and twelve). Here we also have the transmission of karmic memory of an intellectual nature.

The Astral Body This is associated with the heart chakra, which develops between the ages of twelve and sixteen. Like the chakra to which it belongs, its functions are love and compassion and our ability to relate to others in an atmosphere of unconditional love. It also begins to deal with our spiritual life, allowing energy from the earth to rise through it and energy from the cosmos to descend through it, bridging the human and the Divine. Here we also have the chance to deal with 'negative' emotions such as jealousy and judgment. It appears as clouds of pastel colour (often with masses of pink when the person is feeling love) and extends to about 35–55 cm from the physical body. At this level we also move from group consciousness towards unity consciousness. It is to our astral body that we go when we dream and that we use as a vehicle during out-of-body experiences. At our transition we remain in our astral body until our ascension on to the mental plane

The Etheric Template This body is associated with the throat chakra which develops or is activated between the ages of sixteen and twenty-one. Its functions include communication, sound, truth and integrity. It follows the contours of the body and is blue, shimmering with silver. It extends to about 55–75 cm from the physical body.

The Celestial Body Related to the brow chakra, the celestial body is sometimes activated between the ages of twenty-one and twenty-six but often much later, and is comprised of shafts of sparkling pastel light extending outwards to about 90 cm. Its functions include vision and celestial love.

The Causal Body This auric body, connected to the crown chakra, is sometimes developed between the ages of twenty-six and thirty but often much later, and sometimes not until shortly before death. The causal body is golden and shimmering, extending to about 120 cm around the physical body. Its function is our connection with the Divine. The crown and root chakras open on to this level. Laid within the matrix of the causal body are bands of denser energy that relate to past-life issues. They are often called past-life bands and they remain there until we resolve the karmic issues we came to deal with, finally dissolving as we make restitution or do the work that frees us from our karmic obligations.

Our Journey Back Through the Soul Planes

On its way back to the material plane, the soul visits every one of the seven soul planes again, and at each level, with the help of the angels of that plane, using the substance of that level of consciousness, we build one of our auric bodies. The causal body is formed first at the highest level, then the celestial and so on, down through the lower planes. Eventually, on the lower vibrations of the etheric plane, we form our etheric body – the exact double of our physical body and the etheric matrix upon which physical cells will finally manifest. As we evolve through various lifetimes, our energetic bodies become finer and stronger. Rather as in a physical training programme, our weaknesses and strengths are refined at every level as we incorporate new experience, and in each successive lifetime we are therefore prepared to extend ourselves further by accepting new challenges. Once our etheric body is prepared and we are energized and filled with light, we are ready to await birth. The soul now hovers around the chosen mother and father awaiting the moment of conception.

WAMBACH'S STUDY

In Helen Wambach's study (see page 24), not every soul wanted to come back, some showing resistance and ambivalence. This is supported by past-life work. In Dr Wambach's sample 81 per cent said they chose to come back while 19 per cent said that they were unaware of having a choice. Many in this sample reported having sessions with a pre-birth counsellor in the hope of setting and achieving goals. Most reported that their purpose for reincarnation was to learn about love rather than to develop talents or acquire wealth, status or power, whilst 28 per cent said they had come back to teach humanity and help develop higher consciousness.

The Experience of Conception

At the mystical moment of conception, the vital essence of the mother and father unites. The soul which is to incarnate hovers close by so that in that moment the etheric body of the foetus can be transferred to the mother and the template is set for the development of the physical body. The soul can sense the consciousness of each of the parents and their feelings at that moment of conception and continues to be aware of all the energies in and around the womb throughout the pregnancy. The events experienced at conception are those that have been chosen and are part of the karmic agenda and set the stage for later life. Should the mother be shocked and hurt, for example by rape, the child feels this. Should she not want the pregnancy, this is also recorded and may result in long-lasting feelings of rejection, which must be either integrated or overcome. Similarly, feelings of love and joy are registered and become some of the earliest memories of this lifetime.

Living in the Womb

Since the embryo shares the blood and nerve supply of the mother, everything that happens to the mother, consciously or unconsciously, happens to the child also. Her feelings and desires are clear to the developing embryo throughout the pregnancy, and also to the hovering soul. Sometimes the foetus appears able to pick up the feelings of the father too, which suggests that there is consciousness beyond the blood and nerve supply. The moment of confirmation of the pregnancy is a milestone in foetal development, and again, the reaction of the mother to this news can greatly affect the unborn. Any thoughts of disappointment or wanting to abort the foetus will leave a lifelong impression. For some the time *in utero* is a time of oneness, harmony and bliss. For others it's a perilous time, with attempts to abort, anger and resentment at carrying the child, and sometimes verbal, emotional or physical violence towards the mother.

As the soul continues to work with the mother to raise her vibration so that it may enter, the soul is also lowering its own vibration. Several of the 'symptoms' of pregnancy are due to this manipulation of energy. Occasionally two or more foetuses have chosen to occupy the same womb simultaneously. The souls here often have a joint purpose, sometimes to help each other and sometimes so that one may escort the other to the point of incarnation but then leave quite quickly when the mission is complete. This often accounts for one twin being stillborn or dying very shortly after birth. The twin that survives may have feelings of grief or insecurity which are part of its first lesson of the new lifetime. Sometimes there has been reluctance to reincarnate on the part of the surviving child, hence the escort. From the time of quickening (the moment when the mother can feel the baby move) the soul may start to enter the growing body of the child intermittently. This may continue up to birth or later. Sometimes, in past-life work, the person will remember actually being in the body of the growing foetus and then quite quickly being outside the mother again. Some people can actually describe events and conversations that they heard while inside the womb.

Where for any reason there is termination of pregnancy, the hovering soul is ready to reabsorb the etheric body which was placed with the mother. The pregnancy may have been part of the mother's learning experience and was never intended to go to term.

BIRTH

Birth has been referred to as beauty in its purest form. However, it has also been said that birth is a kind of death, as we leave the bliss and expanded consciousness of the interlife, with its close, accessible relationships to our guides, the angels and ascended masters, to enter once again the restrictions of the human body and the pain and trials of human experience. At the onset of labour many events occur to set in progress the process of full incarnation. The soul – its vibration now lowered to the point where it will be able to enter the body without damaging it, and the vibration of the mother and the baby's body raised to meet it – is hovering closely and is fully aware of all the physical and emotional responses of the mother. The physical body of the baby is also suffering both physical pain and anxiety as it begins to be forced down its traumatic journey through the birth canal. At this time there is activation of karmic memory and the karmic patterns of the past imprinted on the etheric body of the foetus. Depending upon the reactions of the mother and its own karmic memory, the child may see this process as one of rejection and expulsion, with consequent feelings of shock, rejection and abandonment; or as a move into freedom and loving welcome, in which case the feelings will be of warmth and nurture. Either will have a major effect throughout life on the way we feel about ourselves and also on how we handle the ending of relationships, the former causing us to react with insecurity, dependency, entrapment and possessiveness. In one study the majority of people who were regressed to the time of birth reported feelings of deep sadness on being ejected from the birth canal.

One of the most beautiful passages about birth comes from *Benjaya's Gifts* when the soul of the child talks through his grandmother about his birth. He reports coming from the darkness into the light of the new world 'with spinning motions as the brain connected to the eyes and the mind was reborn'. He then talks of his every cell being motion suffused with sound: 'And within that sound was heard the call of my mother, a call unceasing with wonderment, not from the lips but from the heart I heard that sound . . .' Then talking of the first touch from his father: 'I experience electrification as the life current runs between us in our first earth embrace. Time stood still as soul touched upon soul.' Isn't that beautiful?

IMMEDIATE POST-BIRTH PERIOD

We have already discussed birth in Chapter 2, so let's confine ourselves here to the process of incarnation. Although, as we've seen, the soul may have entered the body of the foetus intermittently during the latter part of the pregnancy, there is sometimes reluctance to enter until the moment of birth. Finally, however, it enters through the crown chakra and opens the central channel as it moves through the body towards the root chakra. The root chakra begins its activation immediately and develops maximally during the first few months. Although over the next few weeks the soul may again leave from time to time, which may account for the infant's prolonged periods of 'sleep', eventually it comes to rest. Occasionally there is reluctance to incarnate due to a variety of reasons, perhaps the most common being past-life death trauma, but in normal circumstances the soul is in full residence after the first few months.

POSTSCRIPT

Here we are, back where we began, the soul once again starting its journey in a new lifetime. But of course we are *not* back where we began. The soul has experienced much and has incorporated new wisdom and understanding. Some karmic obligations have been discharged and new ones added; new relationships have been forged and others concluded; missions have been accomplished and new ones accepted. Underlying the whole process, however, is the continuing journey of the soul in its earnest desire to perfect its growth and finally fulfil its desire to be reunited with the Beloved, the Divine. Wherever you are on your journey, I wish you joy, passion and adventure and finally a safe haven once more in the body of the Beloved. I shall meet you there . . .

✿ AFFIRMATION

I rededicate this day to love and healing, to learning and teaching, to my higher good and the higher good of all. I acknowledge my mission and open my heart with unconditional love that I may fulfil the intention of my soul.

✿ MEDITATION

This meditation is to honour your journey thus far and all of those who have aided you in your many lifetimes. It is a good meditation to use as part of your daily prayer – I usually bring my morning meditation to a close with this since I see it as a loving statement of gratitude and dedication. If you were adopted, perhaps you would like to do this meditation once for your natural family and ancestors since they are the ones you chose as a biological family, then again for your adoptive parents, since they are the ones you chose to be nurtured by.

Prepare for your meditation as usual.

Now take a deep breath and close your eyes. Once again breathe out and as you do, allow your body to relax, let your shoulders fall and let your chair take your weight. Let anything you don't need simply flow out of your root chakra to be neutralized by the earth. Take another deep breath and this time as you breathe out send gratitude to the earth for supporting you and for being an anchor for you in this lifetime and all your previous lifetimes here. Feel a sense of being well grounded and held by the earth. Take another deep breath, and this time bring in some white light through the top of your head and let it fill every cell of your body. Feel yourself cleansing, healing and coming into harmony and balance. Relax and breathe naturally, visualizing your whole aura being filled with light and your chakras aligned and spinning healthily with all the colours of the spectrum.

Relax . . .

Now, in this moment, gently allow your mind to start to travel back in time. There is nothing to alarm you; nothing to harm you. Relax. Allow your mind to wander down through the years, through your adulthood, your adolescence and childhood, honouring yourself as you go, but not actively remembering any of the events. See yourself simply drifting gently back and back until you reach the moment when you were born. Pause for a second or two and give thanks for your life, for this opportunity for growth and learning, for the possibility of coming even closer to the true understanding of who you really are; closer to the possibility of a final reunion with your twin soul and with the Divine.

Gently now allow yourself to go back even further. Back beyond the time of your life as a baby in your mother's womb; back to the moment of your conception. Now pause again . . .

Send gratitude to your mother and your father as they came together by your choice to bring you life. Know that in that moment, even if for only a moment, there was harmony in the union of their essence so that you could be conceived. All was exactly according to plan. Allow yourself to feel gratitude and, if you can, a wave of love.

Now continue on your journey back in time. From a place where you can observe, watch your mother's life unfold back through her young adulthood and her adolescence, back to her childhood and to her birth. See her parents, your grandparents. Pause and give gratitude to them for the birth of your mother. And if you can, send them love. Continue now back down the ancestral line of each of your grandparents, gently now. Give thanks and send love. Stay as long as you wish.

From your same vantage-point take your focus back to your father, and watch his life unfold, back now through his young adulthood, back through his adolescence, through his childhood and to his birth. See your paternal grandparents. Pause and give thanks for the birth of your father. If you can, send your grandparents love. Stay as long as you wish.

From this vantage-point you can now see all the way through time, down and down your ancestral line. Allow yourself to absorb an impression of what your ancestors brought to the final union between your mother and your father. Be aware of the qualities, the passion, the joy, the tenderness they brought. See their work, their struggles, their hardships. Without feeling it, be aware of their pain. Know that all of this came together so that you could be carried on the crest of this wave of humanity into the present. Send gratitude to them all and, if you can, love and forgiveness for anything that you may have judged harshly, anything you may not previously have understood. Send light, love, healing so that your whole ancestral line may be cleansed and healed.

Now, look forward in time . . .

From where you are, look forward, scanning the lives of your parents, and see what they too suffered and enjoyed on their way to coming together in order to fulfil your choice of having them as your earthly parents. Now, if you can, send them loving gratitude for their love on the soul level even if you perhaps didn't feel it on a human level. Thank them for their teaching and for all the things you have shared. Now widen your scope if you can and take in the souls of your siblings whom you also chose.

Now with a single breath, honour them all.

Stay for as long as you wish, then allow yourself to return gently to this moment in time. Know that you are here in your safe place and that you are well grounded. Though all those souls that have gone before you are part of your story, be in this moment. Your angels and guardians are around you. You are safe and protected. Let their love surround you as it will forever wherever you may be. Let their guidance be known to you and trusted by you. Let the love that surrounds you heal you and hold you. Let the breath of God warm you and bring you never-ending life.

Give thanks and when you are ready, come back to a place behind your closed eyes and be fully aware. Take a deep breath and fill your whole being with energy. Gently open your eyes. Stretch a little and have a drink of water. Take your time, then record whatever you wish in your journal.

FINAL PRAYER

By the power of the Divine that is within me, by my will, by my mighty heart and the greatness of my love, I pray that I may receive the highest guidance, the purest healing and the best teaching so that I may fulfil my obligations and bring forth the very best of who I am. In doing so I ask that I may help others to become the best that they can be. I rededicate my life this day to peace, to joy, to love and to my eventual reunion with the Divine. I offer gratitude to all whose souls have played a part in my journey.

EPILOGUE

My hope for you in completing this *Journey of the Soul* is that you have found within you a sense of peace, and also that you have become more familiar with your soul, that you have learned to listen to and with your body and emotions, and that your heart has learned a new and wonderful song. In every moment of our lives we have choices. No matter what has gone before, in this moment you can start to make healthier ones, to resolve outstanding issues, forgive where necessary and let yourself move on. Wherever you find yourself in this earthly life, I hope that you have discovered that there is no need ever to fear your transition, that in fact 'death' doesn't exist and that loved ones you have 'lost' live on and are only a breath away. If you are approaching your own transition, I wish you a gentle journey home. I know that you will be welcomed warmly by those who went before. You are closer to your ultimate goal than those of us you leave behind. I honour you.

There is presently an ongoing revolution in consciousness. As a race, we are completing cycles, balancing our energies and resolving karma as we prepare for a quantum leap in our evolution. The fact that you have been reading this indicates that you are part of that great shift that will bring us all new vision, new peace and harmony.

I thank you for sharing your journey with me, for allowing me to be a fellow traveller even for a short while. You have been travelling with me as I write, and in this endless moment of now, and across the non-existent space between us, I send you love.

APPENDIX 1

ANGELS

Be not forgetful to entertain strangers: for thereby some have entertained angels unawares.

Hebrews 13.2

All of creation is in a state of ascending consciousness, from the mineral world which includes crystals and gemstones, up through the plant and animal kingdom with their nature spirits (including the devas, elves, fairies, undines, sylphs, salamanders, trolls and gnomes which nurture the physical environment), through humanity and eventually to the angelic kingdom and thence to the nucleus of all energy – the divine energy or source which we call God. Religious literature and the mythologies of almost every race on earth have talked of angels, guardians and supernatural entities whose job it is to look after us and to help inspire us, teach us, bring us hope, encouragement and comfort. Saints and poets, mystics and artists have borne witness to the presence of angels and many of us mere mortals have had our own experiences. My own healing and teaching mission was revealed to me by an angel when I was four. There are many books about angels, encounters with angels, etc., and this is merely a brief sketch. I would refer you to the Bibliography for further reading.

Although angels are androgynous beings, we may often

perceive them as having a strongly masculine or feminine energy and project human qualities on them.

THE ANGELIC HIERARCHY

There have been many attempts to categorize the angelic kingdom. It is generally accepted that there are three categories or spheres of angelic beings, and that within each sphere, there are three orders. The highest or first sphere consists of seraphim, cherubim and thrones, all of whom serve as counsellors at the highest level. The second sphere consists of the dominions, virtues and powers, and the third – closest to us in the material plane and acting as heavenly messengers – are the principalities, archangels and angels. Let's look briefly at each.

The Seraphim
These are the heavenly beings that surround the nucleus of energy we call God and which are recognized on the soul planes by their vibration which is expressed as divine music.

The Cherubim
These are beings of light, and though in many ways very remote from us, they still touch our lives with divine light.

The Thrones
This is the lowest order of the first sphere, and the angels here are the guardians of the planets. The earth angel takes care of our planet and helps make us more aware of the need for conservation, ecological awareness, etc.

The Dominions
This is the highest order of the second sphere and the angels here coordinate and govern the activities of all lower orders.

The Virtues

These are almost like the transformers of heaven, beaming out divine energy in a way that helps us raise our vibration and continue to grow spiritually.

The Powers

The lowest order of the second sphere, these beings are the keepers of our collective history, consciousness and the divine plan. The angels of birth and death are of this order. All of the powers work through us to help us raise consciousness and spiritual understanding.

The Principalities

The upper order of the third sphere, these are guardian angels but not of individuals. They guard whole communities, groups, cities, continents, integrating our needs, understanding and tolerance and moving us towards universal peace.

The Archangels

Although there are many archangels, the ones with whom we are most familiar are Gabriel, Michael, Raphael and Uriel. These are angels concerned with human endeavour and are sometimes known as the overlighting angels.

Gabriel has been mentioned in many scriptures. In the Bible, he is reported to have parted the Red Sea so that the Hebrews could escape from the Egyptians, and later he appeared to Mary and her cousin Elizabeth. He is the Spirit of Truth who dictated the Koran to Mohammed and also the archangel whom Joan of Arc claimed as her guide and inspiration. Gabriel is classically associated with winter, the winter solstice and Capricorn.

Michael is reported to have appeared to Moses in the burning bush, to have rescued Daniel from the lion's den and to have warned Mary of her forthcoming death. He has been seen as the Prince of Light fighting against the power of darkness and evil. He is associated with the autumn, the autumnal equinox and Libra.

Raphael is the archangel of healing and is mentioned in the old and new testaments. Classically he governs spring-time, the vernal equinox and Aries.

Uriel, the Archangel of Salvation, warned Noah of the flood, led Abraham out of Ur and gave the Kaballah to the Jewish faith. He is associated with the summer, the summer solstice and Cancer.

The Angels

These are those with whom we are most familiar, being in the order most close to the material plane and most concerned with our individual welfare and daily life. They act as our companions and guides. Within this order are our guardian angels who have cared for us since the moment of the creation of our soul. Though one guardian may work simultaneously with several souls, the angels are neverthe-less always available to guard us, help and comfort us when-ever we call upon them and to offer us guidance to the higher benefit of our soul. They are our spiritual mentors and protectors.

COMMUNICATION WITH THE ANGELIC KINGDOM

It was Audrey Hepburn who said, 'For poise walk in the knowledge that you never walk alone.' How wise. We can always walk with poise, for indeed we are never alone. Like love, the angels surround us constantly and, forever at our service, are always waiting for an opening to flow into our lives though we're often totally unaware of their presence.

Collectively, the angelic beings are entities of light, love and joy, which usually exist in a frequency higher than we are able to perceive with our human senses. The lowest soul plane they occupy is usually the etheric, which is why more often than not we can't see them. Actively calling them brings them closer. They are not usually restricted by our structured world, although sometimes they choose to manifest as physical beings, enriching our lives beyond measure with their expression of divine love so that we in turn may increase our own vibration to benefit ourselves and the world by radiating love, enthusiasm, fun, positivity and clear and undistorted perception. The more we raise our vibration in partnership with the angels, the more those around us are changed merely by our presence. Being in the presence of angels, we experience a sense of lightness, connectedness and security of being held in love. Sometimes we may almost enter into a state of altered consciousness where we hardly need to breathe, time seems suspended and we are fully grounded yet connected with the Divine.

Although we may hear angels talk to us in dreams, meditations and at times of need, or see them in mystical moments, usually we need to raise our vibration in order to perceive them with our senses. Messages may be perceived as insights, inspiration, glorious Ahas, sudden creative ideas and synchronicities. Every single thought, word and deed, no matter how seemingly insignificant, is part of the plan. Every slip of the tongue, every 'coincidence' is part of their guidance. Communication with them is always loving, compassionate and supportive and never carries guilt or manipulation or interferes with our personal will and choice.

Perhaps you could experiment with shifting from your usual way of perceiving stimuli only with your physical senses (note that sometimes you don't even use all of those to their full capacity!). You can then open to a much more exciting way of living where you perceive every single event as part of the divine guidance relayed to us by these bene-volent guides and helpers. Ask that you may receive their guidance and you will, though you may need to practise interpreting their language.

APPENDIX 2

THE ENERGY SYSTEM

There follows a brief sketch of the energy system. I would refer you to the Bibliography for further reading.

THE HUMAN ENERGY FIELD (HEF), AURA OR AURIC BODIES

The aura is that part of our body which is generally invisible to most people, but which can be measured as an electromagnetic radiation. Consisting of seven layers, each associated with one of the major chakras, it is our largest and most sensitive organ, collecting, accurately deciphering and storing information about the outside world, then relaying its impressions to us either as intuition, emotions or physical sensations. It can be torn or otherwise damaged, displaced or clogged with debris from the past, and may remain that way for years unless we actively work to heal it. Parts of it can be lost and we can sometimes have parts of other people's auras lodged within ours. Since it is one of our primary defences, its integrity is extremely important. If it is not in good health, then neither are we. The auric bodies were discussed in Chapter 9.

THE CHAKRA SYSTEM

Within the aura there are the chakras – swirling wheels of

light, constantly in motion when we are in good health. They penetrate the layers of the aura and the physical body, forming intimate contact between the outside world and us. The major ones (we shall deal with seven of them here) are each associated with one of the major glands of the body and also with a neurological plexus. Each has a specific colour, morphology and function, time of maximum development and speed and direction of spin. In good health the chakras are in balance, their energy connected by a central channel that runs from crown to base within the physical body. They are capable of spontaneously opening and closing, their petals being flexible and under our control. However, they may be blocked, underdeveloped or damaged, under- or overstimulated, and we need to balance and develop them if we are to be in good health. Everything about us, from our stamina and energy level to the tone of our skin and the radiance in our eyes, can be improved by working on our chakras.

All the chakras are present in a rudimentary form at birth. Apart from the major ones, which we shall discuss here, there are twenty-one minor ones, and many lesser ones found over joints and acupuncture points. Of the minor ones, those in the hands and the soles of the feet are particularly relevant to healing – the former since we use them to channel healing energy; the latter since we use them both to draw up energy from the earth and discharge unwanted energy to it.

The seven major chakras are:

1. **The root chakra,** situated at the base of the spine, is red in colour and has its primary development from birth to the age of between three and five years old. Its functions include keeping us grounded to the planet and ensuring our survival and stability. It governs our physical reality,

our self-esteem and sense of belonging. It is the chakra of the physical. When it is dysfunctional for any reason, we often suffer depression, a lack of belonging, and may feel so unattached to the planet that we want to leave it. We may therefore dissociate, feel suicidal or temporarily absent ourselves by the use of drugs or alcohol. Physically it governs our lower limbs and external genitalia.

2. **The sacral chakra**, situated in the lower abdomen, is orange in colour and has its first major development between the ages of three to five and eight. It governs the masculine/feminine balance, helps us start to relate to others and helps us be flexible and flowing in all areas of our lives. It is the chakra of emotion. Physically it governs the fluid systems such as the renal system and menstruation, lymphatics and to some extent circulation. Creativity is born here, to be manifested more fully as the throat chakra develops. When it is blocked, damaged, underdeveloped or unhealthy, we become rigid physically, emotionally and intellectually and our sensuality and sexuality are compromised. Fluid retention, menstrual problems and urinary tract problems are common.

3. **The solar plexus chakra**, which is bright yellow, is found in the midline or slightly to the left in the upper abdomen. It develops between the ages of eight and twelve and governs power, potential, prosperity, and will. It also governs the pancreas and the digestive tract. It is here that we hold old feelings such as bitterness, hatred, anger and rage, here also that we develop opinion. This is the first chakra dealing with intellectual issues. Trauma at the time of its initial development may result in digestive problems – ulcers, colon problems, etc. or diabetes mellitus. It is worth looking here to see if cancer is the presenting symptom. Old anger here may result in arthritis. Problems with authority figures, being overpowering or

feeling helpless, having little balance of will and being unable to bring true prosperity into our lives are also solar plexus problems.

4. **The heart chakra** develops between the ages of twelve and sixteen and is found in the centre of the chest. It is green in colour though often as it opens it reveals a pink centre. It has been said that the heart chakra is the lens through which the soul integrates earthly emotions and divine awareness to produce divine integrity. The middle of the seven major chakras, it is in fact the pivotal point of the chakra system uniting our human and divine aspects. Its essence is love and this is its only function. Though there is love at every chakra in some form, here the love is not necessarily focused on a particular person but extends out into the world to embrace the whole universe, although of course we do love those we know intimately with our hearts. Compassion and empathy are also emotions of the heart. Physically this chakra governs the heart, the circulation and the respiratory tract. Dysfunction causes us to have difficulties with intimate relationships, to be unable to feel love and compassion or to empathize, or to be so open that we cannot love objectively and set good boundaries, leading us to burn-out. Cardiac and respiratory problems are common. Healing with love and detachment is a gift of the healthy heart chakra.

5. **The throat chakra** is sky-blue or turquoise when in good health and is situated at the base of the neck. It develops between the ages of sixteen and twenty-one and deals with communication, creativity, truth, integrity and vocation. It governs the throat, neck, mouth, ears and the lower part of the face and all the associated organs including the thyroid gland. Trauma during its time of development may result in communication problems,

thyroid dysfunction, and difficulties in finding our vocation or living within our integrity.

6. **The brow chakra** develops between the ages of twenty-one and twenty-six, although in many people it develops along with the crown only in the final ascent to consciousness shortly before death. Deep indigo-blue or purple in colour, it deals with vision in all its forms – internal vision, visualization, clairvoyance and physical vision. Its gifts include wisdom and understanding and its development allows us to receive channelled information. Problems or lack of development here produce headaches and visual disturbances and prevent us from opening fully to our spiritual gifts.

7. **The crown chakra** is situated above the top of the head and may develop after the age of twenty-six or so, but sometimes not until just prior to death. It is our final ascent to our divinity, giving us a direct access via soul to spirit. The gifts of its development include channelling, healing and knowing beyond faith and understanding.

Dysfunction can occur due to trauma at the physical site of the chakra (for example, injury or surgery); there can also be emotional shock, though most of this is developmental – that is, due to some trauma at the time of development. Blocks, damage and lack of development at any chakra can cause further secondary blocking within the fully integrated system. Learning regularly to scan, cleanse, heal and balance the whole system is essential to thorough healing. Many people embarking on their spiritual journey neglect the lower chakras while searching for the spiritual gifts of the higher ones. This creates problems with grounding and leaves them vulnerable. If we wish to achieve the ideal situation of being ordinary human beings capable of extraordinary powers, then attention to the lower chakras which govern our humanity (what might be called the human–Divine) is as essential as the work on the upper chakras which govern the spiritual (what might be called the spiritual–Divine).

I hope that you will explore your energy system and by doing so expand and extend your whole being.

APPENDIX 3
GROUNDING AND CLOSING DOWN

GROUNDING

Being grounded is very important since if we don't keep our connection with the earth, anything else we do is rendered insecure and without foundation. Also, despite the fact that we may be able to feel wonderful by focusing on our upper chakras, eventually we can become sick and somehow disconnected from the rest of our fellow humans since we don't have the strong robust energy of the earth to nurture us. The energy from the cosmos cannot flow freely either since it has nowhere to ground, leaving us apparently floating out of our bodies and communicating in a way that is fey and appears conceited, insincere and quite off-putting to other people. Our grounding acts a bit like a lightning conductor and renders us much more powerful and real. The exercise that follows can be used whenever you remember to do it, but always after meditation, when you're with someone who is ill or whose energy is disturbed, or when you feel yourself to be under any kind of attack – physically, emotionally or spiritually. Eventually the exercise may only take a second and can be done with a single breath. Note any physical changes as you do it. Sometimes people feel as though their body weight has shifted, sometimes they comment that they feel as though they are resting more on their heels and as though the way they stand has changed. For me there's a whole shift in my body. I feel more solid and yet energized, the earth seems to be coming up to meet me and settle me into it; my centre of gravity shifts and seems to be right down through the centre of me with a feeling of leaning very slightly backwards. Then within a moment I can feel my whole being thrill as the energy from above now courses through me like a breeze bringing me fresh power, and I have a different quality of clarity. It may take you a while to perceive these things – and of course you may react quite differently. But being aware of new perceptions will help you know when you're grounded.

Grounding Exercise

Stand if you can, but if due to some disability that's not possible, sitting or lying will do fine. Energy follows thought, so whatever you visualize will be so.

Make sure that your feet are flat on the floor and bend your knees slightly so that your weight rests in your pelvis. Feel that as you do so, your centre of gravity shifts and you seem slightly heavier (don't worry, you aren't!). In this position, your central power channel will be vertical and your chakras aligned. Now take a deep breath, closing your eyes if you wish, and imagine that breath coming right down through the middle of you. Breathe it out through your root chakra and the soles of your feet where your plantar chakras (the chakras in the soles of your feet) are now opening to the earth too. Imagine that from your root chakra a wonderful ruby-red light spins down and into the earth. Imagine that spirals of light go down into the earth from the soles of your feet also. Feel as though you're sitting on a tripod of light and that you're held comfortably by the earth. Feel the earth almost come up to meet you and hold you as though you were sitting in a comfortable chair. Now take another deep breath and this time bring in some white light through the top of your head and visualize it coming right down through your central power channel and out through your root chakra and into the earth. Feel a wash of clean, fresh energy as it does so and feel that you are now securely held by the earth below and the cosmos above. Just let yourself feel that for a moment, then straighten your legs but hold the connection with the earth. Now scan your body and take note of where and how it feels different. Then relax – the earth will hold you.

Until you become adept at holding your grounding, check as often as it comes into your mind whether or not you feel grounded. If you've been used to only being 'in your head', it might take you a while to hold your connection. And even when we've been working on ourselves for a long time, things can happen that can blow us off course, so it's good practice simply to be more aware.

CLOSING DOWN

In doing our spiritual work, our chakras begin to open and bring in more energy and also allow us to perceive more of the world. In the main, this is a very good thing since it's the interchange between ourselves and the world around us that allows us to collect information, raise our consciousness and grow. However, there are times when wandering around with our chakras wide open is not good for us. If we're with someone whose energy is not very clear, if we're out in the hustle and bustle of city life, if we're in an abusive situation or simply with someone who's unhappy, then there's the possibility that we'll either lose our energy or pick up someone else's. Although I may have some of my chakras wide open when I'm working, there are times when I close them down to protect myself. Similarly, if I'm with someone I love my chakras may be open, but in an argument I may shut down at least some of them for protection, while leaving some open so that I can perceive very clearly just what's going on and what my part in it is. After meditation I usually close down so as to maintain conscious control over my energy system; however, I know that during the course of even the next few minutes, my chakras will be doing what's right and opening to scan my world for energy and information while putting out into the universe whatever I'm creating within myself, and keeping a clear flow of energy through my whole being to nurture and protect me. Eventually our chakras take care of themselves to a large extent. Rather as though if I decide to lift my arm I do so without apparent conscious effort, so my chakras move when they need to without my consciously willing them to do so. But until they're at that healthy stage, practising closing them at will is an essential part of our spiritual routine. The following exercise will help you close down and protect yourself. It need only take a few minutes, and eventually it can be done with a single breath. Remember that your brow, throat, heart, solar plexus and sacral chakras are present at your back as well as at the front of your body.

Closing-Down Exercise

Take a deep breath and close your eyes (you can also do this with your eyes open, for instance in your car, while out shopping or in a meeting) and take your focus to your crown chakra just above your head. Imagine there a white flower with its petals open and, with a thought, let them close. Then drop your focus to your brow chakra and imagine a deep indigo-blue flower there. Let its petals close too. At your throat imagine a sky-blue flower and allow it to close, then drop your focus to your heart chakra. At your heart imagine a green flower with its petals open and, with a thought, let them close. Then move your focus to your solar plexus where you will see a yellow flower. Let it close also.

Come down now to your sacral chakra where there is an orange flower and let its petals close too. Leave your root chakra open to ground you. Scan your aura and your chakra system with a thought. If you feel vulnerable or unsafe anywhere, just check again that your chakras are closed. You can reinforce the whole close-down by imagining that you have a dark velvet cloak with a hood. Put it on and draw up the hood and know you are safe. As an extra precaution if you wish, you can then surround yourself with white light or moving bands of all the colours of the spectrum. Know that you are safe and protected.

BIBLIOGRAPHY

Rosemary Altea, *Proud Spirit*, Eagle Brook Morrow, 1997

William Anderson, *The Face of Glory*, 1996

John van Auken, *Past Lives and Present Relationships*, Inner Vision, 1984

Lionel Bascon and Barbara Loehger, *By the Light*, Avon Books, 1995

Paul Beard, *Living On*, Continuum, 1981

M'haletta and Carmella B'Hahn, *Benjaya's Gifts*, Hazelwood Press, 1996

Joan Borysenko, *A Woman's Book of Life*, Riverhead Books, 1996

J. H. Brennan, *The Reincarnation Workbook*, Sterling Publishing Company, 1989

Dannion Brinkley with Paul Perry, *At Peace with the Light*, Harper, 1995

Richard Carlson and Benjamin Shield, *Handbook for the Soul*, Little Brown, 1995

David Chamberlain and Jeremy P. Tarcher, *Babies Remember Birth*, 1988

Jenny Cockell, *Across Time and Death*, Simon & Schuster, 1993

Dr Brenda Davies, *The Rainbow Journey*, Hodder & Stoughton, 1998

Dr Brenda Davies, *Affairs of the Heart*, Hodder & Stoughton, 2000

Bibliography

Larry Dossey MD, *Recovering the Soul*, Bantam, 1989

Betty J. Eadie, *Embraced by the Light*, Aquarian/Thorsons, 1992

Peter and Elizabeth Fenwick, *The Truth in the Light*, Headline, 1996

Victor Frankl, *Man's Search for Meaning*, Beacon Press, 1992

Gina Germinare, *Many Mansions*, Signet, 1991

Dr Bruce Goldberg, *Soul Healing*, Llewellyn, 1996

Dr Bruce Goldberg, *Peaceful Transition*, Llewellyn, 1997

Migene Gonzalez-Wippler, *What Happens after We Die*, Llewellyn, 1997

Glenda Green, *Love without End*, Heartwings, 1999

Chris Griscom, *Ecstasy Is a New Frequency*, Bear & Company, 1987

Stanislav Grof MD and Christina Grof (eds), *Spiritual Emergency*, Jeremy Physical Tarcher, 1989

Elizabeth Haich, *Initiation*, Aurora Press, 2000

Barbara Harper RN, *Gentle Birth Choices*, Healing Arts Press, 1994

James Hillman, *The Soul's Code*, Bantam, 1997

Deborah Jackson, *With Child*, Chronicle Books, 1999

Robert Keck, *Sacred Eyes*, Green Books, 1998

Lawrence Leshan, *The Medium, the Mystic and the Physicist*, 1974

Lawrence Leshan and Henry Margenan, *Einstein's Space and Van Gogh's Sky*, Macmillan, 1982

Stephen Levine, *Healing into Life and Death*, Gateway, 1987

Joel Martin & Patricia Romanowski, *We Don't Die*, Berkeley Books, 1988

Raymond A. Moody Jr MD, *Life after Life*, Bantam, 1975

Raymond Moody, *The Last Laugh*, Hampton Road Publishing Company Inc., 1994

Melvin Morse MD with Paul Perry, *Closer to the Light*, Ivy Books, 1990

Michael Newton, *Journey of Souls*, Llewellyn, 1994

Dr Christiane Northrup, *Women's Bodies, Women's Wisdom*, Piatkus, 1995

Karlis Osis PhD and Erlendur Haraldsson PhD, *At the Hour of Death* (third edition), Hastings House, 1997

Terry and Natalia O'Sullivan, *Soul Rescuers*, Thorson, 1999

M. Scott Peck, *People of the Lie*, Rider, 1983

Jenny Randle and Peter Hough, *Life after Death and the World Beyond*, Piatkus, 1996

Mirella Ricardi, *African Visions: The diary of an African photographer*, Cassell, 2000

Sogyal Rinpoche, *The Tibetan Book of Living and Dying*, Harper, 1992

Ronald Russell, *The Vast Enquiring Soul*, Hampton Road Publishing Company Inc., 2000

David Schiller, *The Little Book of Prayers*, Workman Publishing, 1996

Anne Sheffield, *How You Can Survive When They're Depressed*, Three River Press, 1998

Tom Shroder, *Old Souls*, Simon & Schuster, 1999

Kathleen Dowling Singh, *The Grace in Dying*, Newleaf, 1999

Ann Smolin and John Guinan, *Healing after the Suicide of a Loved One*, Simon & Schuster, 1993

Malidoma Patrice Some, *Of Water and the Spirit*, Arkana, 1995

Julie Soskins, *The Wind of Change*, Barton House, 1990

Ian Stevenson, *Reincarnation and Biology: A contribution to the etiology of birthmarks and birth defects*, Praeger, 1997

Wistancia Stone, *Invocations to the Light*, Blue Dolphin Publishing, 2000

Lorna Todd, *A Healer's Journey into the Light*, Bantam, 1995

Kenneth L. Vaux, *Will to Live, Will to Die*, Augsburg Publishing House, 1975

Bibliography

Thomas Verney, *The Secret Life of the Unborn Child*, Dell, 1981

Neale Donald Walsch, *Conversations with God Book 1*, Hodder & Stoughton, 1997

Neale Donald Walsch, *Conversations with God, Book 2*, Hodder & Stoughton, 1999

Neale Donald Walsch, *Conversations with God Book 3*, Hodder & Stoughton, 1999

Brian L. Weiss MD, *Many Lives, Many Masters*, Simon & Schuster, 1988

Brian Weiss MD, *Messages from the Masters*, Warner, 2000

Joel Whitter and Joe Fisher, *Life between Life*, Warner, 1986

For workshops, seminars, conferences, training or healing – whether you wish to attend as a participant or engage Brenda to teach – please contact her on her website: www.brendadavies-collection.com

INDEX

Index

Index

Index

Index